D1484556

RECKLESS ROAD

VIP ONLINE PASS

GUNS N' ROSES

BACKSTAGE

CERTIFIED ENHANCED ¥ FIRST EDITION 2007

ADMIT ONE

ADMISSION PRICE: FREE! WITH REGISTRATION OF THIS BOOK

GNRO-92P7-N80X

sec.   row

RECKLESS ROAD

Guns N' Roses
and the Making of
Appetite for Destruction.

By **Marc Canter**
with **Jason Porath**

additional photographs by
Jack Lue

For orders and information, please contact:

Shoot Hip Press

Tel. (toll free) 1-877-241-4473
Email: info@shoothip.com

Website: www.shoothip.com

This publication has free additional images, audio, video and information online.
REGISTER THIS BOOK TODAY FOR FREE at www.recklessroad.com or www.enhancedbooks.com

Enhanced Books is an online hub for anyone with an interest in books. Enhanced Books provides the owner of this book with a page-for-page digital companion copy, DVD-like digital extras and a social network to connect with other readers.   Using a secure and unique identification method, Enhanced Books turns every book into a key that unlocks a broader experience for book readers online. Register today for your free access.

Although the author and publisher have made every effort to ensure accuracy and completeness of information contained in this book, we assume no responsibility for errors, inaccuracies, omission, or any inconsistency herin. Any slights of people, places or organizations are unintentional.

ISBN-13: 978-0-9793418-7-8
ISBN-10: 0-9793418-7-6
LCCN: 2007932752

CREDITS

BASIC BOOK CONCEPT AND STORY: **Marc Canter**
PHOTOGRAPHY: **Marc Canter**
SELECTED PHOTOGRAPHY: **Jack Lue**
SECTION TEXT, INTERVIEWS AND ADDITIONAL STORY: **Jason Porath, Courtesy of Real Deal Entertainment**
BOOK LAYOUT AND DESIGN: **Steven Slomkowski**
PHOTOGRAPHY IMAGING: **Two Cat Digital**
BOOK PRINTING: **Quad Graphics**
ONLINE PARTNER: **Enhanced Books**
TECHNOLOGY PARTNER: **Concrete CMS**
COVER DESIGN: **Steven Slomkowski**
RR MICROSITE: **Michael Hatchwell**

ACKNOWLEDGEMENTS

Special thanks to: Axl, Slash, Duff, Izzy and Steven for being so photogenic and fun to shoot, Genise Schnitman for helping me find the words for the first manuscript, Kim Dermit for also helping with some of the words, Farhad Shahkaram and Rene Diaz for helping me develop all of the photos, Jack Lue for all the photos from the shows while I was video taping, Robert John for the back cover photo and some of the photos in the flyers all his time, Marc Leoncavello for his time in helping me with all of the copying of the memorabilia, my wife, Leisa Canter, for sleeping alone for fifteen months while I was working on this book, Alex and Gina Canter for being the best kids. Alex, thanks for all your help with the transcriptions from all the shows, Gina, thanks for being a wiz on the MAC, Del James for his encouragement and support, Jason Porath and Steven Slomkowski for making this book happen, Carrie Small Laskavy and "My" Michelle Young for some of the missing memorabilia, Chris Amouroux and Leonard McCardie for some of the extra photos, Elizabeth and Alan Canter, my parents, for allowing me to use their station wagon to lug around Slash's equipment in 1983 for late night rehearsing until 3 am, Jacqueline Canter-Schnitman, Dr. Rand Schnitman, Gary Canter, Pamela Forester-Valente, ESQ., and Ron Schneider. A special thanks to all the people who shared their memories and contributed their voice to this book (see Cast of Characters).

FROM THE PUBLISHER

When this project came to us, my only recollection of the band was from glimpses I could recall seeing on MTV in the mid '80s. Working on "Reckless Road," I have of course become very familiar with GNR, 20 years later. Sit and listen to "Appetite for Destruction" and you'll know why it is considered one of the greastest albums of its genre and if you are not already a fan, like millions of people worldwide, you might just become one like me.

My job as the publisher and senior designer was to keep things real, avoid sensationalism and let the story tell itself without judgement. It doesn't matter whether you like, appreciate, respect or loath the story of these five guys. But, something very special did happen and it's very, very rare. My hat is off to Axl, Slash, Izzy, Duff and Steve. I wouldn't have had the guts or talent. You guys did.

Through this visual chronology it's easy for the viewer to witness the emergence of the iconic Guns N' Roses that we all know. I'd have to say, that I've been inspired by their journey to reach further in my own creativity and professional aspirations. To the fans, I hope most of you love this book, like I do. It's hard to please you all, but we've done our best.

Special thanks to: Jason Porath for shaping a great story and never giving up, Austin Chester who inspired me to dream and is a most remarkable friend and human being, Dianne Slomkowski; I don't have the words to say how precious you are to me, my brothers and sisters; Robert, Donna and Kevin, and our small, smart and loyal group of investors (Bernie, Jonas, Tom, Ken, Dana, Tim & Katherine, Austin, Xander, Anne, Arnold, Jason, Zu)

Steven J. Slomkowski
Publisher

AXL ROSE "Victory or Death:" The tattooed motto on Axl's arm accurately describes his all-or-nothing approach to music and life. Axl was born and raised in Indiana, like his former band mate Izzy Stradlin. He left Indiana to escape a somewhat destructive lifestyle, having no outlet in a small town for his youthful energy and aggressive personality. Determined to become a great songwriter and a kick-ass rock-n-roll frontman, he hitch-

a Olympic-class inebriate. With the success of Guns N' Roses, Slash established himself as a world-class guitar virtuoso, bringing the **Les Paul** guitar back to life and is known for infusing hard rock and blues into his music. He has been a childhood friend with Marc Canter since grade school.

IZZY STRADLIN Izzy was born and raised in Indiana, where he went to high school

hiked across the country to Los Angeles in 1984 and started several bands including Rapidfire, Rose, which later became Hollywood Rose, with Izzy, and after combining forces with Tracii Guns, Rob Gardner and Ole Beich, formed Guns N' Roses. After some disagreements with Tracii, Axl and Duff invited Slash and Steven to join Guns N' Roses for a Troubadour show in 1985, followed up by a tour of the Northwest. Slash and Steven accepted the invitation and the two events helped solidified the band into the "Appetite for Destruction" lineup. Axl is known for his strong stage presence, dedicated work ethic and vocal range. He contributed lyrics and melodies that shaped some of the best work Guns N' Roses produced and as their frontman never failed to captivate audiences whether they were playing small Hollywood clubs or the largest stadiums in the world.

SLASH Slash is known as a force of nature as a guitar player and one of the most recognized musicians in the world. He began playing in his early teens, borrowing a six-string acoustic from Steven Adler's grandmother. He was a quick learn and having been raised in and around the music business, he knew that rock n' roll was his destiny. He started the bands Tidus Sloan and Roadcrew and played for Hollywood Rose, Black Sheep and eventually stuck as the lead guitar for Guns N' Roses. As a band leader, Slash was active in every aspect of living the rock n' roll dream: a tireless ticket salesman for gigs, a demanding musician who expected the most out of his fellow band mates and

with Axl. Izzy began to play as a drummer, eventually took up guitar and decided that rock n' roll was his dream to pursue. He left small town America for Hollywood and started playing in different bands until Axl joined him in L.A. and together they formed Rose. After a few incarnations of Rose, renamed Hollywood Rose and the New Hollywood Rose, Izzy left the band citing creative differences with a new guitarist named Slash. Izzy joined the band London for a short period, but rejoined Hollywood Rose for reunion shows and continued playing with Axl when L.A. Guns and Hollywood Rose combined to form Guns N' Roses. Izzy is an accomplished songwriter and contributed lyrics and melodies for several Guns N' Roses songs and had a big influence on the look and sound of the band, which was drawn from his admiration of bands such as Hanoi Rocks and the Rolling Stones. Since his departure from Guns N' Roses in 1991, he has released seven solo albums.

DUFF MCKAGAN Duff began his musical journey in dozens of garage and club circuit bands in his home town of Seattle, Washington. He played several instruments, but focused mainly on the bass guitar. The music scene in Seattle during the early 1980s was too small for Duff and he knew Hollywood was the place to pursue his dream. He answered a classified ad in a local paper in Los Angeles for a bass player, which led him to a meeting with Slash and Steven Adler at Canter's Deli. Over pastrami sandwiches and a few beers, supplied by

Marc Canter, they decided to try playing together as Roadcrew. It only lasted a few rehearsals. Coincidentally, Duff moved in to an apartment across the street from a house where Izzy was staying, struck up a friendship with the visionary musician and they started playing together. Later, when Guns N' Roses reshuffled their band member lineup, Duff reunited with his former Roadcrew band mates, Slash and Steven.

Appetite, tours the world playing songs from "Appetite for Destruction" to sold out crowds.

MARC CANTER Marc grew up with Saul Hudson, a.k.a. Slash, and built a solid friendship with him during their years together in public school. They befriended each other on a BMX practice course in Los Angeles, where Slash impressed Marc with his daring

Greenberg playing drums. Together they formed Roadcrew in 1983, which only lasted a few months. When Slash and Axl met and decided to play together, Ronnie was questioned about his vision for the band. Although Axl admired him as a bass player, he thought Ronnie's inclinations leaned toward heavy metal and didn't think he was right for the band. Slash asked him to leave as the new Hollywood Rose was forming and

Duff described the first rehearsal as the "Appetite" lineup of Guns N' Roses this way: "It was, "lightening hit ting the place." Duff was a grounding force for Guns N' Roses and actively participated in songwriting. He stayed with the band until 1998.

STEVEN ADLER Steven became friends with Slash as a young teenager and they shared a passion for music. Together, they began experimenting with different instruments, and Steven gave Slash his first guitar, an acoustic six-string that his grandmother owned. At that time, Steven also played guitar and even tried singing, but realized his talents laid elsewhere. Once he discovered the drums, he knew he had found his calling. It took some time before Steven became proficient; he taught himself how to play and discovered how to achieve a unique double bass sound that remains his signature contribution to the "Appetite" lineup of Guns N' Roses. Once he felt confident enough, he invited Slash to listen. Slash was impressed and decided to give Steven a shot in Roadcrew, replacing Adam Greeenberg. Steven followed Slash whenever he could throughout different band changes, but it was his willingness to substitute for Rob Gardner at the last minute for a Guns N' Roses Troubadour gig in 1985 that solidified his future as the band's drummer. The meteoric rise to success of Guns N' Roses took its toll on Steven and he slipped further into drug addiction. His performances, both onstage and in rehearsals, became too unpredictable for the band. He was fired during the recording of Use Your Illusions 1 and 2 and replaced by Matt Sorum. His band, Adler's

tricks and bold moves. When Slash started playing guitar, Marc was equally impressed with his dexterity and marveled at the speed at which Slash learned the instrument. As a teen, Marc was an avid, almost obsessive, Aerosmith collector. Once he had a feeling that his friend Saul was going to succeed as a guitar player, Marc turned his hobby for collecting into documenting: he photographed, and in some cases audio and video taped, every gig Slash played from 1982 – 1987. Marc unknowingly captured the rise of one the greatest rock bands of an era. Since Marc had a "real" job, managing the family business, he helped the band anyway he could. When Slash, or any member of Guns N' Roses, needed help with flyers, ads, demo tapes, food, or equipment Marc provided. He is a family member of one of the most famous delis in world, Canter's Deli, home of the Kibitz Room, which continues to be a hot spot for emerging Hollywood bands. Marcs' photos appear in the album covers of "Appetite for Destruction" and "Live Era '87 – '93."

JACK LUE Jack Lue grew up with Marc and Slash. He shot the earliest group photos of Guns N' Roses and covered the gigs when Marc began videotaping. One of his photographs is on the back cover of "Live Like a Suicide," and several appear in the album artwork on "Appetite for Destruction" and "Live Era '87-'93."

RON SCHNEIDER "Ronnie" Schneider began his musical journey with Slash at Fairfax High School. He joined Tidus Sloan as a bass player, with Slash on guitar and Adam

he was replaced by Steve Darrow. However, Ron remained good friends with Slash and Axl when Guns N' Roses formed and he was asked to become their equipment tech. Ronnie worked as a roadie with Guns N' Roses for several years, touring the world and witnessing their supersonic rise to success. He left his position with the band in 1988 to pursue his own musical career.

ADAM GREENBERG Adam went to Fairfax High School with Slash and was invited to become the drummer for Tidus Sloan by Slash and Ronnie Schneider. It was in Adam's garage that the three budding rockers cleared some space and began jamming cover songs from AC/DC and Black Sabbath. Adam's mother was very supportive of her son's musical ambition, but never failed to voice her opinion when the music got too loud. When Tidus Sloan ended and Roadcrew began, Adam followed but was unexpectedly replaced by Steven Adler, a moment he remembers as being devastating. He continued playing, but nothing worked like it did with Slash and Ronnie. A year had passed before he checked out Slash and Steven in thier new band Guns N' Roses and when he heard them for the first time, he knew his replacement happened for a good reason.

CHRIS TORRES Chris bounced around from band to band, just like everybody else. Chris and Slash's mothers were best friends, so when Roadcrew needed a singer, Chris got the job. Roadcrew never lasted very long, and Chris continued to pursue music while going to high school and preparing for college. It was a passion of his, but when he saw Axl and the "Appetite" line up play, he knew making it in the music business was not his calling. He observed the insane commitment, tenacity and drive Guns N' Roses had to make it and realized he did not have it. He stopped singing, went to school and works as a professional in Colorado.

CHRIS WEBER Chirs Weber went to Fairfax High School with Slash, but they never played together even though their paths often crossed. When Chris was sixteen, he was introduced to Izzy in the parking lot of the Rainbow Bar and Grill by Tracii Guns. It was there that they hopped in Chris's car and listened to cassette tapes of Hanoi Rocks and the New York Dolls, that defined the style they wanted to model. Chris and Izzy found much in common and Izzy suggested including his friend Bill Bailey, a.k.a Axl Rose. When Axl arrived in Los Angeles, they formed Rose and moved into Chris's parents house. There they wrote several tunes together, Axl putting lyrics to the melodies and riffs Izzy and Chris were creating. One day, Axl was singing Nazareth's "Hair of the Dog" in the shower with a high-pitched voice and suddenly Chris and Izzy recognized the sound they were looking for. They encouraged Axl to use that voice, which became his signature sound. Chris played many of Hollywood Roses's first shows prior to his departure in 1984. He contributed to the song "Anything Goes" which appears on "Appetite for Destruction", as well as "Reckless" and "Move to the City," both of which appear on the GN'R Lies album.

STEVE DARROW Steve Darrow had seen Izzy around the Sunset Strip music scene for at least a year before they officially met through a classified ad that Izzy had placed. The ad called for a musician that had "hair, flash, glam and vogue." They immediately recognized in each other a common style and sound and begin rehearsing together once Rose was formed. Steve began by playing drums, but his skill wasn't up to the quality Izzy and Axl were looking for and they sought out a replacement. In the meantime, Steve joined Kerry Doll and started playing bass. When Kerry Doll and Rose played a double bill, Izzy and Axl realized how good Steve had become as a bass player and invited him to join Rose/Hollywood Rose. Steve played in Hollywood Rose until the band broke up after Izzy joined London and Axl joined L.A. Guns. At one point as Hollywood Rose, Steve was the only member of the band that did not graduate to the Guns N' Roses "Appetite for Destruction" lineup. Ultimately, Steve was drawn to a heavier sound than Hollywood Rose and moved on to play bass with other bands.

WILLIE BASSE A mentor to many, Willie has been responsible for nurturing budding Hollywood musicians for many years. He owned several rehearsal studios and always seemed to draw the biggest crowds for his after hour parties. He founded the band Black Sheep and they hired Slash, after auditioning Tracii Guns and C.C. DeVille, He

was proud to work with Slash and tried to block his decision to join Guns N' Roses, by ratting on Slash to his mom. A list of his protégés include James Kottak, Randy Castillo, Paul Gilbert, Kyle Harrison, Mitch Perry and Marshall Harrison.

DANNY BIRAL It was in Danny's mother's station wagon that the infamous Northwest Hell Tour began. The car broke down in Fresno on the way to Seattle and left the band stranded in the desert with nothing but the clothes on their backs. Although Danny was not a musician, he was a very close friend to Slash and the band. When Tom Zutaut and Geffen Records signed Guns N' Roses, they singled Danny out as a bad influence and told the band to keep their distance from him.

ROBERT JOHN Robert John was a construction worker in Los Angeles who had a passion for photography. He knew Izzy from the music scene in Hollywood and was introduced to Axl. Izzy and Axl invited John to take pictures of the band, and upon the first viewing of Robert's work, Axl liked what he saw. Axl and Robert quickly became friends and Robert was invited to quit his day job and start as the band's official photographer. From 1986 until 2001, Robert followed the band everywhere they went, and photographed their finest performances and their most intimate moments offstage. In 1993, Robert published a very successful photography book called "Guns N' Roses: The Photographic History," that chronicles their rise to fame. Robert has photographed numerous bands for countless magazines and album covers.

ADRIANA SMITH-DURGAN Adriana was a stripper at the legendary Seventh Veil on Sunset Boulevard and loved hanging out with her rock n' roll boyfriends. Like their other stripper friends, she gave the guys a bed to sleep on, a refrigerator full of food and plenty of alcohol. The parties at her apartment always ended with late-night balcony dives into the swimming pool. Adriana and Steven Adler formed a close friendship that became an on-again, off-again intimate relationship for a few years, which fell apart soon after Adriana returned from a trip to New York with Axl, Slash and Izzy. She was invited to hang out while "Appetite" was being mixed. One night, Axl asked her to record some "environmental" sounds for "Rocket Queen," and she acquiesced, albeit with a guilty conscience. Although the song was not written about her, she takes pride in being the "Rocket Queen" on the album.

PAMELA JACKSON MANNING Pamela was the ultimate Guns N' Roses cheerleader. She was a Hollywood stripper who befriended the band as they were climbing their way up the club circuit on the Sunset Strip. Like other stripper friends, Pamela provided sustenance, such as food and shelter, when the band needed it and eventually she became part of their act on stage. She was known for her sultry moves while

her and Axl pretended to have sex on stage, grabbing the attention of even the toughest crowd. As a friend, she would often sit in on rehearsals and watched songs develop from their inception.

MICHELLE YOUNG Michelle is the inspiration for the song "My Michelle" and was a junior high school friend of Slash, Ron Schneider and Tracii Guns. She met Axl one day at Slash's house and they became very close, intimate friends. Michelle was a constant companion of Guns N' Roses and was considered one of the gang. She helped the band out with whatever resources she could find; a car to drive them to gigs, money to buy food or a supply of stimulants to liven up the party. She is most fond of her memory of Axl playing "November Rain" on the piano in the auditorium of her junior high school, where they broke into one night.

DESI CRAFT Desi and Izzy met in Hollywood when Desi approached Izzy believing he was a member of the band Hanoi Rocks. They fell in love, moved in together and sold drugs to support the band. Desi, a dancer and choreographer, began stripping at clubs in Hollywood as a way to support herself and Izzy's musical interests. She brought her club act to Guns N' Roses gigs and never failed to arouse the audience with her dance number to the Rolling Stone's, "Jumping Jack Flash." Her relationship and affiliation with the band ended when they signed with Geffen Records; she was underage and they wanted to avoid potential legal liabilities. Tom Zutaut also knew she was the one supplying heroin to the band.

VICKY HAMILTON Vicky had a history of managing glam metal bands, such as Poison, Faster Pussycat and Stryper before accepting the job of managing a group of musical misfits named Guns N' Roses. Between December 1985 and May 1986, she was instrumental in booking gigs for the band while they were emerging on the Sunset Strip circuit and made sure they were visible to prospective A&R representatives around town. Vicky facilitated a meeting between the band and an A&R representative at Geffen Records named Tom Zutaut, which led to the signing of the band by that label. Vicky let Axl and Slash live at her apartment for a short time; a time she remembers as both the best and worst time of her life. Later she was hired by Geffen as an A&R representative, managed a number of successful bands and now runs her own music management company, Aesthetic V.

TOM ZUTAUT Tom was known as one of the top A&R representatives in Hollywood and was responsible for discovering some of the most successful rock n' roll acts of the '80s and '90s. He launched the careers of Motley Crue and Dokken while working at Elektra Records and he was hired by Geffen Records to bring in the next big thing. He learned about Guns N' Roses from a tip by a friend who worked at a record store in Hollywood called the Vinyl Fetish. He witnessed the frenzy Guns N' Roses generated with their live performances and after meeting Axl, he believed he was looking at the future of rock n' roll. He signed the band to Geffen Records and tolerated their indulgences as long as he, and Geffen Records, could handle. Through his dedication to the band, his love of their music and his vision to usher in the greatest rock band "since the Rolling Stones or The Who," Tom succeeded at corralling the band long enough to record "Appetite for Destruction." The success of the album is due, in large part, to Tom's effort and commitment.

MIKE CLINK Mike Clink was an accomplished engineer who started at the Record Plant studios in New York City, where he began to record with a roster of artists including; Metallica, Jefferson Starship, Heart and others. His work on the UFO records, particularly the live album "Strangers in the Night," caught the attention of Tom Zutaut and Axl Rose, who considered him a candidate to produce and engineer "Appetite for Destruction." Mike recorded "Shadow of Your Love" and the band was immediately satisfied, offering Mike the job after nearly seven months and several producers who auditioned. It was Mike's easy-handed approach to collaboration, as well as his no-nonsense discipline that provided just the right balance for Guns N' Roses. The success of "Appetite" put Mike on the map as a producer and he has since produced artists such as Aerosmith, Motley Crue and Sammy Hagar. He is known for capturing the best live performances from the artists he works with. Mike has become somewhat of a legend for his work on "Appetite" and continues to receive praise for his work from every generation that discovers the album. Mike continued working with Guns N' Roses and produced every subsequent album after "Appetite," with the exception of "Chinese Democracy."

STEVE THOMPSON When it comes to mixing and engineering music, Steve is known for his Midas touch, something David Geffen recognized in Steve when he first began working. Geffen provided Steve and his partner Mike Barbiero with a steady stream of opportunities with emerging bands, but it wasn't until Guns N' Roses came along that Steve emerged as a great mixer. Steve and Mike Barbiero took the studio tracks that Mike Clink recorded and mixed the album to perfection with Axl, Slash and Izzy. They became good friends and the band enjoyed their collaboration with their new mixing team. Steve has become one of the most sought after mixers in the music industry, winning several Grammy's and awarded diamond status for records he's mixed that have sold into the tens of millions.

MIKE BARBIERO Mike was working with Steve Thompson as a mixer on a variety of albums for Geffen artists when Tom Zutaut contacted him to mix "Appetite for Destruction." Originally, Tom wanted Mike and

Steve to produce the album, but a conflict of schedules forced them to pass, an opportunity that Mike regrets to have passed up. Since teaming up with Steve Thompson in 1984, Mike produced three multi-platinum albums for Geffen artist Tesla, a six times platinum, Grammy award winning album for Blues Travelers, a Grammy award winning album by Ziggy Marley and other assorted platinum recordings.

SPENCER PROFFER Spencer was hired by Tom Zutaut and Geffen Records to produce a few song demos soon after Guns N' Roses were signed to the label. Spencer had a history of using creative production techniques and shrewd marketing tactics to propel artists to stardom and his client list ranged from Tina Turner to Quiet Riot. Guns N' Roses rehearsed at his Pasha Studios in Hollywood where they worked together for several weeks and recorded versions of "Sweet Child O' Mine" and "Nightrain." Spencer produced a few demo tracks, but their relationship ended abruptly when Spencer dropped the project due to an offensive ultimatum presented to him by Axl. The band remembers not being too pleased with his work anyway. However, their contract with Spencer included studio time to produce their live album, "Live Like A Suicide," and it was recorded there without Spencer's participation.

MANNY CHARLTON Manny was the lead guitar, songwriter and producer from the hard rock band Nazareth. In their quest for the right producer, Tom Zutaut and Axl, being big fans of Nazareth, invited Manny from Scotland to audition and record some demos with the band in Los Angeles. Manny's goal was to capture the best live recording he could using a two-track system and then give his assessment of how the record should be engineered. They recorded over two dozens songs in two days, known as the Sound City Demos. But Manny sensed their dissatisfaction with the process, partly due to their unfamiliarity with each other and partly due to their difference in age. Manny returned to Scotland, after the short but productive session in Los Angeles to complete a Nazareth album he was producing and never heard from the band again. Manny is proud of the recordings he captured and believes the final versions of the songs that made the track list for "Appetite" bare a resemblance to the demos he produced.

DEL JAMES Del moved to L.A. in 1985. While looking for a place to live, he met Axl and Wes Arkeen. What was to be a casual drink turned into a weekend of music, fun and debauchery. Del and Axl formed a strong bond that is unbroken to this day. Del has authored a horror novel titled "The Language of Fear," which contains the short story "Without You;" the basis for the "November Rain" video. He also co-wrote "The Garden " from "Use Your Illusion I." Del was the project coordinator on the "Live Era 87-93" recording. He continues to tour with GNR to this day.

PHOTO: ROBERT JOHN

CAST
CHARACTERS

ANYTHING GOES

WELCOME TO THE JUNGLE

CONTENTS

ITS SO EASY

*Ain't Going Down Never released this song can be heard on the Guns N' Roses Pinball machine.

FOREWORD

Mark and I became friends when I was stealing his mini-bike.

I probably came up with some stupid excuse and managed to soften the blow a little bit and then we managed to get into a normal conversation. We started to hang out. We did fifth grade, sixth grade, then seventh grade and junior high school together and we were just really good friends -- all the way up until now.

He's my best friend; one of the only good friends that is consistent. I can't nail it down in a word what makes Marc the person that he is -- he is just a character unto himself. He is a really good, loyal friend and we had a lot of common interests: I was into bikes and he was into bikes. A lot of the same stuff that I got into, he was already into.

Marc was always good at taking pictures. He always kept a lot of pictures. As we got older, Marc turned into a big fan of the band Aerosmith, and he got into collecting their magazine interviews and photos and any kind of rarities he could find. So I guess at one, point he started to put a scrapbook together of stuff that I was doing when I started putting bands together. He always had a camera around. Mark has been working on the peripheral forever and I just never really paid much attention to it because he just always kept shots and kept scrapbooks of everything. Its Marc's nature and it's great. I wish I were like that. I would have a clearer memory of my past.

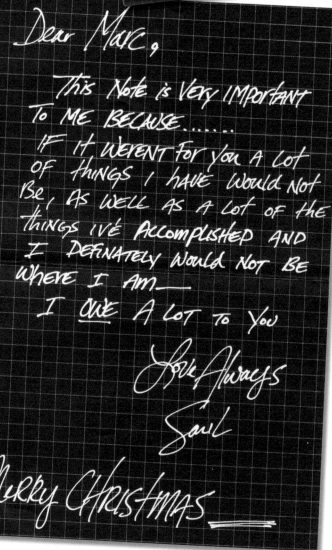

MARC C.

from: SLASH

Dear Marc,

This Note is Very IMPORTANT TO ME BECAUSE.......
IF IT WERENT FOR YOU A Lot OF things I HAVE WOULD NOT BE, AS WELL AS A Lot OF the things IVE ACCOMPLISHED AND I DEFINATELY WOULD NOT BE WHERE I AM___
I OWE A LOT TO YOU

Love Always
Saul

Merry CHRISTMAS

CHRISTMAS NOTE FROM SLASH

There isn't a better person to actually release any material having to do with the coming together and history of Guns N' Roses and where it went and what was going on behind the scenes.

SLASH

I met Slash and Steven [Adler] at Canter's restaurant. It was the first time I had ever been to Canter's. I'm sure I met Marc that night or within a very short period of time. When Guns N' Roses formed, Marc became like a sixth guy in the band. He was always around and he had unlimited access to the band, especially in the early days. He was really the only guy who cared about the band outside of the guys in the band. I think he believed in us from the beginning and had a much broader view of what the band was about than we had from the early stages. He documented the whole thing, tirelessly. He was a guy, to all of us, who meant stability. He had a life in L.A.; a legitimate life, with a family and a business that had been around forever. Living the nomadic lifestyle, that was our life for a couple years, Marc would always come around and you'd get a little piece of stability from him.

When the band did break and we got a deal and a record, Marc was a guy that was always there. He was there from the beginning. A lot of people jumped onto our bandwagon later on, and Marc, of course, wasn't one of those guys. He was a guy who would shoot straight with you and that meant a lot to us because later on we didn't have a lot of people, maybe no one, that would shoot straight with us. Marc saw through all the bullshit and he was there.

DUFF MCKAGAN

We had no money, but we had good friends like Marc. Nobody has been there long enough, cared for us, believed in us, or got pretty deep with us. The dude was always there. Look at this book he put together. It's beautiful. It's amazing. The tickets, the posters, the flyers; he was there and got it all. Marc was always supportive and really the only one who believed in us. If we were hungry, if we needed anything like stings or sticks, Marc would get them. The first Guns N' Roses banner we had, Marc put together and bought for us. I remember going to Canters and getting knishes and gravy. He is just a great person and a great friend. He was the most responsible out of all of us and he cared. And his wife used to cut my hair. He was our stability. He was there for us. And he kept the pictures. No one could do this better than Marc. Nobody!

STEVE ADLER

"Marc Canter - without you?"

from "Appetite for Destruction" credits

I actually said it out loud to Slash that I was starting a project.

1981 is when I first realized that I wanted to document this project, or at least with Slash at that time. I said, "Wouldn't that be neat if we could start documenting this right now, and every time there's an event just capture it. I mean what does it cost to put a TDK tape into, what is it a dollar? And a roll of film, it's not that much." I never knew it would grow into something like this.

I first met Slash in 1976 when we were in the fifth grade and we became good friends. At that time, I noticed that he had a great talent for sketching on school projects.

By 1978 we were riding bicycle motocross. The tricks that he performed were ahead of the time. Slash was a star. Camera flashes would go off when he took his jumps. He approached bicycle motocross with the same style and flash as he did everything else, including the guitar, which he took up in 1980.

By 1981, he was flying again, but with guitar and I would always push him to learn tough solos. He understood how to get the right tone.

THIRD STREET SCHOOL
GRADE 6
MR. BERTELL
1977

THIS PAGE ABOVE: SLASH IS THE SECOND KID ON THE LEFT IN THE THIRD ROW OF OUR SIXTH-GRADE CLASS PICTURE. I'M THE SHORT GUY IN THE FIRST ROW IN FRONT OF THE TEACHER.

LEFT: THROUGHOUT THE 7TH GRADE, SLASH AND I USED TO RACE AT THIS DIRT TRACK ON THE WEEKENDS. NEAR VICTORY & BALBOA.

NEXT PAGE:
TOP RIGHT, SLASH CAME UP WITH HIS OWN MEANS OF ATTACHING HIS GUITAR TO HIS AMP; IN THE PICTURE, IT'S POSSIBLE TO SEE HOW HE TOOK APART A GUITAR STAND AND FIXED PARTS OF IT TO THE AMP TO SUPPORT HIS FAVORITE GUITAR, THE B.C. RICH MOCKINGBIRD

SLASH IMPROVISING A BICYCLE MOTOCROSS JUMP AT THE LA BREA TAR PITS, 1978

In trying to contribute to his success, I always helped out in any way I could. I would help him buy guitar strings, I'd help him with the effects that he might be interested in. He worked a lot, like twelve-hour days at a clock company and he got by on very little wages, but he did buy his own guitars. The twelve-hour days at a clock company supported his guitar habit.

Slash wanted to play the bass, but when his teacher, Robert Wolin, pointed out that the bass had four strings, whereas the guitar had an alluring six, Slash characteristically went for the more challenging instrument. A quick study, he didn't need many lessons to master the basics and achieve his own expressive style. He had a lot of respect and

admiration for Wolin's playing and credits him with inspiring his own ambitious approach to the instrument.

When Slash hooked up with Axl, because of the chemistry they had, I knew that if they could stay together they would go places. In June of 1985, when Guns N' Roses were together with the Appetite for Destruction line up, songs started to pile up quickly. They were the perfect team of songwriters and they were all living together at that time. Slash knew what to do with whatever Izzy and Duff came up with and Axl knew what to do with whatever Slash came up with. At that point, I helped the band with some money for flyers, advertising, food and other odds and ends. Later that year, as the band became a better draw in the Hollywood scene, better backing soon arrived.

I took the photographs, audio and video taped the shows, and collected the memorabilia including ticket stubs, newspaper ads, press clippings, set lists, show fliers, and just about everything else from every performance that Guns N' Roses did from their very first gig until the recording of Appetite for Destruction.

My goal here is to let everybody that likes this band -- or even if you don't like the band -- see the making of one of the greatest records ever made. It shows how the band came together and how their style emerged. I want to share that with the world; let you see what I was lucky enough to witness. I was there and witnessed the making of Guns N Roses.

It took me fifteen months and over three thousand hours to complete this book. It covers over fifty performances, thirty of them prior to their being signed by Geffen Records. Between Jack Lue and myself we somehow managed to shoot just about every performance. Through this book you will see how it all came together. The goal was to use as many photos as I could, so the reader could feel the flow of the live shows. And when the reader is finished reading this book I want them to feel that they were there, right next to me. That's my goal.

I am pleased to be working with **enhancedbooks.com** because it gives me the opportunity to give the audience the audio, the video clips, the extras that didn't make it into the book. It's really going to jump right out at you. You're

going to open the page and you're going to see and hear exactly what I saw.

If you ask me, I guess I'm still documenting. Anytime something comes around with Guns N' Roses on the cover, I'm buying it no matter what. So, I guess I never stopped.

Enjoy the show,

MARC CANTER

August 2007

ANYTHING GOES

"They were trying out bands like they were trying on clothes."

VICKY HAMILTON

Launching a successful rock group in the early eighties required three ingredients: a dream, some talent, and die-hard ambition. The origins of Guns N' Roses can be traced to a handful of friends with similar taste in music, clothing, girls and drugs, and a collective fantasy to be the next Aerosmith, Zeppelin or Stones. Bands made their initial mark by clearing a garage, jamming cover tunes and playing underage parties. The real dream, however, required talent and skill that matched ambition, and players not up to par had to go. It wasn't personal; it was business.

For those who remained, a frontman and a few original songs were required to break out of high school keg parties and climb the Hollywood club food chain. Promiscuity ruled, as members of one band played sessions with others; everyone trying to find the right combination that could take over the Sunset Strip and land the coveted record deal. Band loyalty was achieved by growing a fan base or through the impenetrable bonds that formed while living subsistence lives together in L.A.

DUFF THIRD FROM LEFT IN SEATTLE
BAND "TEN MINUTE WARNING"

PHOTO: CM GARRETT

> "All we wanted to do
> was play music, jam,
> have fun and be in a
> band. That's what
> we lived for."
>
> - STEVEN ADLER

SLASH The first thing I did as soon as I could put three chords together was start a band. At a really young age, I was going around trying to find people to form a group and I was probably a little more ambitious and focused then most of my peers. It was difficult, but eventually I started meeting people that were into playing music. I was in and out of different, thrown together groups -- I guess you could call them garage bands.

CHRIS WEBER When we were in high school, bands were mainly formed by friends. There was always a drummer, because there were no lack of parents who were stupid enough to buy drum sets for their kids. The garage would end up being the rehearsal room for many budding young bands. Then there was the singer; the charismatic, cool kid. Mostly they couldn't sing for shit, but sometimes a great singer actually emerged. Then there was me, and what seemed like a million guitar players, all practicing their Jimmy Page, Eddie Van Halen or Jimi Hendrix solos. Two or three guitar players would hook up and the least talented one would be urged by the others to play bass. The band was formed, except for the name. Bands broke up before playing one gig because no one could agree on the name.

ADAM GREENBERG I was initially approached at Fairfax High School in the courtyard by two guys. I'll never forget it. They were both wearing long black, trench coats and they both had hair in their eyes and one of the guys was Slash. They said, "We understand you are a drummer, do you want to get together and play?" I said, "Sure." There were so many many musicians at that school and it was just amazing. It was almost like going to rock n' roll school. And across the street from Fairfax High was a Chinese restaurant called Helen's, where you could get fried rice and a coke for two bucks. And a lot of musicians would hang out on that corner and decide whose house we were going to go play at. At any given time, we'd get in a car, a truck or a bus and we would go to someone's house and jam there because their parents were at work. I got to play with all different types of people and styles: jazz, rock and punk. There were so many drummers, bass players and guitar players. It was incredible.

MARC CANTER You might have your guitar at school, playing it at lunch on the schoolyard. Or you hang out with a certain crowd that likes the same music you like, or dresses the same way you do and you find out who plays what. Maybe it's a t-shirt someone is wearing. And you get together and start to jam in what you would call garage bands. You don't book a rehearsal, you just find a garage and you play. There is no singer; you just jam cover songs. The band picks a few songs they are into and they jam on it. It was a matter of searching and finding the right people that were not only into the same things, but that were serious about it.

ADAM GREENBERG We went into my mom's garage and made some room: pushed everything into the back corner in a little area where we could set up and play. Eventually, it evolved into a bigger area. Slash, Ron and I started playing parties. We didn't even have vocals; we just started out playing cover tunes. We sat down and made a list of cover tunes we liked and we played them. We played AC/DC's "Back in Black" and Black Sabbath's "Heaven and Hell," and those are the two songs I remember we played the hell out of back then. Eventually, we slipped in one or two originals, then three or four. We liked playing in front of people. We liked being showmen. When you're a kid, you're so happy to be able to express yourself; to play an instrument, play rock n' roll, and have a group of friends that share the same likes. It was wonderful.

RON SCHNEIDER I got hooked up with Slash at Fairfax High School around 1981. Musically, we clicked right away. We played cover songs -- Zeppelin, Aerosmith, Black Sabbath, and some blues -- as we didn't have any originals yet. At fifteen or sixteen years old, we were just getting into playing music, just learning our craft, but we clicked. The first incarnation of our band was called Tidus Sloan. I remember jamming on "Heaven and Hell" for a half an hour and Slash was all over the place. It was really, really cool. We rehearsed three or four times a week in this garage and had no singer. We played a handful of parties in people's living rooms, backyard keg parties and built a little following. We played at our high school, at lunchtime on the quad. It was a big stage and kids would come. It was all about being in a band, having fun, partying, trying to be cool, fit in and do our thing.

MARC CANTER The only way to start playing the clubs and stop playing parties was to get a professional singer and somebody that had some stage presence. You needed people who were just going to do it; who would quit their day job and just play music. Once you've made the decision, you just stayed on track and sought out the people around that were in the same frame of mind. Slash made that decision early on. He knew he was going to be a musician one way or another. He choose guitar playing as a career. He was the only one that was one hundred percent diving in, not knowing what would happen. He practiced twelve hours a day, living, eating breathing guitar music.

RON SCHNEIDER In putting a band together, if you've got a visionary, a songwriter, that's great. You're always going to have that one person who's going to be the driving force. Look at Led Zeppelin. Jimmy Page was the driving force of Led Zeppelin. He produced everything, he wrote all the music and he knew what he wanted. If you have two visionaries and you've got input coming from two different angles, you're going to have a clash of the Titans. You're going to get a lot of head-butting because one guy wants to be the leader more than the other guy. You're always going to have to deal with one weak link, or that something that isn't working right. It was discouraging to have to get auditions going to find another drummer or guitar player, especially when you go through thirty guys and they all suck. But then, out of nowhere, somebody walks in and it's like, "Wow, this totally melds together."

MARC CANTER Los Angeles in the mid '80s seemed to be a place where anybody across the country could just drop themselves off on a Greyhound bus and go through the channels to see what they could become. There was a destiny factor to it. You are in the middle of the Sunset Strip and between the Troubadour, the Roxy and the Rainbow, you meet people who are there to get a band together and play, especially at the Rainbow. The Rainbow was the biggest turning point for all the bands. That's where they ate, hung out and where most of the connections were made. There was a lot of band hopping going on at the Rainbow. It was like a meat market for musicians.

DUFF There was nothing in Seattle. There was a huge recession, no jobs, no money and newspapers blowing down the street in downtown. I was too young to get really bummed out about any of that. It was just a time to go. It was a perfect time for guys our age to move. We were like nineteen years old and didn't really care if we had a pillow, or anything to eat. It was all about the music and trying to make something happen.

VICKY HAMILTON So many of the kids who were into the Sunset Strip music scene and trying to start a band were not from California. They moved here and they didn't have a background on each other and there were so many of these hard rock, hair metal bands to select from in the early eighties. If they were sporting the same band T-shirts or the same kind of stud jacket, Concha belts and service

clothes, they found a way to get together. The camaraderie began with a shared interest in the genre of music that they liked and the time they spent together hanging out on the Sunset Strip and at shows. But when personality conflicts arose, off they went to start or join the next band.

MARC CANTER I've seen a lot of different musicians over the years, especially during that time in the early eighties, who were members of three different bands at one time. If things didn't work out, they just moved on. Each time, they were looking for something that suited them.

DUFF Punk pretty much had died and when everybody was searching for a thing to do musically.

STEVEN DARROW Bands during the

L TO R RON SCHNEIDER, ADAM GREENBERG, SLASH COURTESY OF ADAM GREENBERG

early to mid-eighties were basically struggling to get their own version of whatever was the big movement at the time, whether it was commercial metal, or Motley Crue/ACDC/Hanoi Rocks part two or Aerosmith part three. There were only so many people that could play together. Out of a dozen people you might find six bands, with one or two guys at the core. Some of them were competitive, and some of them would try to help each other out by volunteering to play the opening act or something, but most of the time it was competitive like, "We're about the band, we're about the team!"

VICKY HAMILTON I don't' think the loyalty came until time was spent with each other. The life experiences they had together were what bound them. A cama-

raderie begins where they say, "We are the band that's going to make it." Then there is the music they share in common and when they start attracting fans, that seals the deal.

RON SCHNEIDER You knew you were on to something if you were packing clubs and you were selling out shows. Why would you want to break that up if it was working? You'd work even harder to try to get signed. If you're still playing the Troubadour after three or four years and you're not signed, then something's wrong. Then I'd say it's time to call it quits. But if something happens for a band between six months to a year of forming and you get picked up and put out a record, you would probably stay together. Everybody wanted to get signed. Everybody wanted a record deal. We wanted to become rock stars. I think that's what was driving everybody back then.

ADAM GREENBERG We just wanted to play and grow. We wanted the lifestyle. We wanted to be rock n' roll. It's an attitude; a way of life. You have to live it, breathe it, eat it, all day and all night. I wanted to live that and live it with my friends.

STEVE DARROW The dream was basically the chicks, the limousines, the champagne -- the jet-set lifestyle -- not living in a room with four guys. We wanted the penthouse apartment in Westwood or off the Sunset Strip and none of that was happening for us. We had little moments of it; you know we'd go to parties with those people and we'd hang out at the Rainbow, and we'd go backstage at certain gigs, but it was getting fewer and farther between, compared to the people who actually lived that dream.

VICKY HAMILTON Most of the bands were after the success: the fame, the money, the cars, the chicks with the boob jobs, the strippers, the designer drugs – all the perks that success brings. The odds of that happening were finding a needle in a haystack and threading it.

One out of a hundred hit that success.

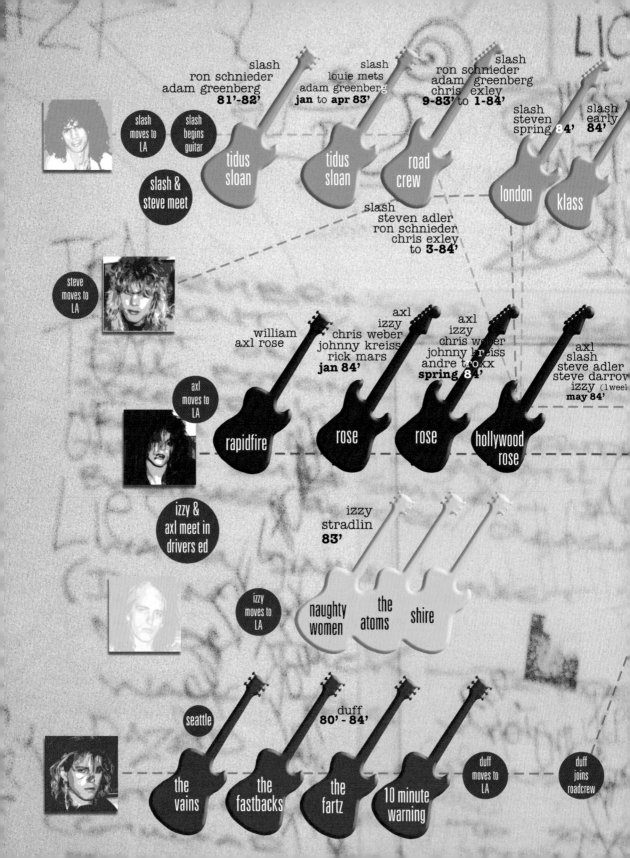

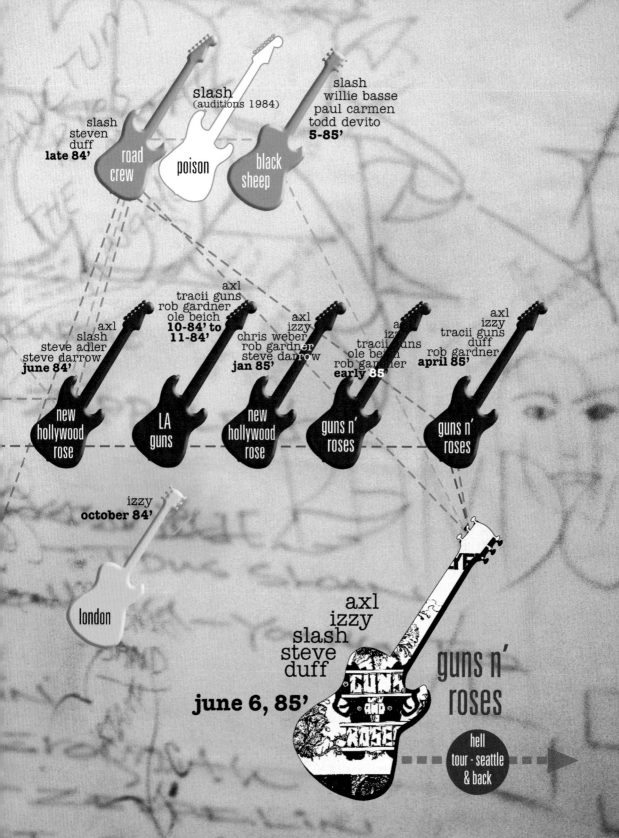

slash
(auditions 1984)

slash
willie basse
paul carmen
todd devito
5-85'

slash
steven
duff
late 84'

road
crew

poison

black
sheep

axl
tracii guns
rob gardner
ole beich
**10-84' to
11-84'**

axl
izzy
chris weber
rob gardner
steve darrow
jan 85'

axl
izzy
tracii guns
ole beich
rob gardner
early 85'

axl
izzy
tracii guns
duff
rob gardner
april 85'

axl
slash
steve adler
steve darrow
june 84'

new
hollywood
rose

LA
guns

new
hollywood
rose

guns n'
roses

guns n'
roses

izzy
october 84'

london

axl
izzy
slash
steve
duff

june 6, 85'

guns n'
roses

hell
tour - seattle
& back

BAND MEMBERS:
Slash - guitar
Adam Greenberg - drums
Ron Schnieder - bass
Chris Torres - vocals

TIDUS SLOAN

SUMMER 1981

FROM LEFT TO RIGHT: ADAM GREENBERG, SLASH, RON SCHNEIDER (BACK), CHRIS TORRES THIS PHOTO WAS TAKEN IN OCTOBER OF 1983

SLASH DREW THIS FLYER; HE SIGNED HIMSELF "SAUL" AT THE END OF THE POSTSCRIPT. HE MADE THE FLYER FOR THE GIG ON THE NEXT PAGE, TOP.

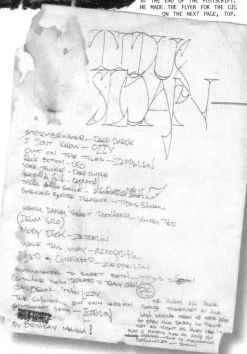

Slash had been playing guitar for about two years when he formed Tidus Sloan and he was playing a B.C. Rich Mockingbird guitar in those days. Tidus Sloan never started with a vocalist.

Tidus Sloan's first gig was a birthday party for a girl who went to Fairfax High School. The cops showed up during Aerosmith's "Walk This Way" and shut down the party because of complaints about noise.

Tidus Sloan used to rehearse in the garage at drummer Adam Greenberg's house. Adam's mom, Shirley, would come out and scream, "It's too loud and I can't stand the noise!" Slash later named his tattoo after her.

ADAM GREENBERG We always cranked it up to the limit. When Slash got his amp, he would really fire it up loud and see what

kind of feedback he could get. Whenever he did that, my mom would come out and bang on the door and say, "It's too fucking loud. I can't stand that fucking noise. The feedback is killing me. You have to stop it. Turn it down!" That was my mom. She is the coolest. It would just drive my mom and the neighbors crazy. She let us play in the garage and do what we wanted. Sometimes she'd pick me up at 2am, if I couldn't get a ride. She was a big supporter and she loved Ronnie and she loved Saul. She was cool, she was hip, she knew what was going on and she supported whatever I wanted to do.

TIDUS SLOAN
FALL 1981

PRIVATE PARTY AT ERIC MILLS HOUSE

Eric Mills was a friend of Slash and would later sing back-up vocals on Guns N' Roses cover of Fear's "I Don't Care About You" on the 1993 album The Spaghetti Incident. This party took place when Eric's father was out of town. The foot-long rolling paper that came with Cheech n' Chongs's classic seventies album "Big Bambu" was used to roll a gigantic joint – a party highlight. It was passed among the musicians and guests and lasted the entire length of the band's performance.

EARLIEST EXISTING PHOTO OF TIDUS SLOAN. SLASH IS VISIBLE BEHIND RON SCHNEIDER, CENTER AND ADAM ON DRUMS IN THE BACKGROUND

TIDUS SLOAN
MARCH 1983
PARTY AT SEYMOUR CASSEL'S

With their new bass player, Louie Metz, the band was back together. This gig was a birthday party at Seymore Cassel's house for Matt Cassel's sister, Dylin. There was a saxaphone player that jammed with the band by the name of David White. It was Seymour who gave the name Slash to Saul Hudson.

THIS SHOT WAS TAKEN AFTER THE PERFORMANCE AT SLASH'S APARTMENT ON WEST KNOLL NEAR LA CIENEGA AND MELROSE. I'M IN THE CENTER AT THE BOTTOM AND SLASH'S BROTHER IS SEATED AT THE FAR LEFT.

DAVID KUSHNER, DIRECTLY IN FRONT OF SLASH, CURRENTLY PLAYS WITH VELVET REVOLVER.

SET LIST
*Metal on Metal
*What A Change
Rats Ass Rock N Roll
What Your Doing (by Rush)

*THESE TWO SONGS WERE WRITTEN
BY RON SCHNEIDER

FAIRFAX HIGH SCHOOL
JUNE 4 1982

Before the band went on, Slash asked the crowd of about two hundred "Do you know the name of this band?" The crowd roared back "Tidus Sloan!" "Rat's Ass Rock N' Roll" was a rockabilly song.

WEDDING PARTY
JULY 15TH 1982

Tidus Sloan performed at a wedding party for a friend's relative. Almost everyone got drunk and trashed the guest house they were staying in. During the formal wedding party, Marc Mansfield (a friend of the band's who later became a roadie for Guns N' Roses) stood up and peed into the pool in view of all the elderly guests. Word spread that Tidus Sloan were pigs.

After that night's performance, Tidus Sloan – that incarnation – fell apart.

SLASH APPEARS AT THE EXTREME LEFT OF THE SNAPSHOT; THE BLOND IS MELISSA FISCHER – SLASH'S HIGH SCHOOL GIRLFRIEND; SEATED BESIDE HER IS MICHELLE YOUNG. POOL-PEER MARC MANSFIELD IS SEATED AT THE REAR NEAR THE COFFEE MAKER.

A CLOCK MADE BY SLASH FEATURING HIS OWN DRAWING. AND A TIDUS SLOAN MATCH COVER.

ROADCREW
SEPTEMBER 1ST 1983

BAND MEMBERS:

Slash - guitar
Adam Greenberg - Drums
Ron Schneider - Bass
Chris Torres - Vocals
Steven Adler - Drums (joins later)

RON SCHNEIDER Tidus Sloan was sort of short-lived. I never really got a clear definition of what that band name meant. One night, Slash called me up at like two in the morning and said, "hey check it out, I gotta talk to you." So we met and went to Canters for some coffee, and he goes, "Listen, I want to change the name of the band." And I was like, "Ok, what are we changing the name of the band to?" And on a piece of paper he had written out, in different styles, the name Roadcrew. And I was like, "Roadcrew?" The only thing I could think of was the Motorhead song "Road Crew", or "We Are the Road Crew." I had to sit on that one for a little while and kick it around. I was like, "Yeah, Road-crew! That works. I dig that. Roadcrew." So Slash, Adam and I trudged around for a little bit as Roadcrew.

AFTER FINALLY BEING EJECTED FROM THE GREENBERG FAMILY GARAGE BY ADAM'S MOM, ROADCREW IS SHOWN REHEARSING AT PROGRAMMER'S STUDIO — THE CHEAPEST COMMERCIAL REHEARSAL SPACE IN TOWN. IT WAS LOCATED AT THE CORNER OF HIGHLAND AND SELMA.

LEFT TO RIGHT: RONNIE, ADAM AND SLASH

SLASH REALLY ENJOYED COMING UP WITH ROADCREW BAND LOGOS SUCH AS THIS ONE.

When the Fire Dies

When the fire dies
And you have left my side
You'll feel the cold in my eyes

there will be no happy returns.
this time

Time ago   Lies and reasons
Young hope i know   excuses
where did it go

I've seen you smile
But not for me
we will see speak what will be will be

All these changes
Always rearanging
Just what are we saving
Cant you see
the fires Dying

                           the fire has died
Slamming Doors   but did our love subside
Cant take much more   Was it really there in the first
What am i here for   did you really care   place
                           i feel nowhere
I hear you scream(ing) Just what Do want from me
Whats here for me
Just leave it be

Chorus/ what have we done
         where did we go wrong
     tell me what is happening please

At left is another icon for Roadcrew by Slash.

MARS STUDIO
REHEARSAL
OCTOBER 15 1983

After rehearsing for two months, Roadcrew found a singer. His name was Chris Torres. His mom and Slash's mom were good friends. This was the first time Slash worked with a singer.

CHRIS TORRES I went to grade school with Slash and our mom's were best friends. I hadn't seen Slash in five or six years and he came to see me in my band at the time to see if I was interested in singing for his band. I joined Roadcrew as the singer with Ron and Adam. We had a blast and it actually clicked. Slash hated that I wore spandex. He wanted us to be all blue jeans and flannels, so I went with that. We would rehearse every week and it became a big party. Steven joined and eventually it stopped working out for Slash. We just weren't good enough and he was looking for something else.

MARC "When The Fire Dies" was an old Tidus Sloan tune. Slash later wrote some lyrics – which were about his ex-girlfriend Melissa Fischer (they were on and off for about five years) – and they worked with the old tune. This was the only song that Slash would ever sing solo on start to finish. Slash usually didn't do vocal chores.

"Roadcrew Eats First" was a song Slash wrote about a fourteen-year-old girl that Slash and Ron had encountered one night at Pan Pacific Park.

NOVEMBER 15 1983

ROADCREW

THIS IS SLASHS ORIGINAL DRAWING FOR HIS NOW FAMOUS TATTOO AND MASCOT

PHOTOS COURTESY OF: JOE KORNBRODT AND JAMIE GREENE

MARS STUDIO
DECEMBER 21 1983

Roadcrew's first show was a Christmas party held at Mars Studio. All the songs played that night were Roadcrew originals. Steven Adler, an old friend of Slash's from Bancroft Junior High School showed up at the Mars party. They hadn't seen each other for a few years.

CURLY JOE'S STUDIO
NEW YEARS EVE 1983

TIDUS SLOAN AND PYRRHUS
2 Live Bands   Kegs
Friday May 22
615 N Orange Dr
Time 7:30
Hear the sounds of Rush, Zeppelin, Sabbath, Aerosmith, & Hendrix
Admission: Free

KICK IN THE FUCKING NEW YEARS PARTY EVE
4 LIVE BANDS - INTRODUCING ROADCREW (FORMALLY TIDUS SLOAN)
WITH SPECIAL GUESTS
SHYST
PYRRHUS
WARRANT   LIVE
STARTS AT 7:00 PM / FREE DRINKS
LIMIT AT 400 PEOPLE BE EARLY!   AT CURLY JOE'S STUDIOS
ADMISSION $2.50   No EXCEPTIONS!   1984 N. MAIN ST.
THE ONLY PARTY YOU WANT TO BE AT NEW YEARS EVE
SAT. DEC. 31st

PYRRHUS
CURLY JOE'S PARTY, 12-31-83
LEFT TO RIGHT: RICK MARS, MIKE JAGOSZ,
ROB GARDNER, TRACII GUNS

Slash organized this entire gig, putting together four bands and charging a cover. Shyst was a band Ron Schneider used to play in during the Tidus Sloan days, when Louie Metz was in the band. Pyrrhus was Tracii Gun's first band. Warrant, after several personnel changes, made it big many years later. This was the last Roadcrew gig with the existing lineup.

SLASH MADE THE BACKDROP FOR THIS GIG.
HE ALSO CREATED THE DRAWING ON THE BASS DRUM.

LAWS OF ATTRACTION

Were it the simple laws of attraction that brought Guns N' Roses together? Slash places a classified ad for a bass player and Duff answers. Izzy discovers a drawing of Aerosmith and traces it to a music store where Slash worked. Duff moves into a new pad across the street from a hangout of Axl's and Izzy's.

The eventual merging of the Appetite line-up of Guns N' Roses can more easily be attributed to chaos theory than a straight forward chronology. Their music, as individuals, was becoming more dynamic and more defined: Slash wrote more original songs, Izzy began to model his look and sound after Hanoi Rocks and Axl became a prolific writer of lyrics. But their efforts to keep a band together kept failing. It didn't take much to upset the balance between a group of talented and hungry musicians; personality clashes, power struggles over emerging differences in style, or the inevitable no-show at rehearsal due to a narcotic hangover. Quitting was often easier than sticking it out. And sometimes, individual opportunities to join other bands with more traction often preceded band loyalty, even at the expense of friendship or playing music that mattered the most. Just like in the city they played, unpredictable seismic shifts brought an end to one opportunity and created another.

RON SCHNEIDER I wanted to get into more of the metal scene and I jammed with some other guys and nothing ever really clicked the way it clicked when I was working with Slash. So we tried again, and it was still Roadcrew, but this time we decided that something wasn't working and that something was Adam the drummer. So in comes this kid with really long blond hair and the super double bass drums and this guy had the look, he had the drums and he could play the heavy metal beat. That was guy Steven Adler.

STEVEN ADLER I gave Slash his first guitar. We met at Bancroft Junior High School and I used to bring him over to my grandmother's house where we put KISS records on and I played the Ace Frehley parts. I knew two chords and two scales on the guitar. The guitar was cheap, but because Slash was so natural and talented at it, he learned ten chords within a week and was playing songs. It was too difficult and too complicated for me and I couldn't sing, so I picked up the drums. When I finally felt that I was good enough, I had Slash meet me over at La Cienega Park. And I said, "Dude, I want to play

for you. I'm ready to go. This is it. It's time for us to do our thing." So I set up my drum set and played for him. He said, "'Alright! Let's do it. Let's go."

SLASH Steven Adler was actually the guy that started me playing guitar in the first place. So when I started playing guitar, he started playing drums and we had an ongoing relationship that went on for years.

MARC CANTER Steven wanted to join Roadcrew. He was very impressed with Slash's playing and had just moved in with an old friend of his and Slash's named Marc Mansfield. Slash went to check out Steven's playing and was blown away by his fast double bass drums and put him in the band. Slash then wrote a bunch of songs especially for the double bass drums.

ADAM GREENBERG Steven had resurfaced on the scene after not being around for a long time. He had improved greatly. He had gotten a handle on double bass drumming and catching a closed cymbal. He had taken some lessons and he was good and he was flashy. Slash and Steven had played together once to see what it would be like and I guess it worked out. I remember that I had a phone call with Saul and we talked about it. That is when the transition occurred. He had replaced me in Roadcrew. I remember I was bummed. We were kids and things have to change and evolve in order to become what they are supposed to become. But it was devastating. It took me a while to get over that, but once I did, I realized this is what had to be.

DUFF When I met Slash, it was when I answered an ad in The Recycler and I came to Canter's. I had like short red and blue hair and I met Slash and Steven. That night we went back to Slash's mom's house, the bottom basement room in West Knoll, and he showed me all these Joe Perry pictures. This guy started playing guitar and I'm lookin' at him, this kid, thinking, "Yeah!"

SLASH Duff came out from Seattle and answered a Recycler ad I had in the paper. Steven and I met Duff at Canter's and we decided to start something.

MARC CANTER The only problem was that Chris's singing didn't fit in with the new songs. Now Roadcrew was without a singer. The songs were fast and heavy. With the right singer, this could have been a great speed-metal band. Duff didn't stay in Roadcrew for long, and Slash realized

that he was not going to be able to make Roadcrew happen.

CHRIS WEBER My friend Tracii Guns and I were hanging out at the Rainbow Bar and Grill and he introduced me to Izzy. I was only sixteen. Izzy and I sat in my car for a couple hours, listening to tapes he had in his pocket. He'd say, "this is what I want to sound like" and he'd put in a copy of a Hanoi Rocks album or a New York Dolls album. Littered around my car were the tapes I listened to: Led Zeppelin, Judas Priest, and Aerosmith. He'd say "Yeah, that stuff great, but I want to look like this" and he showed me a picture of Hanoi Rocks. Done deal; I was sold. We jammed for a day or two, and then Izzy mentioned he had a friend from Indiana who had just moved to Hollywood.

We drove over to an old, crappy apartment building on Whitley in Hollywood. We took the gated elevator to the roof and got out. I could see, way across the roof, something shining in the sun. We walked over and lying on a small towel, on the burning tar roof, with long red hair and skin as pale as a piece of paper was "Bill." We went down to Axl's girlfriend's apartment, laid around, talked and played songs on an acoustic guitar. That was the beginning.

When I first met Axl at that apartment, I didn't think much of him. He could sing, but his voice wasn't unique. Axl said he had learned to sing in the choir and, at that time, he only sang his stuff in a smooth baritone voice. Then a week, or so later, Izzy and I heard Axl sing "Hair of the Dog" by Nazareth while in the shower. Izzy and I looked at each other and said, "That's it! That's the voice." We asked Axl if he'd consider just singing in that voice and he said, "fuck yeah." The rest is history.

At some point, Axl moved in with my parents and I and after a while, so did Izzy. That's where we wrote all our early songs. We wrote music and rehearsed during the day and we'd go out to the clubs at night. By this time, Izzy had created an image for the band and Axl and I were both spraying our hair to the roof with Aquanet Extra Hold. Izzy made Concho necklaces and wristbands and sold them for extra money. We'd be all clad in tight black jeans, Concho belts, Capezio shoes and bangles all the way up your arm.

The band was originally called AXL and Bill was still called Bill. AXL was the name he wanted for the band. After a couple of shows, the first one being at the Orphanage in the San Fernando Valley, Axl and Izzy got into an argument.

CHRIS WEBER A few days later, Axl wanted to bury the hatchet and start playing again. Izzy said he'd only do it if we called ourselves "Rose." We changed our name and played under the name Rose, until we discovered there was another band called Rose. So, we changed our name to Hollywood Rose.

STEVE DARROW Izzy and I actually ran into Duff in the parking lot of the am/pm across from the Whisky. And Izzy said, "I think I know that guy. I think I met that guy at a party or something." Duff had just moved into town from Seattle and was playing with this guy Michael McMahon in a power-pop band. Izzy started talking to him and asking about what his situation was. Duff described the kind of music he was looking to play; Stones, New York Dolls, Hanoi Rocks. Izzy was impressed and probably thinking in the back of his head that if things don't go well with me, he would definitely call Duff because he wanted to create exactly what Izzy had in mind.

DUFF Izzy was more in my vein; he was more punk rock. I'd never hung around anybody my age with long hair and who was into Wasp and bands like that. It was all kind of a learning experience for me. Seeing Axl sing for the first time with Rose, he was wearing Chaps. The whole thing, the whole experience was pretty kick-ass.

SLASH Izzy came down to the Hollywood music store where I used to work because he'd seen this drawing that I did, which I gave to Marc. It was a picture of Aerosmith and it was photocopied a bunch of times and was spread around the neighborhood. Izzy got a hold of one and came to my store to ask where he could get one. It was the weirdest thing. So Izzy and I struck up sort of a relationship and he played me some demos of his band with Axl. At one point, Steven and I went to Gazzarri's to go see Izzy's band and to see Axl because I wasn't looking for another guitar player, I was looking for a singer. I had no intention of working with another guitar player at the time. Although nothing happened at the moment, it was sort of destiny that we'd run into each other later on down the road.

MARC CANTER Slash heard that there was a great singer in a band called Rose. Slash and I went to see Rose at Gazzarri's. Axl and Izzy had lots of energy and a great stage presence. After the show, Slash said, "I would love to get Bill in my band." Axl was still going by the name Bill at the time. Slash and Axl talked and decided to try to work something out.

DESI I remember when Slash came and auditioned. He came to the apartment where Izzy and I were living on Orchid. Izzy had me hide in the hallway while they talked and played, but I peaked through a crack to see. I remember seeing his high-top sneakers and his guitar case and I knew he would be hired. Our apartment was the central hub for the whole band. We kept the beer there.

STEVEN ADLER I remember when we first met Axl. Slash and I went to see Axl and Izzy's band Rose at Gazzarri's. I met Axl and he didn't have the make-up or the hair all done up so I didn't quite recognize him. Once I did recognize him, I said, 'Dude, weren't you the singer from that band last night? Well, you're fucking great." He then introduced me to Izzy.

RON SCHNEIDER Slash brought Axl over to my house and said, "this guy is really cool. You gotta check this guy out." And I wanted to hear Axl sing, so he brought a tape of what he was doing and

it completely blew me away. It had this big double bass drum, a lot of attitude, fast and heavy. I was like, "Whoa! I've never heard anything like this!" I had never heard anybody sing like this guy. Axl started asking me questions about where I wanted to see the band go, and in what direction. He was interviewing me and was trying to feel him out at the same time. Slash called me a couple days later and said, "Axl thinks you're a really cool guy and you're a good bass player, but I think we're going to be looking for

SPRING 1985, GUNS N' ROSES
WITH AXL ROSE AND TRACII GUNS
PHOTO: CHRIS AMOUROUX

somebody else that wants to move in the same direction that we're going in." I was a little hurt, but I said, "That's cool, I'll find something else to do." And that was pretty much the end of my partnership with Slash as far as playing in a band together. We had a good three or four year run.

MARC CANTER Steve Darrow was a bass player in a band called Kery Doll, which used to gig with Rose/Hollywood Rose. When he joined up with Slash, Izzy, Steve Adler, and Axl, the New Hollywood Rose lineup was complete.

ADAM GREENBERG When they started playing together with Steven, he had a big honking set. He had double bass and a lot of toms and cymbals. When they finally got together with Axl, Duff and Izzy, they had taken all these pieces away from him and they said, "Listen, you have to get down basics: bass, snare, floor tom, cymbal, high-hat, a ride and a crash and that's it." The first time I went to see Guns N' Roses, he had that minimal set.

DESI No one could stand how Steven played because he had so many drums. One day we were in a rehearsal studio and someone got Steven to go outside. They locked him out and smashed every drum, except the basic four that they

needed. He was screaming because he could hear all his drums being broken and smashed up, but it worked out for the better. Once they got rid of the excess, played perfectly, he had more drums than he could handle.

STEVE DARROW At one point we got a rehearsal together with Slash, Izzy, Steve Adler, Axl and I. And it sounded really good. Slash had added a whole other dynamic, in contrast to Izzy's stuff that was simple, straight-ahead, and fast. Slash thought this would work, that we could be great. We had a few rehearsals, probably about once a week at best. It wasn't anything steady and none of us had a lot of money.

MARC CANTER The first time The New Hollywood Rose jammed together was at Fortress Rehearsal Studio in Hollywood. "Anything Goes" was the first song they played. The lyrics were different from those that were eventually recorded, and the song was played much faster with double bass drums. Izzy didn't seem very happy working with Slash and Steven – he had a problem with the fact that Steven played double bass drums – and soon quit to join "London," a band that was then bigger on the Los Angeles scene. The New Hollywood Rose started rehearsing at Shamrock Studio because the sound system there was much better. Axl began putting lyrics to Slash's songs.

STEVE DARROW Izzy faded out again. He was out of the picture and was looking to do something else. He ended up joining the band London right after Hollywood Rose. Axl was the one who got the ball rolling again. Izzy was more the glam kind of flash-talker, and Axl was like, "Let's do all that same stuff, but I want to make it more street, more denim, you know straight-up Nazareth-meets-Motorhead-meets-Aerosmith." And he was convening with Slash more. Axl and Slash were bouncing sounds and riffs off each other. The next time we got together, it was basically the same lineup except for Izzy. It was really cool. A lot of old songs that Slash had put his influence on were a lot more dynamic, flashier and more complex. From that point, we had- a couple of jams and realized we could do it. Slash knew the owner of this rehearsal place and he booked it from midnight to 3am because we could get it for three bucks or five bucks an hour as opposed to eight bucks. We had these marathon graveyard shift rehearsals. We played until we're really fast, learning all this new stuff and falling asleep while we did it. But we did it!

DESI Axl was working at Tower Video on Sunset when Izzy introduced us, even though there was bad blood between them at the time. Later that night, Axl showed up at our apartment, knocked on our window and said that he wanted to talk. Izzy was ready to go back to Indiana and give it up because he had been out here for five years. The band Hollywood Rose had never been signed and he was ready to give up. **I encouraged him not to give up and Axl convinced him to give it a shot.**

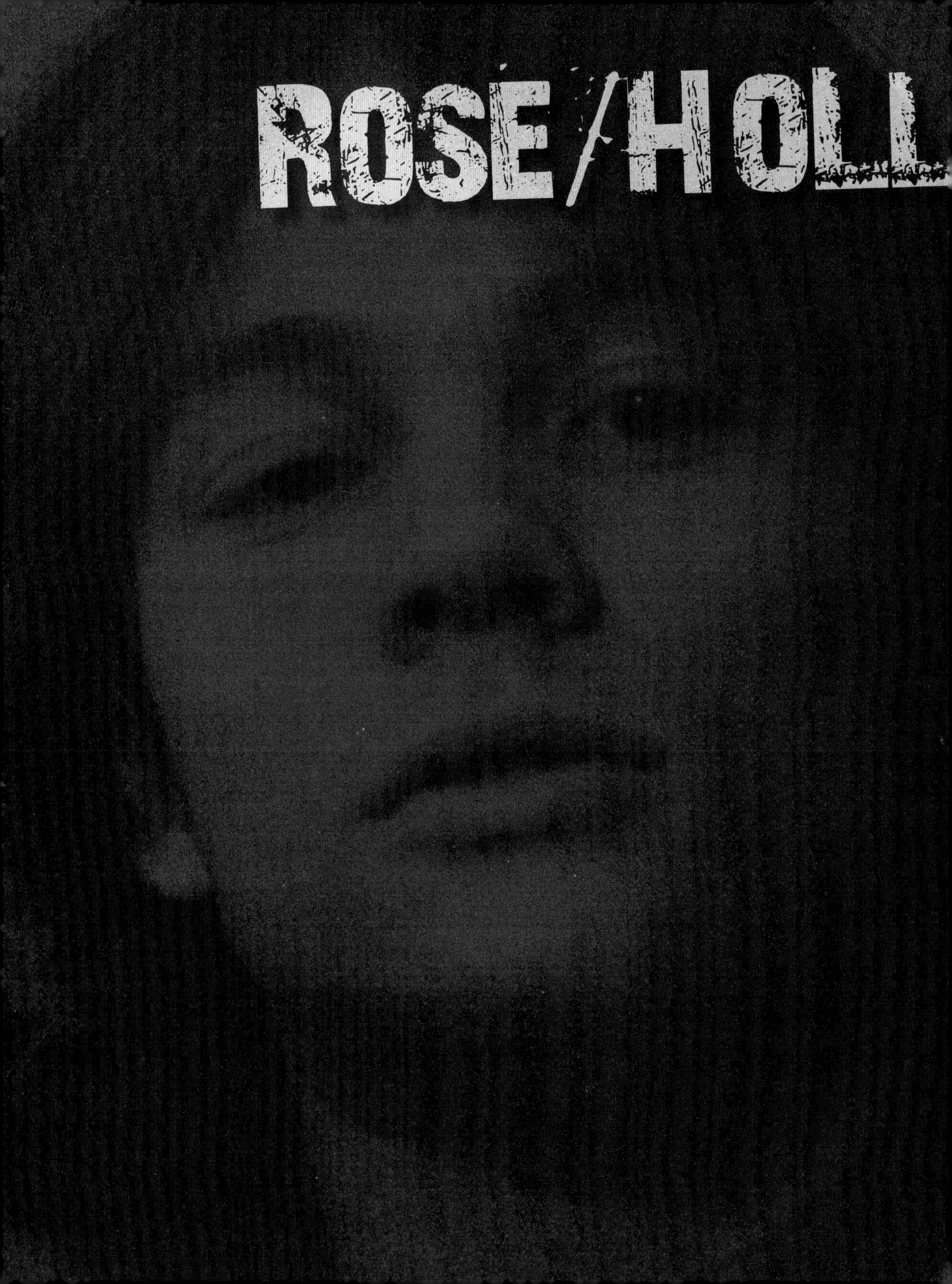
ROSE/HOLL

...YWOOD ROSE
EARLY INCARNATIONS

Axl Roses's first gig in Los Angeles was a Friday night show at the Orphanage in North Hollywood on January 3, 1984, with a band billed as Rose which included Izzy Stradlin, whom he had known in high school back in Indiana and who had settled in Los Angeles some time before.

In these early shows they were generally billed as Rose, but occasionally appeared under the same name Hollywood Rose (it sort of went back and forth for a time).

The flyers and advertisement for some of the early shows are self-explanatory. The flyer (on the following page) for the March 16th show at Madame Wong's belongs to Axl, as he managed to hold on to it all this time despite not having a steady place to live for the first couple of years he spent in Los Angeles. It appears in the video for "Don't Cry."

PHOTO COURTESY OF MICHELLE YOUNG

BAND MEMBERS:

Axl (Bill) Rose - vocals
Izzy Stradlin - guitar
Chris Weber - lead guitar
Johnny Krieff - drums
Rick Mars- bass

IZZY, AXL, CHRIS WEBER
PHOTO COURTESY OF CLEOPATRA RECORDS

ROSE FLYER
COURTESY OF RON
SCHNEIDER

STEVE DARROW

This was the first
performance with
Slash, Axl and
Steven Adler
on stage together.

AXL DREW THE ROSE
AND THE BARBED WIRE.

MADAME WONG'S WEST
JUNE 16 1984

BAND MEMBERS:
Axl Rose - Vocals
Slash - Guitar
Steve Darrow - Bass
Steven Adler - Drums

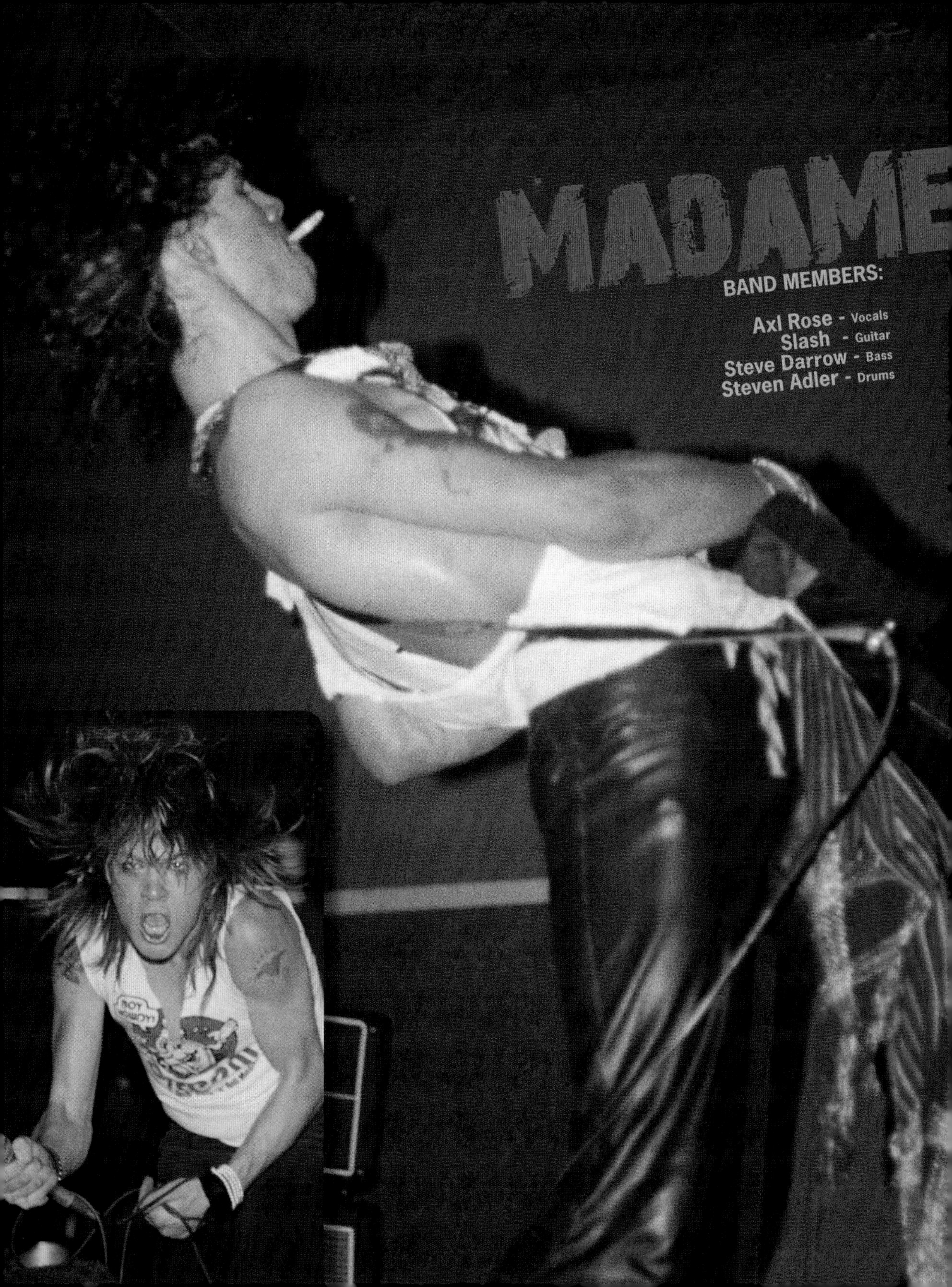

MADAME

BAND MEMBERS:

Axl Rose - Vocals
Slash - Guitar
Steve Darrow - Bass
Steven Adler - Drums

WONG'S EAST

JUNE 28 1984

Axl was working at Tower Video on Sunset around the time of ths show. He eventually became the manger of the store.

He sometimes slept in the parking lot under the stairs after the store closed for the night. He told me that one of his goals was to get a membership at a health club so he could always have a place to shower.

The band used to hang out in the store after closing and watch porno movies while the staff was cleaning up.

While the band was on stage, Axl - for whatever reason broke a glass against a back wall. The band was told they would never play the Troubadour again. Luckily, Steve Darrow knew the booking agent for Poison and was able to get the band back on a bill, opening at the Troubadour on August 29th.

Axl Rose – Vocals
Slash – Guitar
Steve Darrow – Bass
Steven Adler – Drums

NEW TROUBADOUR HOLLYWOOD ROSE JULY 10 1984

COMPLIMENTARY
★ WITH FLYER ★

THE NEW HOLLYWOOD ROSE

AT THE doug weston's Troubadour
9081 Santa Monica Blvd. 276-6168

JULY 10 9:00 PM

TWO DRINK MINIMUM
ENFORCED AT BOX OFFICE

© /84

ORIGINAL ART FOR JULY 10 FLYER.
COURTESY OF DEL JAMES.

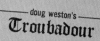

doug weston's
Troubadour

23. SUNDAY THRU THURSDAY THERE IS A TWO DRINK MINIMUM, $4.00 ENFORCED AT BOX OFFICE
24. 22 AND 23 INCLUDE GUEST LIST BUT DO NOT INCLUDE BAND OR CREW.

ORDER OF APPEARANCE	3 BANDS PERFORMANCE TIME	4 BANDS PERFORMANCE TIME	SOUND CHECK
FIRST	9:00		
SECOND	10:30	8:30	7-7:50
THIRD	11:45	9:45	6-6:50
FOURTH		11:00	5-5:50
		12:30	

ANY VIOLATION OF THE ABOVE RULES MAY RESULT IN DISQUALIFICATION OF PAYMENT AND/OR NO FURTHER BOOKINGS.

PRINT BAND NAME _____

DATE: 7/9/54   SIGNED: _____

9081 Santa Monica Boulevard, Los Angeles, California 90069 Phone (213) 276-1158

SLASH'S SIGNATURE ON THE CONTRACT
BETWEEN THE CLUB AND THE BAND.

The band was announced as Rose by the PA person as they took the stage. After the second song, Axl said they were "Hollywood Rose, not just Rose," adding, "This next song is for anyone getting drunk; this song is called Reckless." Using feedback, Slash would create sounds resembling motorcycle gears shifting for the intro to that song.

"Anything Goes" used to begin with a bass intro and guitar feedback. During performances of this song, Axl would introduce the members of the band and Slash would open up and play a five-minute lead with the band backing him up. This is how they did it all the way up until 1987. "Rock N' Roll Survivor" was another Roadcrew tune written by Slash that Axl added lyrics to, while "Rock N' Roll Rose" was a song Axl wrote after playing his first gig in Los Angeles. "Back Off Bitch" was a Rose song and Slash changed some guitar parts. On this evening Axl dedicated the song to "every guy that's got some girl who just bugs the fuck out of them."

MADAME WONG'S WEST

JULY 20TH 1984

HOST:
Would you please give a
warm welcome to Rose

AXL: "Thank you. Good evening everybody.
We are Hollywood Rose -- not just Rose.
This song is for anybody getting drunk.
This song is "Reckless."

AXL: Speaking over Slash's extended guitar
lead in "Anything Goes":
Bass guitar, Steve Darrow. On the drums,
Steven "Kush" Adler.
And on lead guitar, Slash.

AXL: (After "Anything Goes"):
Thank you! I want to thank everyone for
showing up tonight. Our next show is a little
ways a way, at the Troubadour, on August
26th. This is "Rock N' Roll Survivor."

AXL: (Before "Rock N' Roll Rose"):
Our next song is our theme song for
Hollywood Rose.

AXL: This is "Back Off Bitch," for every guy
and girl who just bugs the fuck out of them.

AXL: "Nice Boys, Don't Play Rock N' Roll!"

AXL: This is a Nazareth tune,
called "Hair of the Dog."

**AXL: (at the end of the show)
Thank you. We're Hollywood Rose.
August 26th, at the Troubadour,
complimentary. Thank you
all for coming tonight.**

lineup: Axl, Slash, Steven Adler, Steve Darrow

Cold Hard Cash caused some creative disagreement between Izzy and Axl. Izzy wrote a riff, but decided he didn't like it. Axl liked the riff and insisted on keeping it. It was one of the things that caused tension serious enough to make Izzy decide to leave Hollywood Rose barely a week after Slash and Steven joined. "Hair of the Dog" was an old song by Nazareth, performed by Hollywood Rose with the intro to the Stones' "Honkeytonk Woman." It was a last minute add on to the set list and Axl memorized the song minutes before they went on stage.

Shadow of Your Love
Everything's OK
Reckless
Anything Goes
Rock N'Roll Survivor
Rock N'Roll Rose

Back Off Bitch
Cold Hard Cash
Nice Boys - Rose Tattoo
Hair of the Dog -
Nazareth

NEW HOLLYWOOD ROSE
AFTER HOURS PARTIES
AUGUST 24 & 31st 1984
TROUBADOUR AUGUST 29 1984

doug weston's
Troubadour
9081 Santa Monica Blvd. 276-6168
Presents

DATE AUG 29 1984
TIME 9 PM
COMPLIMENTARY TICKET GOOD SUNDAY THRU THURSDAY, ONLY
NO AGE LIMIT · TWO DRINK MINIMUM · ENFORCED AT BOX OFFICE
COMPLIMENTARY

I missed the August 29th show so I could see Aerosmith in Bakersfield, which is why I have no photographs of this gig.

Although Steve Darrow Booked the show on the 29th, by the time of the event he was out of the band and a bass player named Snake was his replacement.

DOUG WESTON'S World Famous
Troubadour
9081 SANTA MONICA BLVD., L.A. 276-6168

FRI. AUG. 24	**LITTLE TOKYO** ALA CARTE · NETWORK
SAT. AUG. 25	**MEDUSA BLACKSTAR** SLIM WEAPON · HANS NAUGHTY
8/26	GLASS HAMMER · KCORDRAH MONARCH
8/27	AZ-IZ · SARDONYX · AERIAN RAGE
8/28	DWP · RISK · WARRANT
8/29	HOLLYWOOD ROSE · WARNING POISON · ASSEMBLAGE

COMPLIMENTARY WITH FLYER!

THE NEW HOLLYWOOD ROSE

She stepped inside the door
And was luckily laid upon the floor,
She screamed and kicked and raised a fuss,
But was later heard to say—she loved it!

AUG. 29/9:00
AT doug weston's
— **Troubadour** —

PHOTO OF STEVEN ADLER ABOVE
IS FROM JUNE 16th, 1984

HERE YOU CAN EASILY SEE SLASH'S CREATIVITY AND RESOURCEFULNESS. HE TOOK THE FLYER ON THE LEFT AND DREW MORE OVER THE ORIGINAL TO CREATE THE GREEN FLYER IN THE CENTER.

SAT. ONLY
VICTIM · HOSTAGE

SLASH IN TRANSITION

MARC CANTER *I drove* Slash out to Radio City to see Poison. I think Vicky Hamilton was managing them at the time. Matt Smith, the old guitar player was leaving because he got his wife pregnant and wanted to start a family. And Matt really liked Slash and wanted Slash for the job. Poison was an established LA band that could sell out almost any club they played and were getting ready to sign a record deal.

Slash went to three Poison gigs to check out the scene, and the band gave him their demo tape to learn their material. Slash showed up at a rehearsal but couldn't bring himself to join. He didn't like the Silly String act at the end of the show, nor could he stomach saying "Hi, my name is Slash" during the moment of the set when the band would introduce themselves. He hated their image and considered the music lame. C. C. DeVille was hired a few days later.

JACK LUE TOOK SOME SHOTS LIKE THESE DURING THE TIME WHEN SLASH WAS LOOKING FOR A BAND TO JOIN, FALL 1984

THIS WAS SLASH'S PET SNAKE CLYDE.

L.A. GUNS
OCTOBER 5 1984

Axl Rose - vocals
Tracii Guns - guitar
Rob Gardner - drums
Ole Beich - bass

Bloodshot Eyes - L.A. Guns
Shadow of Your Love
Nice Boys
If You Don't Love Me - L.A. Guns
Stick to Your Guns - L.A. Guns
Anything Goes
Heartbreak Hotel

Axl called to ask me to photograph L.A. Guns. I didn't tell Slash - I thought he would be upset that I was helping Axl and Tracii. Tracii and Slash had always been in rival bands beginning in high school.

Slash and Axl weren't talking at the time. In fact, I remember Axl calling Slash around this time and asking him to teach Tracii the new guitar parts to "Back Off Bitch," which Slash had written. Slash blew them off.

I was at a party with Slash, who was depending on me for a ride home and he got drunk. I had to leave at 11:30

to catch the midnight show, so I forced Slash to leave the party early. He really wasn't ready for a car ride. He threw up in my car on the way home, which was only five blocks away. I guess that was my punishment for betraying him. Later, I told him about the show and said that I was spying for him, and that I had gotten a tape of the show and pictures.

ON STAGE ANNOUNCEMENTS

PA: Lets here it for L.A. Guns. Their first L.A. appearance.

After the first song, Axl's microphone went out, prompting a loud "Dammit!" from Axl.

AXL: I want to thank everybody for showing up tonight. We're L.A. Guns.

After "Shadow of Your Love:"

AXL: I'd like to take a moment to thank the band before us – London; this is one of their posters. Axl tears the poster in half, then someone in the crowd yelled "Fuck London." London featured Izzy at the time.

Axl continued:

AXL: We'd like to thank them for fuckin' nothing! This is called "Nice Boys Don't Play Rock N' Roll."

AXL: Thank you! Is everyone having a good time? Let me hear it a little louder! This is called "If You Don't Love Me."

During "Stick To Your Guns," the cordless microphone was on the blink and Axl commented from the stage.

AXL: It sure ain't a lot of fun when somebody fucks with your equipment.

AXL: Thank you. This next song is called "Anything Goes." I think we learned that today.

The band had learned Anything Goes that day at sound check.

SOUND ENGINEER: That's it.

AXL: One more! This is the last song. This is an old Elvis Presley tune. This is "Heartbreak Hotel."

AXL: We're L.A Guns! I'll see you next Saturday night, right here at 12:00am with Ruby Slippers. **Good night.**

L.A. GUNS AT THE TROUBADOUR OCTOBER 13 1984

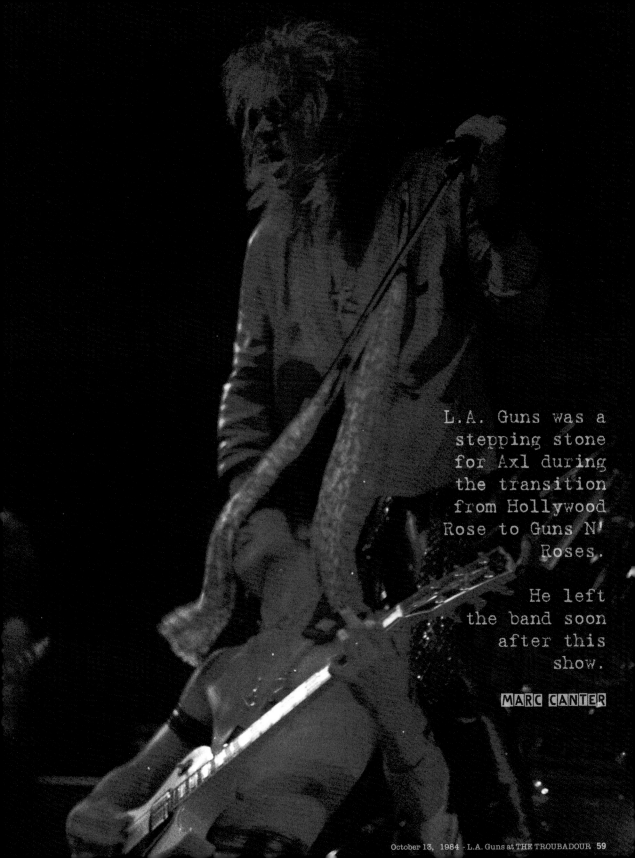

L.A. Guns was a
stepping stone
for Axl during
the transition
from Hollywood
Rose to Guns N'
Roses.

He left
the band soon
after this
show.

MARC CANTER

HOLLYWOOD ROSE REUNION AT THE WATER CLUB

GUNS N' ROSES
TROUBADOUR APRIL 24TH 1985

Axl Rose - vocals
Izzy - rythm guitar
Tracii Guns - lead guitar
Rob Gardner - drums
Ole Beich - bass

Guns N' Roses originally began as a side project of Axl's and Tracii's. At the time the shows were booked and the flyer for them made, it wasn't yet certain who the drummer would be; hence the question mark covering Rob Gardner's head in the photo flyer.

This show was the premiere of "Don't Cry" which was the first song that Axl and Izzy had written for GNR. It was a song about a girl named Monique that Izzy used to date and that Axl was in love with. She's also memoralized in a tattoo on Axl's arm.

Izzy booked a club date in San Pedro during the time he was without a band, having just left the band London. He pulled together a pick-up group comprising of various members of Rose / Hollywood Rose and L.A. Guns for this gig, which became a Hollywood Rose reunion and was billed as such. Axl agreed to do the gig and Slash was willing to do it too, but he couldn't get a night off from his job at Tower Video, where he started working a couple of months earlier. They turned to Chris Weber, the former guitarist from Hollywood Rose.

BAND MEMBERS:
Axl Rose - vocals
Izzy - rythm guitar
Chris Weber - lead guitar
Rob Garnder - drums
Steve Darrow - bass

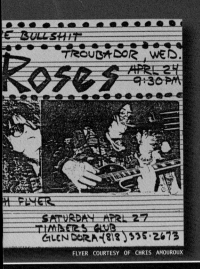

BLACK SHEEP AT THE COUNTRY CLUB MAY 31ST 1985

Slash joined Black Sheep one week before this show.

Guns N' Roses had a show booked on June 6th at the Troubadour, but Tracii Guns had quit the band to start up L.A. Guns again, leaving GNR without a guitar player. A few days before the Black Sheep show, Axl stopped in on Slash on his day job at Tower Video to ask if he wanted to join up with his old pals again. This posed a hard decision. Black Sheep was a big L.A. band on the verge of getting signed. Even though Black Sheep was more of a heavy metal band than a rock n' roll band - that is, musically -- it was less to Slash's taste. Slash's heart wanted to be in Guns N' Roses, but the question was: could they stay together long enough to make it? My wise advise was to stay in Black Sheep, even though I knew that, musically, GNR was a much better match for Slash's style. However, I didn't give GNR more than three months together.

Axl, Izzy and Steven showed up at the Black Sheep show to hang out and try to persuade Slash to join them. A few days later, Slash joined Guns N' Roses.

WILLIE BASSE Tracii Guns and C.C. Deville auditioned for Black Sheep and I said no. I hired Slash. Black Sheep was a musician's band and Slash, even at his young age, could hang with any of the neoclassical guys. He's a serious technical guitar player. We were like Black Sabbath meets Bon Jovi meets Purple; neo-classical rock. It was pretty awesome to have two guys of color fronting a metal band. We rehearsed for maybe a month at the most and it was a really good line up at the time. We only did a few gigs like the Troubadour and the Country Club. When Slash was in Black Sheep he was using a B.C. Rich Warlock and he had Risson amps. I told him, "Dude, you're not going on stage with me with Risson amps," and I got him to go with Marshall.

Guns N' Roses had a gig they were planning to get to in a station wagon to Seattle. I remember calling Slash's mom and saying, "You can't let him join the band. They're all a bunch of heroine addicts." I tried to get her to talk him out of going. Slash told me that his mom didn't speak to him for a year after I called. I was trying to block it but it was fate. He left Black Sheep and joined Guns N' Roses.

WILLIE BASSE - VOCAL
PAUL CARMEN - BASS
SLASH - GUITAR
TODD DEVITO - DRUMMER

GNR FIRST LINEUP

ROCK N ROLL

L.A. GUNS HOLLYWOOD ROSE

L.A. GUNS

PRESENTS THE BAND

GUNS·N·ROSES

IZZY   TRACII   ROB

OLE

AXL

AT TROUBADOR
Tue. MARCH 26
10:00 PM

TWO FREE ADMISSIONS WITH THIS FLYER

JUNE
SIX
1985

First Show with
APPETITE FOR DESTRUCTION
Lineup

GUNS
AND
ROSES

AXL
ROSE

SLASH

DUFF
MCKAGAN

STEVE
ADLER

> ## We had one day of rehearsal. It really was like a synergy. It was like we'd been playing together for years.
> ### SLASH

DUFF Izzy and Axl and I were just like, "Yeah, let's do it. Let's go on the road. Let's do this thing." Tracii Guns and Rob Gardner were more concerned with where they were going to stay or how we were going to get there. They got cold feet at the eleventh hour for doing a tour of the Northwest. Izzy, Axl and I just didn't care. When they pulled out, we asked Slash and Steven to be in the band and the Troubadour was our first gig as a band.

SLASH Rob Gardner couldn't cut it; he was scared to go. I called Steven. He came down and we had one day of rehearsal. It really was like a synergy. It was like we'd been playing together for years.

STEVEN ADLER I guess Tracii Guns and Rob Gardner didn't want to do these shows up north. So Slash calls me and says, "We have two empty shows you want to do them? One's at the Troubadour and we're going to go up to Oregon and Seattle for the others. And I said, "Fuck yeah, of course." The two other guys didn't have it in their hearts to do it and we did.

_____

DUFF The first rehearsal day that we had as the five guys was at a studio in Silverlake. Playing the first few chords was like thunder had hit the room; like lightning had hit the room. That day was probably the most important day of the five of our lives, as players and musicians. It definitely ranks up there because that's when we all knew it was solidified. This was the best band that any of us had come close to being in.

_____

AXL: Thank you everyone for coming out tonight, we're Guns N' Roses.

SLASH (to audience): Come up here closer to the stage. Move your fucking asses!

AXL: Alright, this is "Think About You."

AXL: This is a song about coming to L.A. This is a song called "Move to the City."

AXL (before "Don't Cry"): We're going to slow things down.

AXL: This is our theme song, "Nice Boys Don't Play Rock N' Roll."

AXL: This one is called "Back of Bitch."

AXL (In the middle of "Anything Goes"): I want to take a moment to introduce the members of Guns N' Roses: on guitar here, Mr. Izzy Stradlin; on bass guitar, Mr. Duff Rose; on the drums,

Mr. Steven Adler; and on lead guitar, Slash. This is Guns N' Roses ladies and gentlemen.

AXL: This is our last song people, hope you remember this, "Heartbreak Hotel."

Reckless
Shadow of Your Love
Jumpin' Jack Flash
Think About You
Move to the City
Don't Cry
Nice Boys
Back Off Bitch
Anything Goes
Heartbreak Hotel

HELL TOUR SEATTLE

SLASH It was just a conversation for a few days and then it became a reality -- all of the sudden we were going to Seattle. We did the Troubadour show, packed up an Oldsmobile and a U-Haul and set off. It was Duff, Izzy, Axl, Steven and myself, and we set out to do this Northwest tour of Seattle and Oregon.

DUFF It wasn't just Seattle -- it was a whole west coast tour starting in Seattle and coming down. There was Portland; there was Eugene; there was a Sacramento gig; and there was a San Francisco gig. I had toured in a punk rock band so I knew the clubs and the club owners and I booked this tour. So a few days after our first show at the Troubadour, we were playing our first gig on the west coast "Hell Tour," as it was later dubbed.

SLASH Duff had booked us in all the clubs he was familiar with, from playing in the bands he was in like The Fastbacks. So he booked us gigs in Sacramento and a couple gigs in Oregon and a couple gigs in Seattle. We got as far as Fresno and the car broke down.

STEVEN ADLER We were in Danny Birall's car and we had a U-Haul and his car broke down. We were determined and that wasn't going to stop us from doing any shows.

DANNY BIRALL I stole my mother's gas card to get us there. It was a 1977 green Pontiac Catalina. At that point, it was a pretty solid running car, but I was young and was probably taking a lot for granted when I loaded up seven people plus a U-Haul and thought I could make it to Seattle. I remember arguing with everybody. I wanted to get out of town early in the morning, but nobody could just get their shit together. It was taking forever to get everybody rolling. We finally drove out of L.A. and things seemed kind of nice. At that point, everybody was happy; everybody was excited. There were the inevitable fights about what was going to be played on the tape deck.

As we started to get into the Grapevine, there was a problem. The transmission was slipping as we were going up the hills. I didn't really say anything, but I knew there was going to be a problem. Finally the transmission just slipped and it wouldn't catch. We were stuck; really stuck. There was nothing where we were and nobody was stopping to help. I had a Triple-A card, but there wasn't a telephone in sight.

We realized that the car would run if there were nobody in it. Imagine, there I am, putting along at five to ten miles-an-hour, which is about as fast as the car would go before the transmission would slip, and the band was just sort of walking behind. This went on for miles. I was impressed with how they just walked. At that point, it came to a head. They were just like, "Fuck this!" So they grabbed their guitars out of the U-haul, left all the equipment, the amps and everything else, and they decided they were going to hitch.

SLASH We took the guitars out of the U-Haul, told the crew guys to get the car fixed and meet us up in Seattle. We sort of canned all those other gigs because

we knew it was going to take us a while to get up there. So we took the guitars and stood on the side of the road and finally got picked up by a semi-truck. Try to picture us, knowing what we look like, and then picture us on the side of the road with guitar cases wanting a ride. It made visions of The Hitcher seem like a cakewalk. We rode with this guy and we were all in the cab and I don't know how many miles we went. This was the first time I was ever exposed to somebody that lived on speed.

> It was just a conversation for a few days and then it became a reality -- all of a sudden we were going to Seattle.
>
> **SLASH**

STEVEN ADLER I asked all these truck drivers if they could give us a ride to Seattle. And I got a truck driver who said, "Yeah, no problem." So we left all the gear except the guitars, my sleeping bag and we hopped into this eighteen-wheeler.

SLASH We had stops here and there, but we didn't have any money, so we would go into these patches of land that were off to the side of the road where people were growing agricultural crops and we would steal food – onions, carrots and shit like that. Finally we sort of burned out on one driver and then we'd go out on the highway hitchhiking again.

DUFF We were eating onions from the onion fields outside of Bakersfield on the side of Interstate Five (I-5) because we were hungry. Just being out there was pretty cool. This old Mexican farmer picked us up in a small pickup and we all got in the back. The truck was so beat-up and rundown that the bed started rubbing against the back tires. It started smoking and he said, 'I'm sorry, I can't take you guys.' We were stuck on I-5 in the middle of nowhere.

STEVEN ADLER This Mexican guy and his kid picked us up. We didn't go further than twenty-feet because he had a low rider and we were so heavy in the back of the truck that it was scraping against his tires and it was smoking. He gave us a ride to Medford, Oregon. We were hitch-hiking on the freeway again and these two hippy-chicks gave us a ride.

SLASH We just kept inching our way towards Seattle. Two chicks picked us up and put us in the back. It wasn't a truck; it was like a pick-up with a cab over the top. We piled in there and they drove us to Oregon. From there, one of our friends from Seattle came and got us. He took us to this guy Donner's house, who was a good friend of Duff's, and we just partied like crazy. The next day we showed up at the venue and used the Fastbacks gear and played our first set. The club didn't want to pay us, for whatever reason, so we cornered the manager in his own office, bolted the door, and threatened him within an inch of his life. Then we got paid. We got a ride with one of Duff's friends all the way back to Los Angeles.

STEVEN ADLER It wasn't hell, it was fun -- it was great, it was exciting, it was an experience. And we actually played a decent show.

DUFF When we got back from the Hell Tour, from that shared experience, we knew that we had each other's backs. **At that point we knew we were a band.** We were ready just to fuck up L.A. Finally, all of us had a solidified band and that was very important. It was very important to the credo of Guns N' Roses. We were like a little family. We were like a little gang of five musicians. We had each other.

SLASH Having everything that could possibly go wrong, go wrong, and survive it, and to actually make it to Seattle to do our first show; nobody I knew could've handled it and we had the best fucking time.

"That trip really cemented the camaraderie between the five of us and that was it; that just set the whole pace for everything."   SLASH

THIS PHOTO WAS TAKEN IN CANTER'S
DELI RIGHT AFTER THE BAND'S RETURN
FROM SEATTLE. THEY NEEDED
NEW PUBLICITY AND FLYER SHOTS.

WELCOME TO THE JUNGLE

"It was about having a good time;
partying, drinking, being on stage on
the Sunset Strip, getting your band out
there, and letting people know
who you were."

RON SCHNEIDER

Original, dangerous, rebellious, fierce, transcendent; whatever qualities described the music and attitude of the newly cemented Guns N' Roses, they still had to play by the rules of the Sunset Strip like everyone else. In the 1980's, the Sunset Strip was a thriving, micro-music eco-system, teaming with glam, sleaze and punk rockers; all attempting to bait an audience, land a deal and enjoy the bounty with bacchanalian delight like their rock n' roll predecessors. The Strip (giving its name to the street in Las Vegas) consisted of a small circle of established music venues, either on or adjacent to Sunset Boulevard, each run by eccentric impresarios. They presided over their clubdoms like mini-mafiosos; idiosyncratic personalities who could position bands in favor or ban them on a whim. Whether their power to make or break emerging bands was real or imagined, collectively, they were responsible for launching some of the greatest rock n' roll acts of the twentieth century. They flaunted their claims-to-fame with signed photos, memorabilia and ticket stubs adorning the walls of their clubs and enjoyed the popularitiy it brought them.

Although club owners could always bank on a thirsty crowd for Friday and Saturday nights, they lost money during the week. Therefore, Pay-to-Play was introduced in the 1980's: an insurance policy to cover the costs of operation during down time. It required that bands slotted to play during weeknights collect a minimum cover fee by pre-selling tickets to their own gigs. Club owners shifted the financial risk of running a club to the band, taking advantage of favorable supply-and-demand conditions. The more tickets sold, the better favor would be gained and a plum spot on the weekly line-up assured. If the band caused trouble, however, and cost the owners more than they brought in, getting blacklisted was almost guaranteed. This

could be achieved by trashing dressing rooms, bar fighting and assaulting patrons. If a band was banned from enough clubs, they could kiss their dream of a record contract goodbye.

There was both an art and a hustle to promoting a club gig, especially when it came to flyering. Slash and Axl would cruise the Sunset Strip, tacking flyers up on every telephone pole and covering up their rivals' flyers in the process. They gave out tickets like candy on the street to anyone who crossed their path in an attempt to raise the minimum amount to play. When they fell short, friends of

Eventually, we were accepted as being destructive, but profitable.

SLASH

the band (like Marc Canter) often stood outside the clubs on the night of the show and sold tickets one-by-one. When that failed, someone had to pony up the remaining amount or the band didn't go on. If you wanted the dream, these are the clubs you had to play.

STEVE DARROW As far as the club gigs went, the main places you wanted to play were the clubs on the Sunset Strip or The Troubadour. The Troubadour was the place where you had to play to make it and be somebody. You would hand out your flyers and say, "Here come see our band three weeks from now at the Troubadour on Tuesday. You want to buy a ticket?" And most people would go, 'Well, I don't know if I can make it." You'd say, "Well just buy a ticket and that way you'll make it for sure." It was a hustle. If you were a new band without a giant following and wanted to book a gig at a club, you were faced with this stair-step hierarchy. You never really realized it until you tried to infiltrate the clubs and get in with the owners. Then the owners introduced what was coined 'pay-to-play.'

MARC CANTER This was the heyday of the pay-to-play bullshit when Los Angeles promoters would have the

bands themselves shoulder the financial risk of their gig, by either taking on the burden of selling a certain number of tickets themselves or simply forking over the required amount out of their own pocket. They would essentially force the musicians to take on the risks that had generally been considered the reason for club promoters in the first place.

STEVE DARROW Here is how it worked: you sent in a package with your demo tape, waited a couple of weeks and if they called you back, they would slot you in on a Tuesday night at 7:30pm with five other bands after you. Pay-to-play required that you bring fifty people and each of those fifty people had to buy two drinks. If you weren't old enough to consume, you would have to buy a ticket equal to the value of two drinks. That was a lot for a seventeen-year-old kid to shell out.

RON SCHNEIDER Anything over 100 tickets was yours to keep. The more people you brought into a club on a Thursday night, the more power you demonstrated to the club that you could bring in a draw. The bigger the draw, the more booze they would sell, which means the more money you're going to make. Instead of closing a gig at 11:45pm on a Thursday night, you would start climb up the ladder and move up to a Friday or Saturday night. There was a clear motivation for bringing people to the show: you wanted that plush spot.

VICKY HAMILTON It was pay-to-play, and obviously the club promoter wanted the band that had the biggest draw and, "the sexiest chicks at their shows," as Bill Gazzari once said.

SLASH Guns N' Roses went through a period of pay-to-play for a while in the beginning. I used to work at a newsstand up on Fairfax and Melrose and when I got the tickets, I gave them out to as many people as I could. We never paid for a gig ourselves, but we pandered them to everybody. I was really good at it because I was working a job where I came into contact with so many customers everyday. I was a pretty restless member of the band when it came to promotion and managerial things, because I never really slept. This thing was twenty-four-seven with me, everyday! And that was a good quality to have.

MARC CANTER Slash was working at Centerfold Newsstand, on Fairfax, off Melrose. A short time later, he was fired for conducting band business on company time.

RON SCHNIEDER There was big competition out there. You walked around and handed out flyers. It was seven days a week, twenty-four hours a day. Wednesday night at 11:30pm doesn't mean your at home in bed. You had to be out there and flyering. That's what you did. You would post flyers on the Strip and then some other band came along and put up their flyer right over yours. Big rivalries between bands flared up and it either ended up in a fistfight on the Strip or some drawn out drama.

CHRIS WEBER To get future gigs you had to draw a crowd. That's where the girls came in. You'd flyer all night and flirt with the girls. You'd say, "Come meet me at the gig and we can hang out after the show, and, oh, bring five or ten friends with you." And these girls would come. They'd drive from San Diego or Riverside just to hang out with a young, penniless rocker who basically said the same line to ten or twenty other girls. If you, and your band mates all did the same thing, you'd get a crowd, and another gig. Flyer and flirt, you had to be consistent.

SLASH We did that until we were such a huge draw that we didn't need to do that anymore. Then, those people that we used to give tickets out to expected to be on the guest list. So we ended up having a huge guest list for a gig at the Roxy, but we did make the promoters money.

STEVE DARROW Then you're going up the ladder. And eventually if you keep selling tickets and bringing in people, then they'll give you a headline slot on Monday or Tuesday which is still better than nothing, but it's still a Monday or Tuesday. After all that, you turn around and you've got four other new bands below you that are competing for your slot. It was a lot of work.

DUFF There was a lot of politics with the Troubadour. There was an older woman that ran the Troubadour and she could ban you. This woman was not somebody you would necessarily fuck with. You had to get on her good side. The Whisky was closed at that point and the only place for us to play on the strip was the Roxy and those gigs were few and far between. The Roxy gigs were legitimate gigs compared to the Troubadour, where you could always manage to get a spot -- maybe not a weekend night, but a Monday or Tuesday. At the Troubadour, we had to pay for lights and sound, which was a racket.

STEVE DARROW If you wanted to have a dressing room you had to pay another thirty bucks; if you wanted to use the light man you had to pay another thirty. It was like buying a car with all the secret add-ons that they don't tell you about. Essentially, the supply and demand was enough that clubs could get away with doing that.

SLASH In the early days we had our regular shenanigans as a band and were a little offensive to club owners. We definitely weren't invited back for gigs because they just had no viable reason to invite us back. It probably cost them money just to have us around. But we turned the tables on that eventually. We were starting to bring in a following, so they couldn't ignore us. **Eventually, we were accepted as being destructive, but profitable.**

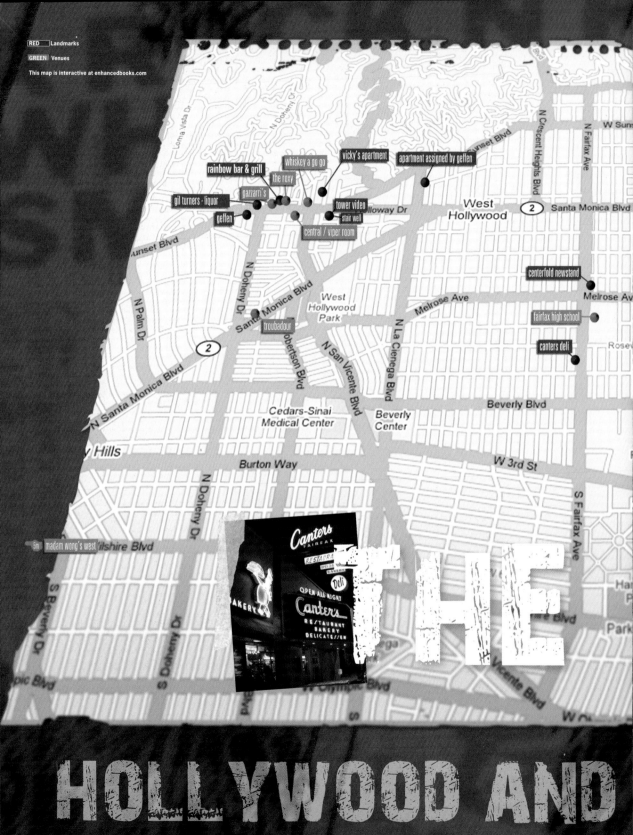

rainbow bar & grill

whiskey a go go

vicky's apartment

apartment assigned by geffen

the roxy

gazzarri's

gil turners - liquor

tower video

stair well

geffen

central / viper room

West
Hollywood

centerfold newstand

fairfax high school

canters deli

Santa Monica Blvd

N Crescent Heights Blvd

W Sunset

N Fairfax Ave

Melrose Ave

Rosew

Roseve

N Doheny Dr

Loma Vista Dr

loway Dr

Sunset Blvd

N Palm Dr

Santa Monica Blvd

N Doheny Dr

West
Hollywood
Park

troubadour

Robertson Blvd

N San Vicente Blvd

Melrose Ave

N La Cienega Blvd

Beverly Blvd

Beverly
Center

N Santa Monica Blvd

Cedars-Sinai
Medical Center

W 3rd St

y Hills

Hills

Burton Way

S Fairfax Ave

Har
P

Park

madam wong's west

S Beverly Dr

S Doheny Dr

ilshire Blvd

Blvd

ga

lvd

pic Blvd

W Olympic Blvd

Vicente Blvd

W

THE

HOLLYWOOD AND

raji's

Hollywood & Highland Center

fortress / programmers studio

club lingerie

Wood Blvd

Hollywood Blvd

Hollywood Blvd

W Sunset Blvd

W Sunset Blvd

N Gardner St

gardner studio

stardust

N La Brea Ave

N Highland Ave

N Gower St

Vine St

Fountain Ave

Plummer Park

hell house

2

shamrock studio

Hollywood Forever Memorial Park

mars studio 1.5m

st. andrews - .5m

pasha studio

Melrose Ave

Melrose Ave

N Rossmore Ave

Rosewood Ave

Beverly Blvd

Wilshire Country Club

Beverly Blvd

madam wong's east .5m

acific

l Park

N Gardner St

S La Brea Ave

S Rossmore Ave

S Wilton Pl

kfc - slash steals marc's bike

W 3rd St

Hancock Park

W 3rd St

JUNGLE

SUNSET BLVD

THE SUNSET STRIP

ROCKHARD ATTR.

PRESENTS

PLUS
SPECIAL
GUESTS

GUNS &
Showtim

Tickets Available at Tic
Box Office Day of Show
BROUGHT TO YOU
ATTRACT
PRODUCED BY VIC

GUNS 'N' ROSES
FRI. JUNE 28

STARDUST BALLROOM

AT SUNSET & WILTON

SHOWTIME: 8:00pm

THE UNFORGIVEN
THE JONESES

STARDUST
JUNE 28 1985

On a bill with four bands, GNR was billed at the bottom, which meant that they would go on first. This was the least desirable slot.

SET LIST:
Reckless
Shadow of Your Love
Jumpin' Jack Flash
Think About You
Move to the City
Don't Cry
Nice Boys
Back Off Bitch
Mama Kin
Anything Goes
Heartbreak Hotel

This was the first time the band performed their cover of "Mama Kin."

Slash sold most of the tickets to this gig himself which meant 50 tickets at $6 a piece.

AXL: *I would like to welcome everybody here. Were Guns N' Roses. And this is "Shadow of Your Love."*

AXL: *I would like to welcome Desi. This is "Jumpin' Jack Flash."*

AXL: *We got a show coming up on July 4th at Wong's East, and at the Troubadour, July 20th, with Jetboy and the Joneses. This is "Think About You."*

The sound system went out just before "Don't Cry."

SLASH: *(before playing "Don't Cry")* Yo, this place has cockroaches going through the PA system. I wanna thank everybody who forked out the money to buy tickets in advance, that was really cool.

AXL: This is a song for everybody that's got someone on their mind who just bugs the fuck out of them. This is "Back off Bitch."

AXL: Lets see if you know this one. "Anything Goes."

AXL: We would like to take a minute to introduce the band. On the guitar, Mr. Izzy Stradlin. On the bass guitar, Mr. Duff Rose. On the drums, Steven Adler. And on the guitar, Slash.

AXL: Last song people.

AXL: *(After "Heartbreak Hotel")* Thank you. Good fucking night.

THE FIRST BACKSTAGE SHOTS EVER TAKEN OF GUNS N' ROSES WERE ALL SHOT BY JACK LUE

Set List

Reckless

Shadow of Your Love

Jumpin' Jack

JULY 4TH 1985

MADAME WONG'S EAST

Very few people showed up for this show and the band was late going on.

SLASH: (after "Reckless") Man, you've got to get up to the front. You can't just fuckin' sit there. Move your asses.

Flash

Think About You

Move to the City

Don't Cry

Nice Boys

Back Off Bitch

Mama Kin

Anything Goes

Heartbreak Hotel

AXL: We can't see any of you people because of the lights. We don't know if you're there. We're Guns N' Roses. I'd like to thank everyone for coming down on this fuckin' Fourth of July.

IZZY: (After "Jumping Jack Flash) You like that, huh. Come up front and get fucked up with us.

AXL: This is a song dedicated to anybody that got tired of wherever the fuck they were and moved to a big city such as L.A. This is called, "Move to the City."

AXL: We've got a slow song for ya. This is for all the girls out here in the audience tonight. This is called, "Don't Cry Tonight."

AXL: You wanna rock n' roll? What was that? (announcing) "Nice Boys Don't Play Rock N' Roll."

AXL: Thanks a lot. Thanks for everybody coming down.

AXL: This is "Heartbreak Hotel."

SLASH: No.

AXL: Alright, this is the last song. We'll give you, "Anything Goes."

DUFF: Thanks a lot, good night.

AXL: Thank you.

Then they did "Heartbreak Hotel," but they had only gotten three quarters of the way through the song when the sound man cut the PA system. The band had already gone on long past their allotted time. But they wouldn't stop. They pulled together and finished the song without the PA system.

That was the last time the band played at Madame Wong's East.

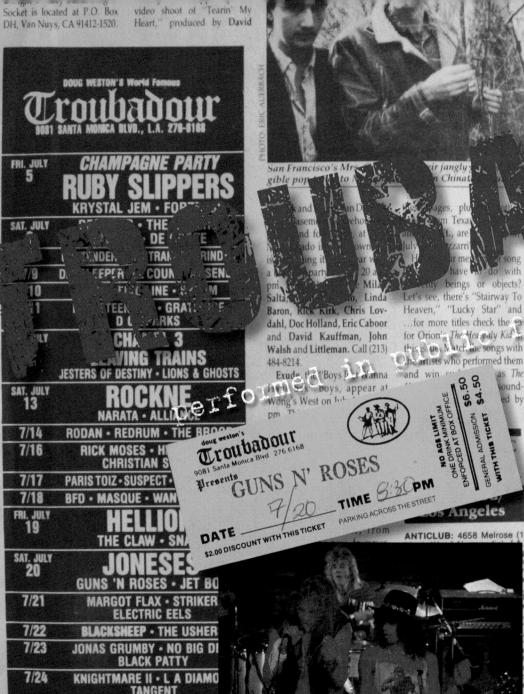

Socket is located at P.O. Box DH, Van Nuys, CA 91412-1520.
video shoot of 'Tearin' My Heart," produced by David

PHOTO: ERIC AUERBACH

DOUG WESTON'S World Famous
Troubadour
9081 SANTA MONICA BLVD., L.A. 276-6168

FRI. JULY 5	**CHAMPAGNE PARTY** **RUBY SLIPPERS** KRYSTAL JEM · FORT...
SAT. JULY	... · THE ... DE ... TENDER · TRAN... GRIND...
7/9	D... KEEPER · COUNT... SENE...
10	...F... LINE · ...UM
11	...TEEN... · GRAT... ...E D O... PARKS
...LY	**CHA... 3** ...AVING TRAINS JESTERS OF DESTINY · LIONS & GHOSTS
SAT. JULY 13	**ROCKNE** NARATA · ALLIA...
7/14	RODAN · REDRUM · THE BROO...
7/16	RICK MOSES · H... CHRISTIAN S...
7/17	PARIS TOIZ · SUSPECT · ...
7/18	BFD · MASQUE · WAN...
FRI. JULY 19	**HELLION** THE CLAW · SNA...
SAT. JULY 20	**JONESES** GUNS 'N ROSES · JET BO...
7/21	MARGOT FLAX · STRIKER... ELECTRIC EELS
7/22	BLACKSHEEP · THE USHER...
7/23	JONAS GRUMBY · NO BIG DI... BLACK PATTY
7/24	KNIGHTMARE II · L A DIAMO... TANGENT
7/25	ST. VALENTINE DEFIANT · DARK ANGEL
FRI. JULY 26	**ONEXCEL** NEON CROSS · FLASH BARRA...
SAT. JULY 27	**LEATHERWOL...** STIFF · LAAZ ROCKIT

UPCOMING: 8/2 HANS NAUGHTY 8/3 ABATTOIR
8/9 WARRANT 8/10 ANTIX

doug weston's
Troubadour
9081 Santa Monica Blvd 276-6168
Presents
GUNS N' ROSES

NO AGE LIMIT ONE DRINK MINIMUM ENFORCED AT BOX OFFICE

GENERAL ADMISSION $6.50
WITH THIS TICKET $4.50

DATE 7/20 TIME 8:30 PM

PARKING ACROSS THE STREET

$2.00 DISCOUNT WITH THIS TICKET

performed in public fo...

San Francisco's Mrs... ...eir jangly ...uin-gible pop... ...to M... ...in Chinat...

...k and ...an D... ...ages, plu... ...uth ...asemen... ...reholu... ...om Texa... ...nd fo... ...e, at ...am... ...ut., are ...ado i... ...own july ...zzarri... is ...ding it... ...ar wi... H... ...ir me... ...er song a ...ur party... 20 at ...have ... do with pm... Mila... ...ny beings or objects? Salta... ...o, Linda Let's see, there's "Stairway To Baron, Rick Kirk, Chris Lov- Heaven," "Lucky Star" and dahl, Doc Holland, Eric Caboor ...for more titles check the p... and David Kauffman, John for Orion? The Heavenly Kid? Io... Walsh and Littleman. Call (213) this is... Match... ...e songs with 484-8214. ...e artists who performed them and win ...u... ...as The Exude, the 'Boys ...wanna H... ...ound-...a... ...x boys, appear at ...d by Wong's West on ... pm T...

...os Angeles

ANTICLUB: 4658 Melrose (1...

Network to form Nasque. This new band also features drummer Ross Cristao, formerly with Thrust. Also in the lineup is guitarist Dale Fine. The band

Hollywood. (213) 413-9111. 7/6: Rick Spadoni, singer/guitarist, Pepe Hill, blues singer/guitarist, Lorin Paulsen, comedy, Don Mar, singer-songwriter/guitarist. 7/13: Ruth Hurtz, singer/songwriter, guitar/pi-

OUR

"Welcome to the Jungle" was the first time at this show.

SLASH: *"Welcome to the Jungle" is an introduction to Guns N' Roses. That's the first song where Axl wrote lyrics and helped me to write. I had the riff part of it.*

AXL: *I consider the song to be the most representative. I wrote the words in Seattle. It's a big city, but at the same time it's still a small city compared to L.A. It seemed a lot more rural up there. I just wrote how L.A. looked to me. If someone comes to town and they want to find something, they can find whatever they want.*

IZZY: *It's about Hollywood streets: true to life.*

Reprinted from Geffen Press Kit

SET LIST
Reckless
Shadow of Your Love
Welcome to the Jungle
Jumpin' Jack Flash
Think About You
Move to the City
Don't Cry
Nice Boys
Back Off Bitch
Mama Kin
Anything Goes
Heartbreak Hotel

PHOTO BY JACK LUE

PHOTO BY JACK LUE

PHOTO BY JACK LUE

Before the band went on, someone in the crowd yelled, "Fresh from detox!" This was in reference to the band's flyer for this show.

AXL: We're Guns N 'Roses, everybody!

The band tore into "Reckless." During "Nice Boys (Don't Play Rock N' Roll)" a stripper emerged from the audience, climbed on stage, and danced.

AXL: Was that a surprise? It was a surprise to me.

AXL: I wanna thank everybody for coming down here. We've got Jetboy and the Joneses coming on after this. This is an old song, "Jumping Jack Flash."

AXL: I wanna thank some people. I'd like to thank Marc Canter, Jack Lue, I'd like to thank Chris Amouroux. I'd like to thank Wendy and Fiona, and our roadcrew. And Barbie. Alright, this is "Don't Cry Tonight."

AXL: Take a moment to get some fuckin' air. You guys like Aerosmith? Do you really like Aerosmith? How 'bout some

FRESH FROM DETOX

Photo: Jack Lue

GUNS "N" ROSES
'Rehab Show' Sat. July 20
Troubadour
8:30PM
$2.00 off with this ad

For Band Info:
SASE to 9000 Sunset Blvd. Ste.405 W. Hollywood, CA 90069

80 JULY 26, 1985/BAM

first album Aerosmith? We got some "Mama Kin."

AXL: This is our theme song. You get to do anything you want, right? "Anything Goes."

AXL: (during "Anything Goes") I wanted to take a moment to introduce the members of the band. On this side of the stage, on the Les Paul, Mr. Izzy Stradlin. On bass guitar behind me, Mr. Michael Duff Rose. On the drums with the pretty face, Mr. Steven Adler, and on the guitar, to the left of the stage, the one and only, Slash.

AXL: We're Guns N' Roses.
Thank you. Goodnight.

SLASH: Thanks a fucking lot!

PHOTO: JACK LUE

GUNS'N'ROSES
SAT. JULY 20TH
TROUBADOUR 8:30
$2.00
OFF W/ -FLYER-
HAD ONE TOO MANY? DON'T STOP NOW, HAVE ANOTHER FOR TH

THE PICTURE FEATURED ON THE JULY 20TH FLYER WAS TAKEN BY JACK LUE. IT APPEARED ON THE BACK OF THE BAND'S FIRST RELEASE, THE EP "LIVE LIKE A SUICIDE," WHICH WAS RELEASED CHRISTMAS 1986. IT WAS TAKEN DURING A PHOTO SHOOT IN THE ALLEY BEHIND CANTER'S CELI A FEW WEEKS BEFORE THIS SHOW.

UCLA FRAT PARTY

SET LIST

Welcome to the Jungle
Move to the City
Jumpin' Jack Flash
Reckless
Think About You
Nice Boys
Back Off Bitch
Don't Cry
Mama Kin
Anything Goes
Heartbreak Hotel

The night after they played at the Troubadour, the band was asked to play this gig at a UCLA frat party with just a few hours notice. "Welcome to the Jungle" was played a few beats slower than the version that appeared on "Appetite for Destruction."

DUFF: I remember playing this frat party. We played for beer and thirty bucks. I don't remember how it came about. It was just a bizarre gig that we did and ended up having a great time cause there was a lot of beer. We were finding ourselves and finding our songs. Playing them for people under the gun helped the process of writing songs. But, we just wanted to play. We were a band. **That's what we were there for**.

THE SEANCE

JULY 26TH 1985

After this show Axl asked me if I would talk to Slash about not getting drunk before a show.

The lesson Axl learned was: don't play a show at 2:30am unless you want to playing with a totally bombed Slash. Slash's playing wasn't up to par that night and the show was plagued by technical and recreational-chemical problems!

SLASH: *We have a little bit of difficulty trying to get any kind of sound out of this fucking room. So bear with us.*

AXL: *Welcome to the fucking jungle.*

AXL: *Thank you everybody else for putting up with the tin can here.*

AXL: *What the fuck is going on with these drums. Alright, this is called, "Think About You."*

By the time the band played "Move to the City," the heat was awful.

AXL: *Alright, it's a fucking oven in here. While we're burning up, while everybody's burning up, we're gonna give you a slow number in here. This song is called "Don't Cry Tonight."*

AXL: *It's exactly 3 am. This song, is called -- I am gonna dedicate this to some recent situation -- this is called "Back of Bitch."*

Axl dedicated "Back Off Bitch" to Slash, evidently in annoyance at his extremely plastered state that night.

AXL (refering to "Anything Goes"): *It's kind of our theme song. The chorus goes, "four times my way, your way, anything goes tonight." Fucking if you feel like it, yell it any way you want to.*

After Mama Kin, Izzy started to play the intro to "Shadow of Your Love", but they ended up playing "Anything Goes," ending the show with "Heartbreak Hotel."

AXL: This is our last song, fuck this!

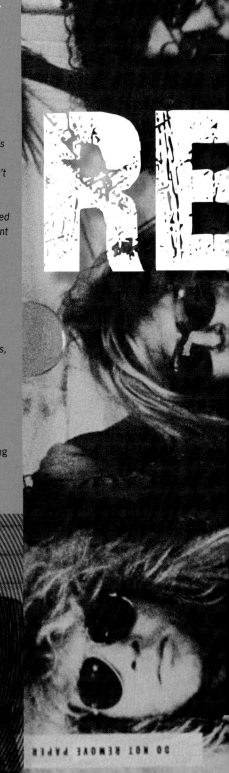

Improvised blues lines
Reckless
Shadow of Your Love
Welcome to the Jungle
Jumpin' Jack Flash
Think About You
Move to the City
Don't Cry
Nice Boys
Back Off Bitch
Mama Kin
Anything Goes
Heartbreak Hotel

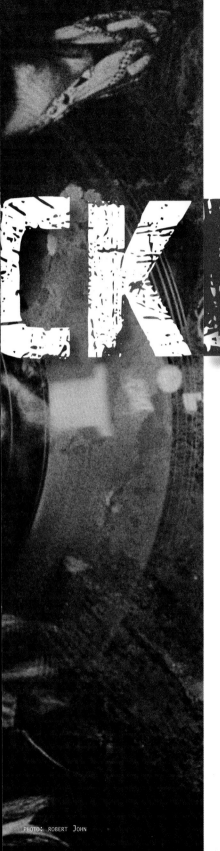

ALL FIVE OF US WENT TO THE SUNSET GRILL AND SPLIT A CHEESEBURGER— CUT INTO FIVE PIECES

STEVEN ADLER

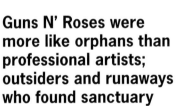

Guns N' Roses were more like orphans than professional artists; outsiders and runaways who found sanctuary in music. Riding on the edge of survival in Hollywood wasn't easy, but it was fun. They fended for themselves for baseline food and shelter on the streets and scraped together money from friends when they needed to fix their instruments. Axl slept underneath stairs behind his minimum wage job at Tower Video. Slash and Steven were lucky if they found a bed and fast food with occasional girlfriends. However, pastrami sandwiches were on the house at Canter's and the drugs and booze came free, since everybody wanted to party with the band.

To most people, the demand of that lifestyle is too much to handle; no predictability, all instinctual. But to Guns N' Roses and other musicians going for broke, it was precisely that impulsiveness, driven by the need to survive, that invigorated their lives and their music.

Survival literally meant making it to the next performance. Writing, rehearsing and performing; they were like children enthralled in play. The child, present to only his activity has no awareness of his need to eat, even when called to eat. Playing music was the source of their sustenance. Food or a place to sleep was just something that kept it going. The only thing that really mattered was music and having a good time.

They developed a tough spirit and a thick skin, letting nothing stop them from playing. Despite empty stomachs, hardcore hangovers and even broken bones, the show went on and they became better players by figuring out ways to play around their pain.

CHRIS TORRES I didn't have that. I was still in high school and here I was staying up until two or three in the morning with these guys and I was still trying to get my diploma. Making it as a singer was secondary for me. I was having a blast and living the life, but I just had other ideas. To me the attitude was Axl. I knew I didn't have it when I went to see Slash and the guys when they were living in the

You had to get a
job, as much as
everybody hated
doing that. My God.
Work? No way!
RON SCHNIEDER

Gardner apartment. They were sitting in this room where they rehearsed and they were pretty strung out on what seemed to be heroin. But, man, when they rehearsed it was just blood, sweat and tears and heart and I just saw the sacrifice it took. They lived for their music. When I saw that I knew I couldn't live like that. That's when I knew I didn't have it, even though I was still in a band. That's how raw and real they were. Their music represented the way they lived.

RON SCHNEIDER You had to live your life. You had to eat white bread and cheese sandwiches, or you'd have to go to the supermarket and steal food just to eat. You'd have to depend on a lot of people to help you get through just to survive. You had to get a job, as much as everybody hated doing that. My God! Work? No way! You borrowed money from people to help you make flyers. You had to do whatever it took. If you want to call it, "paying your dues," that's what we had to do to make it; to get the golden ticket. Then there were the Marc Canters out there that were feeding us or buying us guitar strings, picks or drum sticks.

MICHELLE YOUNG These five guys are homeless. They have nothing. They barely had any food. But they had this music, these instruments and a stage and that's all they needed. They were so secure in what they were doing and sure of themselves.

WILLIE BASSE We all wanted the same thing and we were willing to go to any length to get success in rock 'n' roll and I think if I could draw anything out of that period it would be that spirit and that heart that we all shared together. Everyone was going for it. It was like a do or die rock 'n' roll. All we cared about was music, packing the clubs and living that musical life. I don't think we realized it, but we were hardcore. There was no life but the music.

ROBERT JOHN The art and the music came first with this band, way before the party. They were serious about what they were doing. They were living the lifestyle, but it wasn't a style. They were creating it the way they were living.

SLASH We were all street kids. We were all, individually, very rebellious, so collectively we were a force to be

reckoned with. We had a haphazard way of going about things. The survival of early Guns N' Roses pretty much comprised of little hustling here and there, a lot of really nice girls, a couple of odd jobs and a drive to survive. It was always about the upcoming gig, so whatever you had to do to stay afloat until the next show, you did. We played as many back-to-back gigs as possible. It was really about just having somewhere to lay your head between shows.

PAMELA MANNING The guys were going through some hard times, mostly struggling to get by and going from place to place. They just needed somewhere to crash.

RON SCHNEIDER A couple of guys had girlfriends that took care of them. If you met a girl and she took you home and slept with you and fed you and maybe let you do your laundry or take a shower, you had it made.

STEVEN ADLER If we didn't have a place to sleep that night, we had the rehearsal place to sleep; cockroaches and all! We didn't care. That was it. That was all we wanted to do.

DESI CRAFT Izzy had it made. I had us in a single apartment. The rest of the band members, I can't say exactly what they were doing at night, but certainly it was a struggle. We kept all the gear in our apartment; a big stack of drums the guitars and everything.

SLASH One of us might be lucky enough to find a place to crash and the rest of us would hide behind the bushes. When they said yes, we'd come running out and the next thing you know all five of us would be in there and you'd have to put up with us. We did a lot of partying, since we stayed up all night. It wasn't so much about having a roof over our head, just someplace to go and party. There were a lot of girlfriends and you could find some peace and quiet with them for a second and then it was back on the street again.

Axl and I were being sought by the police for something that we didn't really do, so I asked Vicky if we could crash at her place. It was Vicky and Jennifer Hamilton in a one-bedroom apartment off of Sunset Boulevard and that's where Axl and I lived for a while. We were right across the street from the Whisky. Izzy, Duff and Steve were with their assorted girlfriends. Vicky was great; he was sort of like the- the big den mother.

VICKY HAMILTON Slash called me and said, "Do you mind if Axl sleeps on your couch for a couple of nights because something happened and the police are looking for him?" And I had just gotten a new apartment on Clark Street and I was a little bit hesitant to let him come stay, but I let him come and what was supposed to be a couple of days ended up being several months. Living with Guns N' Roses was probably the best time of my life and definitely the worst time of my life. The funniest part of living with was the fact that "Welcome to the Jungle" was on the answering machine and it played the part where Axl screams, "Welcome to the Jungle, you're going to die," and it just went off constantly, twenty four-seven. Even to this day when I hear that part of the song it makes me cringe. The police broke in my door a couple of times, shining flashlights into the bedroom to see what was going on. There were always a slew of groupies and people partying in my living room. I would barricade myself into one of the bedrooms in the apartment to get away from it.

STEVEN ADLER Axl and I got in a fight the day we moved out from Vicky's and destroyed her apartment, her furniture and the hallway. Axl threw me against this glass coffee table and fire extinguish and destroyed the

STEVE DARROW None of us really had a steady job at the time. I started this job working for the L.A. Weekly, which sounded more impressive than it was. I was basically the delivery guy with a '66 Dodge Van and I could haul a lot of newspapers. I'd deliver them all over Hollywood. So I did it a few times and then realized it was kind of a lot to do by myself. A lot of other delivery guys had kids helping them or they had assistants. So, I'd call up Izzy because he was always like looking for a way to make five bucks.

DUFF I worked phone sales for these Hungarian mafia guys. I was scared to quit that job because I was there since the first day that I moved to Hollywood. I stayed until the time we got signed. We were just making a go of it with the best situations we could create for ourselves.

MICHELLE YOUNG I used to get money and drugs and feed their habits. My dad would always give me money, so I would feed them and take care of them. I would show up and bring them cocaine or Quaaludes or whatever I had. What was mine was theirs. I gave them rides. I took Axl to a lot of shows because he didn't drive. I put them up at my house. I did basically what all the other girls did, except I wasn't a stripper. Our parents weren't around and our friends become our family. I knew what I was doing. I was supporting a good cause. I was helping support these guys because I believed in their music and I believed in them as individuals.

DESI CRAFT We were selling drugs to help support the band. One of our clients was Althea Flynt. That's

something that was tucked under the rug because her sister had always told us that if Larry ever found out who was selling her the heroin, he would kill them. I was always the one that had to go in the house to deliver the stuff because I was a female and it was less threatening, but it was very scary. I was eighteen-years-old, going into a huge mansion with security knowing there was a crazy nut in a wheel chair that's got nothing to lose but shoot somebody.

MIKE CLINK To see the band was to love the band because they were so energetic and so wild on stage. There was nothing that reckless that anyone had seen for years coming out of the L.A. scene or anywhere for that matter.

VICKY HAMILTON There was something sort of dangerous about their performance when you went to see them play live. You weren't really sure if you were going to end up in a riot or if Axl was going to jump off the stage and choke someone. They added a bit of danger to the mix, which is what the kids responded to. You didn't want to keep your eyes open, but you couldn't help but watch.

MARC CANTER Slash was like a monster; you could put two bottles of booze in him and put a blindfold around him and he would still come out and play his part perfectly. Slash played one show with a sprained left finger, a very important finger, and when I still listen to those shows, I realize that there is not one mistake. Whatever demons he may have had, he still managed to make it happen. You couldn't knock him down.

AXL & PHOTOGRAPHER ROBERT JOHN BACKSTAGE AFTER A SHOW AT THE TROUBADOUR ON FEBRUARY 28TH, 1986.

TROPIC CONCERTS AND
7 ELEVEN PRESENT

A SPECIAL EVENT FOR
JERRY'S KIDS

STARRING
POISON
RUBY SLIPPERS
THE JONESES
MARY POPPINZ
GUNS 'N' ROSES

AND VERY SPECIAL
CELEBRITY GUESTS

STARDUST BALLROOM
FRIDAY, AUGUST 30, 1985
BACKSTAGE PASS

Tropic Concerts &

7 ELEVEN

Present

POISON - JONESES - RUBY SLIPPERS
MARY POPPINS - GUN'S & ROSES
AND VERY SPECIAL GUEST!

A spectacular night of "GLITTER-GLAM and ROCK."
As Hollywood and "ROCK-n-ROLL" rally to show there
support with a special ∗ DRESS TO KILL PARTY ∗.

A very special event for

"JERRY'S   KIDS"

August 30, 1985

TICKETS
$10.00 AT DOOR

The New Hollywood Stardust Ballroom
5612 Sunset Boulevard, H
(One Block West of Western)

DOORS OPEN
7:00 P.M.

Among those in attendance were David Lee Roth and Bret Michaels from Poison.

The expression on Bret Michaels face was a mixture of awe and shame when Guns N' Roses did their cover of "American Band," as Poison had played the same song earlier that night in their own set. Axl also changed the lyrics a little near the end: "We're coming to your town, we're going to fuck around," instead of to "party down."

The usual sound problems cropped up:

SLASH: *(after "American Band")* I have no microphone and I have no monitor. Thanks.

STARDUST P.A.: *Ladies and Gentlemen, the new Hollywood Stardust Ballroom is now closed. Please exit out your doors.*

Despite this rather unambiguous announcement, the band started playing Heartbreak Hotel, which was interrupted in the middle of the song when the PA system was switched off.

It's worth noting that the band was actively trying to create their first demo tape at this time. A guy named Raz Cue, who was a backer of L.A. Guns, was helping to finance the demo. I kicked in the final $250 to finish the mix.

DIAMONDS IN THE ROUGH

Photo: Jack Lue

GUNS "N" ROSES

Saturday · August 31st

THE
ROXY
THEATRE

w / St. Valentine

For Band Info:
SASE to 9000 Sunset Blvd. Ste.405 W. Hollywood, CA 90069

AUGUST 31ST 1985

I ended up trying to sell seventeen tickets outside the club the night of the show, and by the time the band was scheduled to go on, I was offering tickets for less than the box office price. They were required to sell one hundred advance tickets for this gig, a considerable number to require of an opening band.

Reckless
Shadow of Your Love
Welcome to the Jungle
Jumpin' Jack Flash
Anything Goes
Heartbreak Hotel

The band was pleased at the turnout and they ended the set within their allotted time. They knew not to screw with the Roxy by trying to extend their set, as they had done at Madame Wong's East and at the Stardust, because it was a premier venue and they wanted to be able to play there again in the future.

DUFF: *Alright, lets do this.*

AXL: *This is "Shadow of Your Love."(after "Welcome to the Jungle") Thank you. Hey, I like this; a nice big fuckin' turnout in here. This is fucking happening. Alright, we're Guns N' Roses. We've got a show coming up September 20th, at the Troubadour. That's with Ruby Slippers, and September 28th at the Street Scene. A lot of people will be there; Poison. Alright, this is "Jumpin' Jack Flash."*

Axl dedicated "Welcome to the Jungle" to anybody moving out to L.A. Slash broke a string on the guitar he was playing, throwing it out of tune. He switched to his B.C. Rich Mockingbird -- the first real guitar he ever owned that he acquired in 1980. He broke a string on the Mockingbird too during Jumpin' Jack Flash," but the guitar remained in tune so he was able to finish the set with it.

SLASH: *Hold on man, we got a tune.*

DUFF: *We've only got 10 minutes, what song should we play.*

AXL: *You want to hear "Anything Goes?"*

SLASH: *Fucking make some noise.*

AXL: *(during "Anything Goes") I want to take a minute to introduce the members of the band. On the guitar, to my right, Mr. Izzy Stradlin. On the bass guitar, Mr. Duff Rose. On the drums, way back there, Mr. Steven Adler. And on the guitar to my left, the gentleman right here, this is Slash.*

DUFF: *(before "Heartbreak Hotel") This is it man, this is our last song, sorry about that. They cut us off short.*

AXL: Thank you very much guys. Rock n' roll, thank you. Goodnight.

Slash with his father, Tony Hudson, backstage after the Roxy show.

DOUG WESTON'S World Famous

Troubadour
9081 SANTA MONICA BLVD., L.A. 276-6168

FRI. SEPT. 6	**BROKEN HOMES** 7th GRADE
SAT. SEPT. 7	**ALISIN** **VOYEUR · LA GUNS**
9/8	SLAVEN · RED RUM DRUNKEN DOGS
9/9	ARSENIK · TRANCE TANK BURIAL
9/10	WORLD SITIZENZ · LOVE CULT HOPE
9/11	DREAM SUITE DETROIT · RAGGED LACE
9/12	GAUNTLET · VELOCITY
FRI. SEPT. 13	*BAD BOYS GIVE GOOD LUCK* **THE JONESES** MARY POPPINZ · PARIS TOYZ
SAT. SEPT. 14	**JADED LADY** NRG · ALLEY BRAT
9/15	AIRBOURNE
9/17	MICKEY KNIGHT HOLLYWOOD HOPSCOTCH SAMARIN
9/18	DAVID SWANSON & RTE. 66
9/19	**NETWORK** MYSTERY · ALIENS
FRI. SEPT. 20	**RUBY SLIPPERS** GUNS 'N' ROSES · SWEET REVENGE
SAT. SEPT. 21	*FAREWELL PARTY* **WITCH · SNAIR** RUFFIANS

UPCOMING: POISON IN ROCKTOBER

EVERY SUN. – THUR. AFTER 12AM
ALL DRINKS HALF PRICE — FRONT BAR ONLY
LADIES FREE EVERY TUES., HOT FOOD NIGHTLY.

doug weston's
Troubadour
9081 Santa Monica Blvd   276 6168
Presents

GUNS N' ROSES

DATE _Fri 9/20_   TIME _10_ PM

$2.00 DISCOUNT WITH THIS TICKET

PARKING ACROSS THE STREET

NO AGE LIMIT
ONE DRINK MINIMUM
ENFORCED AT BOX OFFICE

GENERAL ADMISSION $6.50
WITH THIS TICKET $4.50

"This isn't much, but it's the best I can do. This song is for Barbie. This is "Rocket Queen." —AXL

"Rocket Queen" was played for the first time at this gig and by the time of this show the band was attracting a "draw", audience members who had come specifically to see them.

TROUBADOUR MC: Are you tired of this bullshit? It's time to rock your asses off. Guns N' Roses!

The vibe was great that night. The band and the crowd were in the mood to party hard.

AXL: This next song, is an old mother-fucker by the Rolling Stones. I would like to introduce Desi, My dancing wonder. This is "Jumpin' Jack Flash."

SLASH: You guys gotta give me a break for a second. I gotta tune this fucker.

AXL: We gotta lot of dedications tonight, this song is called "Think About You." One of my best friends is here tonight. We got the Street Scene coming up next weekend going on early. I think it's the 28th at 5:30. There is a rock stage and a roll stage. We're on the roll.

IZZY: Thank you. Thank you very much. I love ya. This is called "Move to the City."

DUFF: Thanks a lot you guys, you're too cool.

SLASH: Alright, listen! I wanna take this time to dedicate a song to somebody. A little while ago, we had a show at the Stardust Ballroom. It was supposed to be a benefit. It was for a muscular dystrophy and somebody who ran the show took off with all the money. I wanna dedicate this song, to um... a girl, who was at the show, and was really disappointed about what happened. So this is something called "Don't Cry."

PHOTO: JACK LUE

AXL: *I wanna dedicate this song to the band Poison. This is called "Nice Boys Don't Play Rock N' Roll."*

AXL: *We're gonna take a small tuning break. We've got a brand new one for you. This isn't much, but it's the best I can do. This song is for Barbie. This is "Rocket Queen."*

IZZY: *You guys are alright.*

SLASH: *This is dedicated to the chosen few. You know who you are.*

AXL: *This is our last song people. We'll dedicate this one to the Troubadour. The only Heartbreak Hotel I know.*

STEVEN: *You guys are happening, give yourself a hand, and a beer.*

AXL: *Alright, the Troubadour. Thank you, goodnight. Street Scene next weekend. Rock N' Roll.*

IZZY: *You're great, I love you all.*

DUFF: *You guys want more?*

IZZY: *Hey hey, wait a minute. We've got time for one more. Well, it's alright, this is for you're mama, I think you know this one.*

DUFF: *What's that, "Mama Kin?"*

IZZY: *Alright, quit fuckin' around*

Reckless
Shadow of Your Love
Welcome to the Jungle
Jumpin' Jack Flash
Think About You
Move to the City
Don't Cry

PHOTO: JACK LUE

WELCOME TO THE JUNGLE

Guns 'n' Roses
Fri. Sept. 20 10 p.m.
Troubadour

PHOTO: JACK LUE

ROCKET QUEEN

They were beautiful,
they were into drugs and
they were naked.

MICHELLE YOUNG

ADRIANA DURGAN

KODAK PX 5062

CONTACT SHEET OF ADRIANA DURGAN FROM AN EARLY PHOTO SHOOT

PAMELA MANNING

Guns N' Roses and Hollywood strippers; the ultimate example of animal attraction and symbiotic relationships.

Serenaded by the music, charmed by the boys and always up for a party, the ladies loved hanging around their rock star boyfriends. For the band, Hollywood nightclub strippers were literally angels in disguise. These benefactresses brought in hard cash, held down apartments and had refrigerators full of food and beer, that is, before the guys arrived. Strippers bankrolled the band and their dream. Sex, drugs and a bed to sleep on, not to mention the occasional limousine after a gig, were all perks showered upon them by the goddesses of Sunset Strip.

They were not prostitutes or pushovers. They were fiercely independent, living on their own terms and earning their keep legitimately. For Guns N' Roses, the strippers acted as champions and cheerleaders, often helping them promote gigs and appearing on stage to liven up the act.

Together, they lived like the stars and starlets they imagined themselves to be and it was likely more real than the lifestyle they ultimately achieved.

ADRIANA SMITH We had the money because we had the bodies and we had the attitudes. We were the girl version of Guns N' Roses. If Guns N Roses had pussies, they would be us. We had a job that didn't require a lot of work. We got off in time to party and that's what we did. We were independent; we were wild; we were reckless and free. And we were young! We always had parties at our house. It was like a place you could take your clothes off and jump naked into our pool.

RON SCNEIDER It was like, wow! These chicks have money and money meant booze. I was called the "lame-broad taxi service." I had a car and I was able to take these chicks to work and pick them up, and they gave me money to do it. They were like my best friends. They loved me and I loved them. They also had apartments. Can you imagine these apartments full of teddy bears that are

hung by nooses in one corner with black 'X's made out of electrical tape on their eyes, a cat box that hasn't been changed in about a month, dishes in the sink with an empty Jim Beam collection and bottles littered all over their apartment thanks to their up and coming rock star boyfriends. We all loved to just hang at their places and jump off the balconies into the pool. And if you were fucking one of them, you'd get to sleep in the bed while everybody else had to sleep on the floor. That means you're not going to have to sleep on your guitar case or under your drum set or in somebody's car. You got in with the strippers and you got a place to crash. Hooking up with them was key.

ADRIAN AND ANOTHER STRIPPER BACKSTAGE

SLASH Strippers were our sustenance for the longest time. We crashed at the stripper's houses and that's where we got extra cash.

VICKY HAMILTON The girls were kind of like the nursemaids for these band guys. The guys were like lost puppies that you left at the vet. You wanted to feed them and help them. They were very generous with the band guys because they made a lot of money.

ADRIANA SMITH We didn't have sugar daddies with big credit cards, and we certainly weren't succumbing to the L.A. lifestyle by getting one who could take care of us. We didn't want that! We didn't want to owe anybody anything. We wanted to make our own existence, and even if we may have been a little sluttish, we weren't whores and we weren't charging money for sex. We were

just being ourselves. We were normal girls. And here come these broke-ass giant turkeys, but they were entertaining. We fuckin' loved those guys! It was unfortunate if you developed a crush on one of them, like me with Steven Adler for instance, because he broke my heart over and over again. They were our friends and they were our family.

DESI CRAFT I was a choreographer and used to dance on music videos, but I had to become an underage stripper. I had to get a false I.D. to keep the band afloat, to keep everything going. It was not really a pleasant experience, but I believed in the band. I believed in what I saw and what I heard. I would always dance to "Jumpin' Jack Flash" from the Rolling Stones, play tambourine and basically go-go dance. I had thigh-high leather boots, fishnet stockings, a little top and go-go girl clothes. When I came out, the crowd would push. I remember once we played this outside fair and the stages were not bolted down. When I got out on stage and took off my long leopard coat, you could feel the stage move, people pushing to get a closer look. It was pretty scary; we were about to be mobbed by 5,000 people. No bands had strippers as part of the act, but it turned out that it brought in flocks of people. People wanted posters of us. Then Axl started getting jealous because he wasn't getting all of the attention. It was quiet and experience. We were happy. I could have been a stupid, ignorant young girl but I wasn't. I knew what I wanted and I wanted to make the band succeed and stand by Izzy's side. I was in love with him.

RON SCHNEIDER It wasn't like we were taking advantage of anybody. They wanted to live that lifestyle as well.

VICKY HAMILTON As a manager, it was kind of interesting for me because I would start to get to know them on a first name basis. It was like, "Hey Lois, hey Barbie," and the bands would look at me like, "how do you know these girls?" I said, "Do you think you're the only band these girls have been hanging out with?" These girls would even go buy the bands limos to drive them to their gigs. It was just insanity.

PAMELA JACKSON The guys were good looking and they were fun to be around. They went to the extreme.

IZZY & ADRIANA

RON SCHNEIDER Eventually, they found their way onstage.

SLASH There were a couple of entertaining gimmicks that we came up to to liven up the show a little bit. We had the idea of having some strippers come up on stage and dance to "Rocket Queen" for a few gigs. They had good moves, these girls. Guns N' Roses was a rock n' roll band but it was a bright and lively kind of gig, and we would try to bring in sleazy elements that we felt comfortable with to sort of liven it up even more. So

that's what we felt comfortable with and people actually seemed to like that because it was sort of pushing the barriers for your average club band. Pamela was great. She was very enthusiastic and did a great job.

PAMELA JACKSON I was just a dancer and we were there to entertain, just like the band. We got real crazy. Axl was a good person to work with. He was just so out there when he sang; the way he would just get so into it. And then the band would just back him and get louder and louder. Then we'd start grooving to the music and before you knew it, the people were hollering, screaming. It was a lot of fun.

ADRIANA SMITH Somebody stole our costumes right before we were supposed to go on stage We went up and just put our t-shirts on and our underwear and Axl was trying to get me to put duct tape over my boobs, but I was too embarrassed. So we just got up there and danced.

ADRIANA

PAMELA Axl and I used to act like we were having sex onstage. We would start grinding, then he would start hollering and that always worked for the sex scene. I remember the crowd hollering and, of course, we wanted to get the crowd hollering more. We'd come over and make sure they would get hollering. We were the cheerleaders.

ADRIANA DURGAN I don't need to close the door on my past, but I need to give it a rose and make it beautiful because it really was. Those were the best, best days of my life. They were like young, innocent, days. I had no responsibility; none of us did. It was a beautiful time. It couldn't have been any better. I have my memories and my experiences from that time and, oh my, how lucky am I that I had those times. It's sad now that we're all so separated.

PAMELA MANNING

STEVE, GABY, SLASH AND ADRIANA

SLASH, DESI AND CLYDE
PHOTO COURTESY OF DESI

DESI

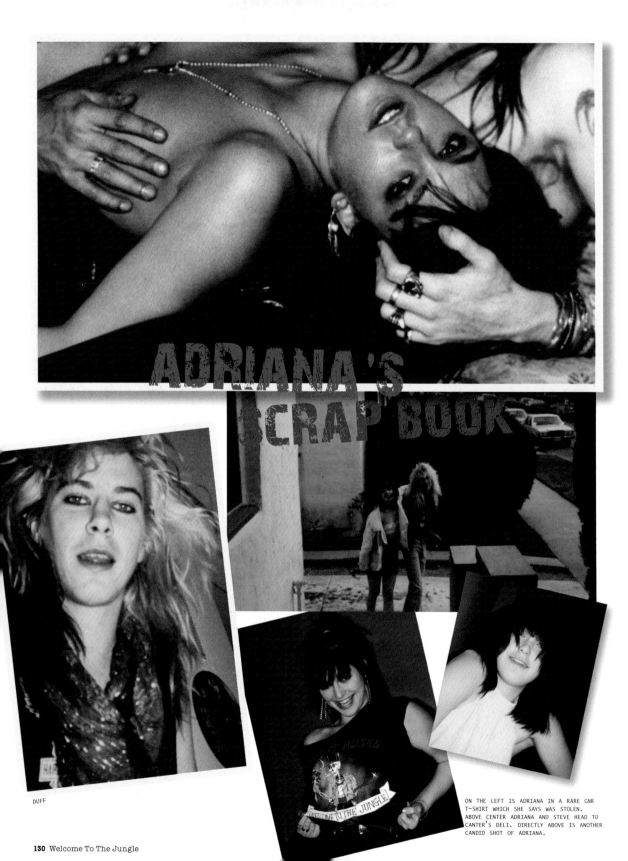

ADRIANA'S SCRAP BOOK

DUFF

ON THE LEFT IS ADRIANA IN A RARE GNR T-SHIRT WHICH SHE SAYS WAS STOLEN. ABOVE CENTER ADRIANA AND STEVE HEAD TO CANTER'S DELI. DIRECTLY ABOVE IS ANOTHER CANDID SHOT OF ADRIANA.

CLOCKWISE STARTING TOP LEFT: STEVE & ADRANA,
STEVE, ADRIANA AND STEVE, IZZY, MODEL SHOT OF
ADRIANA, AXL IN HOTEL ON PHONE WITH SLASH IN
FOREGROUND.

THE CENTER SHOT IS DUFF, STEVE AND MARILYN

8TH ANNUAL
LOS ANGELES
STREET SCENE
SEPTEMBER 28TH 1985

And you're a
Very sexy girl
You can taste the
bright lights
But you won't get there for free
In the jungle
Welcome to the jungle

This was an enormous free outdoor festival sponsored by the city of Los Angeles. Guns N' Roses were scheduled to play at 5:30pm, and the punk band Social Distortion was scheduled to play immediately after them.

The whole festival was running behind schedule and the punk natives were getting restless. Guns N' Roses didn't go on until 8:00pm, and although the punks, many of whom represented some of the harder core elements of L.A.'s punk culture, were still waiting for their band, most were won over by Guns N' Roses's rowdiness, even though some of them decided to spit at Slash. They began moshing and enjoying the show. The event was marked by some technical glitches.

SLASH: *We're Guns n' Roses*

DUFF: *This song's called "Reckless."*

AXL: *Alright, I wanna thank everyone for coming out to the Street Scene. We're glad we finally got to play. This song, is for L.A. This is called "Welcome to the Jungle."*

For half of that song, Slash had a bad guitar connection.

AXL: *Sorry about those technical difficulties. How many people here like the Rolling Stones? I wanna introduce Desi, our wonderful dancing girl, this is "Jumpin' Jack Flash."*

SLASH: *You're wonderful, I didn't even have to take a shower this morning.*

AXL: *This song is called "Shadow of Your Love." This is for all you rowdy mother fuckers out there.*

Reckless   Welcome to the Jungle   Jumpin' Jack Flash

hink About You   Shadow of Your Love   Heartbreak Hotel

This was the
loogie fest.
I stood on the side
of the stage where
the real fucking
loogie army was
for the whole show
and we spit on
each other.

SLASH

AXL: *"Heartbreak Hotel;" how many of you people like Elvis Presley?*

SLASH: *I know these guys in the front just love him. I bet you guys in the front are going to go home and jerk off about us tonight, aren't you?*

AXL: *Alright, this is "Heartbreak Hotel."*

SLASH: *We're playing the Country Club too, so fuckin save up you're saliva you fuck.*

AXL: We're playing the 18th at the Country Club, We're Guns N' Roses. Goodnight.

This is the first
public appearance of
Slash using a
Les Paul.

Purchased at
Guitars R Us, it was
originally owned
by Steve Hunter who
played with
Alice Cooper
and other big
name bands.

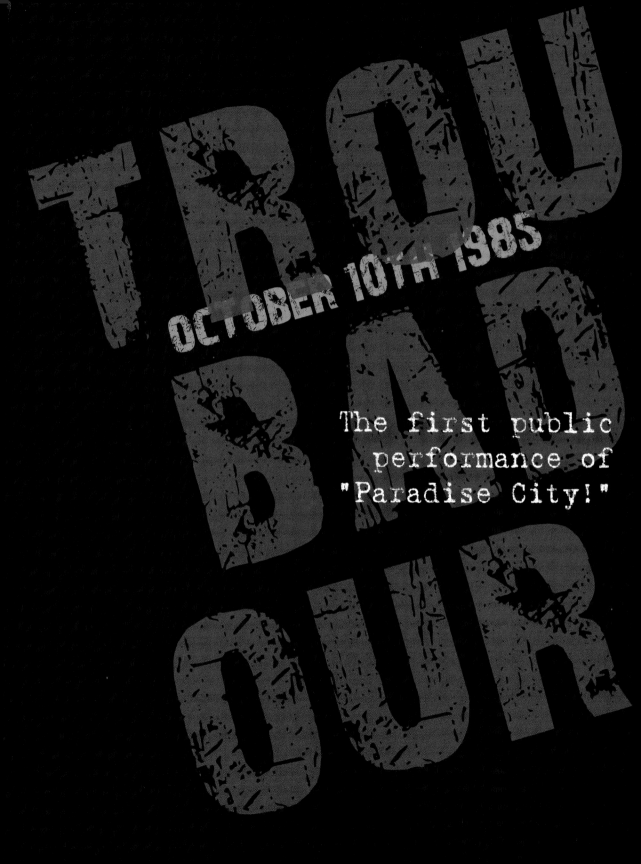

Take me down to
the paradise
city
Where the grass
is green
And the girls
are pretty
Take me home
Oh, won't you
please take
me home

This was a last minute gig;
GNR were asked to fill in
for L.A. Guns, who
had cancelled the
afternoon of
this Thursday
night
show.

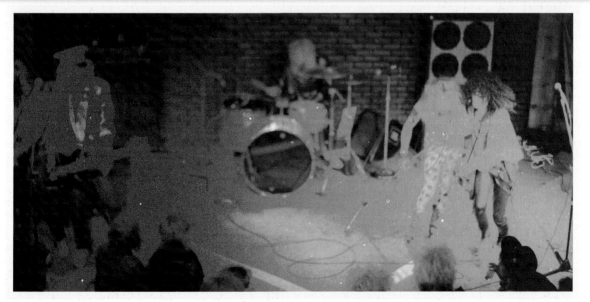

Anything Goes

Heartbreak Hotel

Mama Kin

(Take Me Home To)
Paradise City

this is a partial set
list of the last
4 songs played

PHOTO: JACK LUE

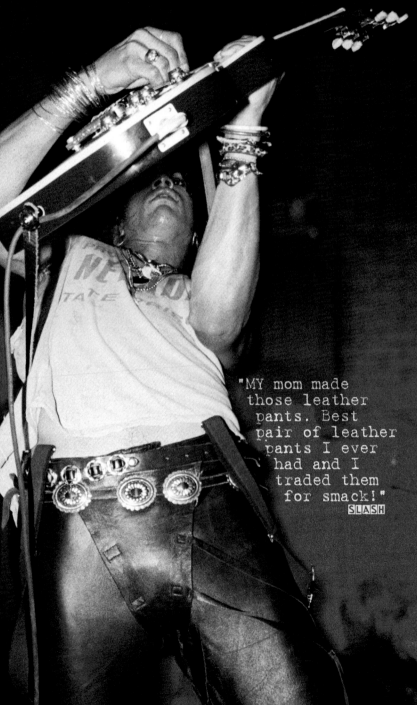

"Take Me Home to The Paradise City" as the song was called at first was brand new.

AXL: Thank you, this next song, is a brand new one, "Take Me Home to the Paradise City."

DUFF: We just wrote this one today so, hey hey.

SLASH: This song is about a half an hour old.

MARC The verse before "tell me who you're gonna believe" had different lyrics than eventually appeared on the album. On this song, Duff sang a lot of the leads toward the end, while Axl filled in the back-up vocals.

——————————————————

*DUFF: The chords to "Paradise City," I wrote the chords to that song when I first moved to L.A., when I didn't know anybody and was feeling a little down. So that kind of came out of reaching for something.

SLASH: The best songs we do, they're collaborations. The best way to do it is to have the whole band sit there and listen to everybody else's ideas, and put it all together to make something that everybody enjoys playing.

DUFF: If one person brings in a song to this band, it always gets raped by the other four people. It always gets changed around to where its Guns N' Roses as a group.

AXL: The verses are more about being in the jungle; the chorus is like being back in the mid-west or somewhere. It reminds me of when I was a little kid and just looked up at the blue sky and went, "wow, what is all this? It's so big out there." Everything was more innocent. There are parts of the song that have more of a down home feel. And when I started putting the overlays of my vocals (I put five tracks on there), it seemed that it came out like some Irish or Scottish heritage. One of the weird things is I had a feeling that it would go over good in Europe.

* Reprinted from Geffen Press Kit

"MY mom made those leather pants. Best pair of leather pants I ever had and I traded them for smack!"
SLASH

I'm a cold case that's
tough
you chair
by me somethin' to

I'll say you at another
time
to the end of
the line

Rags to riches
Or so they say
You gotta
Keep pushin' for the
fortune and fame
You know it's, it's all
a gamble
When it's just a game
You treat it like a
capitol crime
Everybody's doin' their
time
Strapped in the chair
of the city's gas

COUNTRY CLUB
OCTOBER 18TH 1985

The band was paid about $200 for the show. Four years later to the date, GNR played the first of four shows at the L.A. Coliseum opening for the Rolling Stones, for which they were paid $1 million.

Slash looked out at the sparse crowd and said "I can see a lot of people went to see AC/DC tonight."

HEADSHOT PHOTOS OF AXL BY JACK LUE

The band played a very long set at this sparsely attended show. The Country Club had a generous capacity of about 2,500, which was marred that night by water all over the stage.

Backstage, Axl told me "that water was fucked. In the beginning of the show the stage was covered with water. I was bustin' my ass hardcore!"

SLASH: I wanna dedicate this next song to the chosen few who are out there. Every single person knows what this song is about, and everybody who this song is about knows it's about them. This one's called "Back off Bitch."

Axl I'd like to dedicate this next song to a friend of mine that just got back from a long trip. This song is called "Rocket Queen."

The poster text reads:

WRECKLESS LIF[E]

Photo By: JACK LUE

GUNS N' ROSES

ALSO SAN FRANCISCOS' OWN

JETBOY

Fri. Oct. 18th, 10:00 P.M.
COUNTRY CLUB

GUNS N' ROSES — Info. Send S.A.S.E. to:
W. Sunset Blvd., Suite., 405, W. Hollywood, CA 90069
(213) 851-5761

JACK LUE BACKSTAGE WITH SLASH & STEVE

AXL: This is Elvis.

AXL: (after "Heartbreak Hotel") We're Guns N' Roses, October 31, Halloween, with Kery Doll. Thank you very much, good night.

AXL: Do you wanna here something else? You guys like Aerosmith, this song is called "Mama Kin."

AXL: This is a brand new one, this is called, take me home to the "Paradise City." I hope you like to get Funky.

AXL: (After "Paradise City") Thank you, goodnight.

Reckless
Shadow of Your Love
Welcome to the Jungle
Jumpin' Jack Flash
Think About You
Move to the City
Don't Cry
Nice Boys
Rocket Queen
Back Off Bitch
Anything Goes
Heartbreak Hotel
Mama Kin
Paradise City

VOICE
BOX

YOU'RE

The 1980's was the decade of flamboyant rock n' roll subgenres searching for a future. Hair metal, heavy metal, sleaze rock, punk rock, and glam metal were only a few derivatives of rock n' roll that spilled out of the Hollywood club scene at that time.

Although Guns N' Roses would balk at any attempt to be categorized, they modeled their music and fashioned their look from some influential bands that embodied characteristics known as Glam Rock. Teased hair, tight denim, spandex and headbands were all characteristics of glam rock that Guns N' Rose most resembled during the club days and Izzy directly modeled his look and sound after the Finnish group, Hanoi Rocks.

What distinguished Guns N' Roses from the other bands was their insistence that the music come first. Whereas many other bands at that time used their make-up and hedonistic lifestyle to attract a fan base, the music never reached beyond their particular subgenres. Guns N' Roses invigorated rock n' roll with a fusion of punk and blues that appealed to a wide spectrum of rock enthusiasts beyond the Sunset Strip. Punk rockers, metal heads and even fans of Top 40 pop embraced the band equally. They became the bridge to a next generation of rock n' roll artists from the breakthrough acts of the 1970's and 1980's like Led Zeppelin, Aerosmith and Van Halen.

MARC CANTER At that time, the music industry was pretty dead. There was new wave stuff, punk was finished, and hard rock was pretty much out. There was some heavy metal still around, but it wasn't really great. Ratt was the heavy metal band of the year. Aerosmith had just started to come back together but they hadn't put out record yet. I remember driving on Sunset Blvd.

in 1981 or 1982 and no matter what club you were near, punks were in the streets. If you went by Oki Dog on Santa Monica, fifty of them were there and you thought you were going to get attacked. Everybody made it look like they spent six hours dressing up their hair and they looked like they were going to kill you. And then they just disappeared a year later. Every last one of them was gone. The music died.

SLASH We were like the antithesis of what was going on in Hollywood at the time and we were sick to tears of the glam scene and sick to tears with everything that was happening in the 1980's like MTV and Tears for Fears. That gave us the motivation to hang on to what we did. When we arrived onto the L.A. scene, we kicked its ass in a way that nobody else was doing and people could relate to the honesty of the band. It was colorful enough and rough enough and honest and people from all different walks of life were into the band. We had people who were into different genres coming down to check us out, from punk to heavy metal and even new wave and glam people. We started a big buzz and became the biggest band in L.A. It was Poison and us and we hated Poison so that sort of fueled our fire too. We hated Poison so much that we just spent a lot of time touring around the different clubs in Los Angeles just to blow Poison's doors. There were a lot of variables as far what everybody in the band was interested in, but there was a common core: it had

> From the bum on the street to the uptight lady at the office, everybody could relate to their music.
>
> **MICHELLE YOUNG**

CRAZY

to be emotionally expressive. Whatever it was we were playing, it had to mean something. You had to feel it and that was just an unsaid rule. Being categorized, lumped into anything other than the wide-term of rock n' roll was a little too complicated and too knit-picky and it pigeon-holed us into a corner.

VICKY HAMILTON The persona the band took on just developed naturally and it never really changed. They always had an idea of who they were. Obviously, their styles changed a bit, but when I think about Slash; he hasn't changed since the day I met him.

DUFF We didn't feel like we were posers. We didn't feel like we belonged in L.A. to the scene that was going on at that time. I think that feeling was warranted when we would get gigs with punk rock bands and metal bands or nobody. We played Madame Wong's East, which was pretty much a punk rock club then.

RON SCHNEIDER All I can think of is big hair. That's what it was. There were no metal bands playing on the Sunset Strip anymore and Motley Crue, Ratt, Great White, Dokken, and a few others had just come out of L.A. These were all big hair bands with a big sound and a lot of make up. And Poison was another of those bands; wimpy rock with pretty looks.

They looked like girls. In fact, the guys that were handing out flyers for the gigs were prettier looking than most of the girls walking up and down the Sunset Strip. It was just pretty boys trying to be rock stars. GNR was the strongest of the bands that were up there on the Strip. They were considered a glam band because Axl teased his hair, Duff teased

his hair, and some of them were wearing make-up, but the music was heavy and that gave them credibility and balls. They were strong, while every band around was weak.

MICHELLE YOUNG They didn't have to dress in these glam clothes, wear all this make-up or tease their hair. They weren't

So they did what they believed in their hearts was the right thing to do, whether they were going to make it or not.

MARC CANTER

into wearing lipstick and pantyhose and looking the same to promote the band. Granted, they did that when they were on stage but they didn't walk around like that. They walked around with flat hair, duct tape on their boots, duct tape on their pants, ripped jeans and whatever they could put on their bodies.

MARC CANTER So the music industry just needed a big kick in the ass and here come these guys that were here to say, "This is what we're going to do. We were influenced by '60s and '70s music and we're going to do our own version of that. It's what we want to do, not what we think is the fad right now." So they did what they believed in their hearts was the right thing to do, whether they were going to make it or not. It was the music they believed in. And anyone that came to those shows saw that, and felt that, and liked that for what it was. Some bands may have had the look, but they didn't have the sound and they didn't have the songwriting ability. Guns N' Roses was the perfect mix of everything that made

you feel good when you heard it. All five guys were just tearing it up.

ROBERT JOHN With Guns N' Roses, it was just raw talent. They're the only band I've ever seen that wasn't contrived step by step all the way. Is there natural raw talent? Is it a lifestyle? If somebody's got raw talent, they usually can go somewhere with it. These guys did what they did when they wanted to do it and it worked.

DUFF We knew we had the band. This was going to be the band that we had all starved for. This was the band that we had all gone through our separate musical journeys to get to. The music we were writing was absolutely the most important thing and we were thinking of great bands with great lineage like Led Zeppelin.

MICHELLE YOUNG From the bum on the street to the uptight lady at the office, everybody could relate to their music.

FRESH BLOOD

Look out, world! From the sleazy, slimy depths of Hollywood's backstreets crawl Guns and Roses, one bunch'a jokin' no b.s who play unclustered, ballcrushing, (sit) Zeppelin-style rock 'n' roll. With dual guitars, screeching Steve Harris-like vocals and thunderous drumming, these guys are the epitome of young, snotty rock stars. Being bad is a rush," says lead singer Axl Rose. "One time his hippie chick wandered into our studio and started messing with our equipment. She eventually wound up running down Sunset Boulevard in L.A. naked, all dingy, didn't even know her name. The firemen and the cops all came down on us for that." Well, they may have beat the rope rap, but now they're in London recording their hot new vinyl debut for Geffen records-even though these rangdoin party boys just completed a 37-song, two-track recording in just four days. And hey, don't expect any wimpy, limp-wristed love songs either. "This one girl f**ed the whole band, friends of the band, the band next door." Axl says sentimentally. "And two days later she says to me, 'Axl, I'm trying star child.'"

So if you wanna have your brain pulverized like a tiny grape being smashed between Dolly Parton's massive mammaries, you oughta check out Guns and Roses when they come to evade your hometown—but be forewarned, keep the young women at home.

AN EARLY PHOTO SHOOT

In October 1985, the band gathered before Jack Lue's camera again and he shot a series of black and white and a series in color.

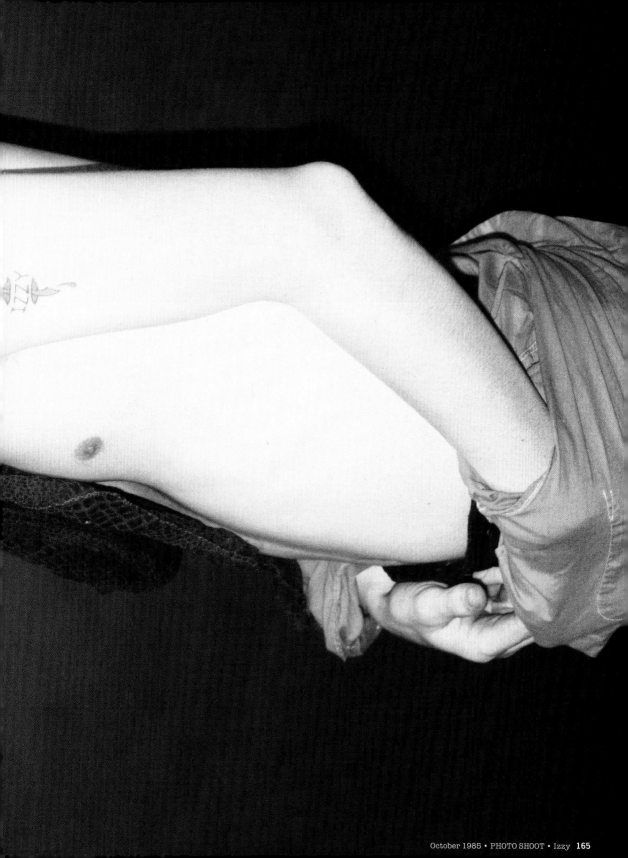

THE REAL "SPAGHETTI INCIDENT?"

GUNS 'N' ROSES w/ DOLL

RADIO CITY

OCT 31, 10:00 PM

HALLOWEEN EVE

NIGHTBEAT

Though all five members of Guns 'N Roses were injured in a recent car crash, they've vowed not to cancel any club dates. The band (pictured here previous to the crash—we think) will play at Radio City October 31 with Doll

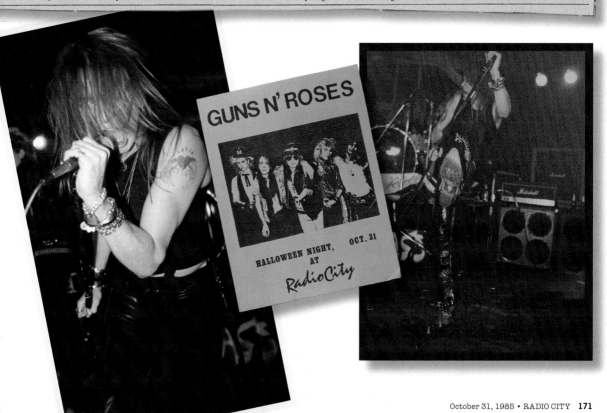

GUNS N' ROSES

HALLOWEEN NIGHT, OCT. 31
AT
Radio City

Reckless
Shadow of Your Love
Welcome to the Jungle
Jumpin' Jack Flash
Think About You
Move to the City
Don't Cry
Nice Boys
Rocket Queen
Heartbreak Hotel

HALLOWEEN NIGHT
DESI, KITTEN WITH A WIP
PHOTO JACK LUE

Once again, the band wrangled with club personnel on this Halloween night gig down in Aneheim, home of Disneyland. This was the same club I had taken Slash to audition for Poison about a year earlier.

IZZY: *What's happening Orange County? Huh.*

DUFF: *We're Guns N' Roses, if you don't already know. This one's called "Reckless."*

AXL: *This next song, I'd like to introduce Desi up here, our dancer. This one's called "Jumpin' Jack Flash"*

AXL: *We gotta "Move to the City."*

AXL: *We're Guns N' Roses. I'd like to thank everybody for coming down here on Halloween fucking night. Happy fucking Halloween. Our next show is going to be at the Troubadour on the 26th with Kix, from New York, and Feline, November 22nd. Alright, this song is called "Don't Cry."*

The main point of contention was the usual sore spot – hassles about continuing their set after the soundman saw fit to cut off the sound.

MC *(signaling one more from the booth):* One more!

AXL: *What's this one more shit. This song is called "Rocket Queen."*

AXL: *Alright, the sound man is having a fit. What do you say?*

DUFF: *We've got one more.*

Taped music was still playing in the background and about a minute went by with the band still on the stage reusing to leave. Finally, the taped music stopped and the band played "Heartbreak Hotel."

AXL: *This mother fucker is called "Heartbreak Hotel."*

AXL: *(After Heartbreak Hotel) Guns N' Roses, November 22nd at the Troubadour with Kix and Feline. I hope you all can make it, thank you for coming down.*

The club made a video of their performance and offered it to the band as a substitute for their pay. Slash, who handled band business, insisted on the cash.

Radio City burned down soon after this show.

PHOTO JACK LUE

PHOTO TAKEN BACKSTAGE AS THE BAND PREPARED TO PERFORM LIVE

TROUBADOUR
NOVEMBER 22ND 1985

This show marked Guns
N' Roses first sold out
performance.

Steven's bass drum pedal broke when the band started to play "Mama Kin" and they simply stopped playing for a moment while Axl told the audience about a temporary delay due to technical difficulties. Izzy started playing a rhythm with Slash supplying some lead licks. Axl told the crowd the half-finished song was called, "Indiana Ain't My Kind of Town" and provided some vocals, some of which were improvised on the spot. Still, without a bass pedal, the band kicked out "Heartbreak Hotel" before leaving the stage.

Axl was obviously pleased at the great turnout: he was enthusiastic and energetic throughout the show, thanking the audience for coming out.

AXL: *We've got a lot of fucking people here tonight. We're Guns N' Fucking Roses.*

AXL: *Hollywood, this is the drug capital of the fucking world. "Welcome to the Jungle."*

AXL: *I'd like to thank everybody for showing up here. If you've been to a Guns N' Roses show, you know what's next. I'd like to introduce dancing Desi. This is a Rolling Stone's song known as "Jumpin' Jack Flash."*

AXL: *We're gonna have a party tonight at (announces the address). This is called "Move to the City."*

AXL: We'd like to make a special thanks to Marc Canter, for the overabundance of fuckin' help he has been. *This song is called "Don't Cry."*

I had just covered the $250 cost of the Guns N' Roses banner designed by Slash, which made its debut at this show.

AXL: *This is dedicated to everybody that thinks this band has a bad attitude. This is called "Nice Boys Don't Play Rock N' Roll."*

AXL: *This is a real pretty tune. For everybody out there that has somebody,*

In keeping with the stripper act on stage, Barbi, a friend of Axl's, danced to Rocket Queen, which had been written for her and about her.

who won't fucking leave them alone, who bugs you a little too much, this song is called, "Back Off Bitch."

AXL: We've got a cover tune for ya'. I think you people like Aerosmith. How 'bout a little taste of some "Mama Kin."

AXL: We've got a temporary delay due to technical difficulties.

Vicky Hamilton came to this show and was so impressed at their performance and their great appeal to the club – they sold out their first headliner show – that she offered her services as their manager. She was experienced at managing unknown bands and had a great track record. She was partly responsible for turning around the fledgling careers of such major bands as Motley Crue, Poison, Stryper and others. Slash had met her about a year earlier when he auditioned for Poison, whom she was still managing at the time. Even though Slash decided he wasn't interested in joining Poison, he considered Vickie a very cool person and knew she was a real player in the Hollywood club scene.

The band met with Vicky and decided to hire her as their manager. Prior to Vicky, a woman named Bridgette that managed the band Jetboy, with whom Guns N' Roses played a number of gigs, manged the band for a brief period of time. But, she wasn't accomplishing much on their behalf and Guns N' Roses ended the relationship. Vicky, on the other hand, had excellent connections for getting and promoting gigs. Her task was to make sure their shows looked and sounded good and, above all, made money. The band believed Vicky's forte was grooming club bands, but realized that if they got signed, she woulnd't be able to manage them at that point. Coincidentally, the label that eventually signed the band, hired her as a A&R scout.

VICKY HAMILTON It seemed like managing Guns N' Roses was a natural progression to what I was doing. I had just gone through something pretty gnarly with Poison, so I had to think about getting involved at that level again with a band.

I was very much in the mix with the A&R people at that time. I shopped Poison, I worked with Motley Crue and Striper, so I was very familiar with the A&R people that were signing those types of bands. I booked some shows for Guns N' Roses at the Roxy and the Stardust Ballroom and I helped them facilitate the Troubadour shows. I kind of brought a higher quality of gig to the band. Guns N' Roses was unique to that time period and very exciting to me.

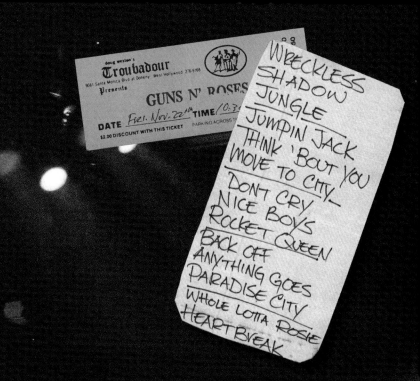

WRECKLESS
SHADOW
JUNGLE
JUMPIN JACK
THINK 'BOUT YOU
MOVE TO CITY —
DON'T CRY
NICE BOYS
ROCKET QUEEN
BACK OFF
ANYTHING GOES
PARADISE CITY
WHOLE LOTTA ROSIE
HEARTBREAK

MUSIC MACHINE
DECEMBER 20TH 1985

Nightrain was performed publicly for the first time that night.

The band debuted a new tune, "Nightrain" that night, with almost everyone in the band contributing to the introduction:

MC: Ladies and Gentleman, please welcome, Guns N' Roses.

DUFF: Alright!

AXL: We're Guns N' Roses, and this is "Shadow of your Love."

AXL: Down here on Pico, in the middle of nowhere. Welcome everybody to the show and "Welcome to the Jungle."

SLASH: Alright, this is a new one that we have, that we pinned at sound check today. This one is called "Nightrain."

IZZY: It's about that cheep shit that everybody drinks.

DUFF: It's a famous past time.

AXL: This song is dedicated to anybody who even resembles an alcoholic. This whole show is dedicated to Debbie.

Axl played harmonica on the intro to Nightrain, which was played much slower than it would be later recorded. The song was still being written, so not all the lyrics that eventually made their way onto the album were sung that night.

AXL: We've got a Troubadour show coming up January 4th with Feline, and we've got another special guest and a show coming up on the 18th at the Roxy, with none other than L.A. Guns. These shows are all dedicated to "Moving to the City."

AXL: I think a lot of you know this song. Ok, this is a special birthday song, for Debbie. This song is called "Don't Cry."

AXL: This song is dedicated to Budweiser. "Nice Boys Don't Play Rock N' Roll."

AXL: Is that something you like to hear. We're gonna lay out some "Mama Kin" for ya.

MC (after "Mama Kin"): Last song.

Several people in the crowd called for "Back Off Bitch!"

DUFF: This is "Paradise City."

By the time of this show the band had "Paradise City" down really tight and that night the song sounded like it had really come together. It would become the band's favorite song with which to close a show.

AXL: (after "Paradise City") Thank you. Goodnight. January 4th at the Troubadour, January 18th, with L.A. Guns at the Roxy.

SLASH I remember; it was, Izzy, Axl, Steven and I walking around Hollywood and we started singing Nightrain and came up with the chorus. We put the song together in a couple days and it became the war cry for the band. Nightrain is immortalized by the actual song, but at the time the song was written, that's all we could afford to drink. We'd get bottles of Nightrain with the few pennies we had and go carousing Hollywood and the Strip. It became a way of life for the band during that period.

RON SCHNEIDER Nightrain was the cheapest, nastiest bottle of wine you could buy. If you had two dollars, you got a bottle of Nightrain. The hangover you would get from that, oh my. You'd drink this one little bottle and you're flying. Then you're throwing up and you're sick as a dog the next day, all day long, going "Oh my God! Why did I do this?" It was a good cheap buzz. That's why all the winos on Skid Row still drink it. I can still taste that shit in my mouth. There was a liquor store right around the corner from the Gardner Street studio that sold Nightrain. There were actually two bands in that location. It was Guns N' Roses in the little room and next to them was Johnny and the Jaguars. It would either be up to us or up to them. We could never afford fifths of Jim Beam or Jack Daniels, just Nightrain.

SLASH Nightrain was the commercially available, tangible product that we could afford at our expense. The other stuff was a little more complicated, but Nightrain was just a simple beverage that we could get with very little money and in great quantity and live on. I think at the time, since we couldn't afford booze and food, it had enough supplements that we could survive on it alone.

*STEVEN: *Great rhythm. "Nightrain" just rocks. Personally, I like the guitar solo in it. I like that part of the song because me and Duff are rockin'. Has more feel to it than just a machine.*

SLASH: *"Nightrain" is just like "Welcome to the Jungle;" it's very indicative of what the band's all about. I remember when it first came together, we'd hitchhiked to the Rainbow and were walking down to the Troubadour and we just started yelling "Nightrain," because we were drinking it.*

AXL: *It's a dollar a bottle, nineteen percent alcohol. Drink a quart of it and you'll blackout.*

IZZY: *We were hanging out at the Troubadour, but it was dead and we just started walking back up to the strip just singing along.*

DUFF: *We were living in the Gardner Street studio, this place where we had one little box of a room. We had no money, but we could dig up a buck to go down to this liquor store where they sold this great wine called Nightrain that would fuck you up for a dollar. Five dollars and you'd be gone. We lived off this stuff.*

SLASH: *It's nothing to do with being a hobo and stealing the midnight train. It's more about the attitude and describing how you feel when you're on it. You feel invincible.*

* *Reprinted from Geffen Press Kit*

We
walkir
levard,
and
out
down t
drin
all
It was
cents f
was all

TROUBADOUR

GUNS N' ROSES

"My Michelle" was performed at this show for the first time and the buzz around GNR was growing loud and clear!

WRECKLESS
SHADOW
JUNGLE

JUMPIN JACK
THINK BOUT YOU
MOVE TO CITY

DON'T CRY
NICE BOYS
BACK OFF

ROCKET QUEEN
NIGHT TRAIN
MICHELE
PAVADISE

ANYTHING GOES

MA KIN
HEARTBREAK

COURTESY
CARRIE SMALL-LASKAVY

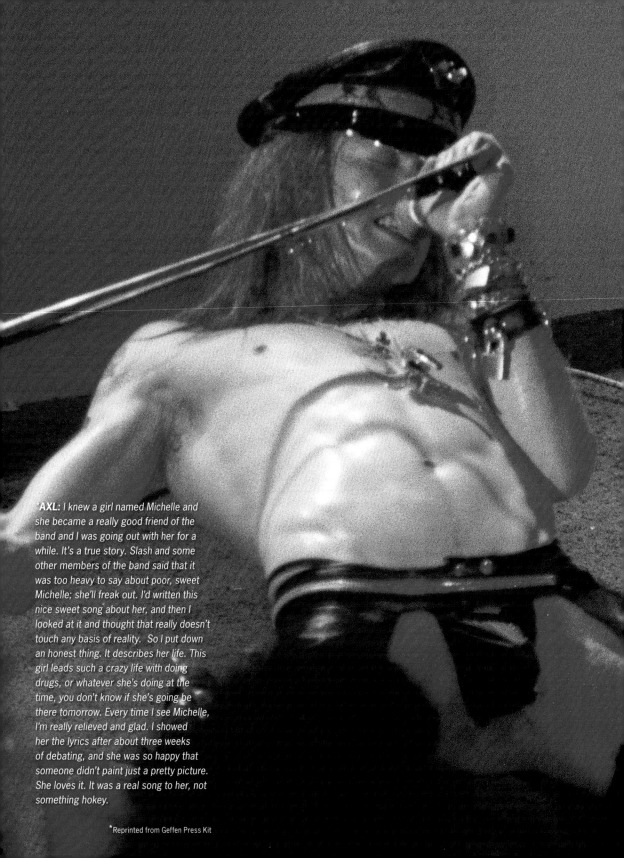

AXL: I knew a girl named Michelle and she became a really good friend of the band and I was going out with her for a while. It's a true story. Slash and some other members of the band said that it was too heavy to say about poor, sweet Michelle; she'll freak out. I'd written this nice sweet song about her, and then I looked at it and thought that really doesn't touch any basis of reality. So I put down an honest thing. It describes her life. This girl leads such a crazy life with doing drugs, or whatever she's doing at the time, you don't know if she's going be there tomorrow. Every time I see Michelle, I'm really relieved and glad. I showed her the lyrics after about three weeks of debating, and she was so happy that someone didn't paint just a pretty picture. She loves it. It was a real song to her, not something hokey.

*Reprinted from Geffen Press Kit

Los Angeles club audiences are notorious for their blasé, undemonstrative attitude.

So when a band appears on the scene and not only begins to attract its own following, but excites club audiences into audible and visible displays of enthusiasm, word begins to get around.

A buzz is born. That is when the guys in suits – the record label guys with the money – start checking things out. The buzz around Guns N' Roses was growing loud and clear around this time.

The band's devotion to good ol' sex n' drugs n' rock n' roll was in ample evidence that night.

SLASH: *Alright, we're gonna do a couple new ones for you. We're gonna start out*

with something called "Rocket Queen," not bad for the fuckin' Troubadour.

AXL: *Alright, this next one is brand new. It's dedicated to alcoholics anonymous. You buy it in your fuckin' liquor stores. It is nineteen percent alcohol and it's called Nightrain.*

SLASH: *We get horny when we're drunk. We start squeezing chicks tits. Well, this is for you. Can I get a fuckin' drink?*

Photo: Robert John/Zimparelli Prods.

GUNS N' ROSES

SAT. JAN. 4 11PM

doug weston's world famous

Troubadour

$2.00 Off With This Ad
"Get Yourself Together, Drink Till You Drop, Forget About Tomorrow, & Have Another Shot"

HAPPY NEW YEAR!
From the boys who brought you the most chaotic shows of 1985.

ALSO APPEARING FRI. DEC. 20 MUSIC MACHINE

For show info send S.A.S.E. to:
Guns N' Roses, 9000 Sunset Blvd., Suite 405, Hollywood, CA 90069

ALSO APPEARING SAT. JAN. 18 THE ROXY

Special Thanks To Marc Canter

JANUARY 1, 1986/BAM 43

doug weston's **Troubadour**
9081 Santa Monica Blvd at Doheny West Hollywood 276-6168

Presents **GUNS N' ROSES**

DATE JAN 4 1986
$2.00 DISCOUNT WITH THIS TICKET

TIME 11 PM
PARKING ACROSS THE STREET

NO AGE LIMIT
ONE DRINK MINIMUM
ENFORCED AT BOX OFFICE

GENERAL ADMISSION $6.50
WITH THIS TICKET $4.50

Troubadour

SLASH: *Make some fucking noise. Not bad for the fucking Troubadour, ha!*

AXL: *This song is for Michelle Young; this song is called "Michelle."*

There were some differences in how the band performed the song that night as compared with the version that would appear on the album. The lyrics in the first few verses – up until the first chorus – were sung with a softer voice, but the music was still the same speed. The lead was the same as it would be on the record. All in all, the song, unfinished as it was, went over well.

MICHELLE YOUNG The song isn't so flattering, but that whole process at that time in my life was awesome. I thought, "Oh my God, this is great," but then there are ramifications of having a song written about you. I know in my heart I'm part of the history. I lived it with them and I'm glad that I did. I'm here and I survived it

Your daddy works
          in porno
Now that mommy's
          not around
She used to love
          her heroine
But now she's
          underground
So you stay out late at
          night
And you do your coke
          for free
Drivin' your friends
          crazy
With your life's
          insanity

along with many others. I would prefer if people didn't know that song was about me, especially since I have a pretty high-powered job and I'm a mom. I meet the occasional person who knows that I'm that person and they'll introduce me and say, "Guess who this is."

Axl announced that "Anything Goes" would be the last song, but the crowd would not be satisfied.

AXL: *Alright, this is our last song, we're gonna do "Anything Goes."*

DUFF: *This one's about your mama.*

SLASH: *Alright, listen, we're gonna do a song real quick before we split, that we left out of the set earlier. It's called "Paradise City."*

SLASH: Alright, man, this is it. We're leaving. Alright Fuckers, "Heartbreak Hotel." I'm sure you all know this one.

THE ROXY
JANUARY 18TH 1986

By now the band was selling out L.A.'s premier clubs. This show at the Roxy, in fact, attracted a far-over-capacity crowd, and Tom Zutaut, the Geffen A&R guy who eventually signed them, arrived late and wasn't able to get in until their set was over.

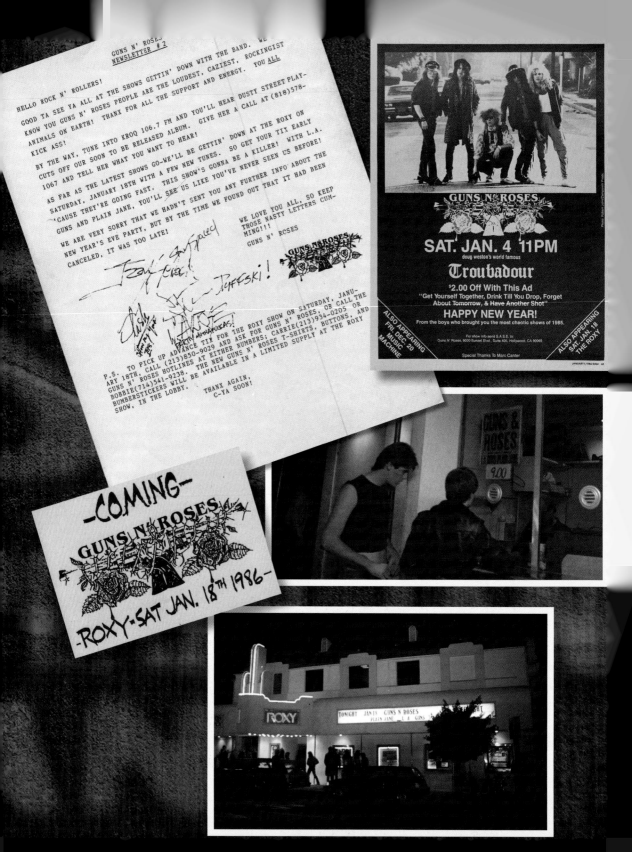

GUNS N' ROSES
NEWSLETTER #2

HELLO ROCK N' ROLLERS!

GOOD TA SEE YA ALL AT THE SHOWS GETTIN' DOWN WITH THE BAND. WE KNOW YOU GUNS N' ROSES PEOPLE ARE THE LOUDEST, CAZIEST, ROCKINGIST ANIMALS ON EARTH! THANX FOR ALL THE SUPPORT AND ENERGY. YOU ALL KICK ASS!

BY THE WAY, TUNE INTO KROQ 106.7 FM AND YOU'LL HEAR DUSTY STREET PLAY- CUTS OFF OUR SOON TO BE RELEASED ALBUM. GIVE HER A CALL AT (818)578-1067 AND TELL HER WHAT YOU WANT TO HEAR!

AS FAR AS THE LATEST SHOWS GO-WE'LL BE GETTIN' DOWN AT THE ROXY ON SATURDAY, JANUARY 18TH WITH A FEW NEW TUNES. SO GET YOUR TIX EARLY 'CAUSE THEY'RE GOING FAST. THIS SHOW'S GONNA BE A KILLER! WITH L.A. GUNS AND PLAIN JANE, YOU'LL SEE US LIKE YOU'VE NEVER SEEN US BEFORE!

WE ARE VERY SORRY THAT WE HADN'T SENT YOU ANY FURTHER INFO ABOUT THE NEW YEAR'S EVE PARTY, BUT BY THE TIME WE FOUND OUT THAT IT HAD BEEN CANCELED, IT WAS TOO LATE!

WE LOVE YOU ALL, SO KEEP
THOSE NASTY LETTERS CUM-
MING!!!

GUNS N' RCSES

P.S. TO PICK UP ADVANCE TIX FOR THE ROXY SHOW ON SATURDAY, JANU- ARY 18TH, CALL (213)850-9029 AND ASK FOR GUNS N' ROSES, OR CALL THE GUNS N' ROSES HOTLINES AT EITHER NUMBERS; CARRIE(213)934-0205 OR BOBBIE(714)541-9238. THE NEW GUNS N' ROSES T-SHIRTS, BUTTONS, AND BUMBERSTICKERS WILL BE AVAILABLE IN A LIMITED SUPPLY AT THE ROXY SHOW, IN THE LOBBY.

THANX AGAIN,
C-YA SOON!

GUNS N' ROSES

SAT. JAN. 4 11PM
doug weston's world famous
Troubadour
$2.00 Off With This Ad
"Get Yourself Together, Drink Till You Drop, Forget About Tomorrow, & Have Another Shot"
HAPPY NEW YEAR!
From the boys who brought you the most chaotic shows of 1985.

ALSO APPEARING FRI. DEC. 20 MUSIC MACHINE

ALSO APPEARING SAT. JAN. 18 THE ROXY

For show info send S.A.S.E. to:
Guns N' Roses, 9000 Sunset Blvd., Suite 405, Hollywood, CA 90069

Special Thanks To Marc Canter

JANUARY 1, 1986/BAM 43

—COMING—
GUNS N' ROSES
—ROXY—SAT JAN. 18TH 1986—

ROXY
TONIGHT JAN 18 GUNS N ROSES
PLAIN JANE L A GUNS

PHOTO BY: ROBERT JOHN/ZAMPERELLI PROD.

GUNS N' ROSES

SAT., JAN. 18th 10:00 p.m.

9009 WEST SUNSET BOULEVARD
LOS ANGELES, CALIFORNIA 90069

ROXY THEATER
plus L.A. GUNS & PLAIN JANE

FOR GUNS N' ROSES TICKET INFO
SEND S.A.S.E. TO: 9000 SUNSET BLVD.
HOLLYWOOD, CA 90066
or CALL 850-9029

TAKE THE NIGHT TRAIN!

I began videotaping the band's live shows at this point, and the tape of this date is the earliest known to exist. The band opened this show by playing a bit of music from the soundtrack of the movie Scarface, from the big shoot out scene near the end of the film, and then put a few minutes of the actual soundtrack tape out over the club's PA system.

The club was jammed for this gig and the band was in a boisterous party mood.

SLASH: *You can make more noise than that, c'mon.*

AXL: *Welcome to the Roxy and "Welcome to the Jungle."*

DUFF: *More monitor for the drummer.*

AXL: *We need some monitor all over the place.*

SLASH: *What's happening Roxy? Make some noise. C'mon. I hope you guys are buying our fucking t-shirts.*

PHOTO COURTESY OF CHRIS AMOUROUX

DURING L.A. GUNS SET, AS THEY BEGAN
PLAYING A COVER OF AEROSMITH'S
"ADAM'S APPLE," AXL JUMPED ONSTAGE
TO PERFORM WITH PAUL BLACK!

AXL: Do you like the Rolling Stones? We've got a little "Jumpin' Jack" for you.

AXL: We'd like to thank Plain Jane. I want you to hang around to see L.A. Guns when this set is over. We're doing a show February 3rd at the Timbers with L.A. Guns and this song is called "Move to the City."

DUFF: We need some monitor for the drummer. He can't hear nothing.

ONSTAGE PHOTOS FROM THIS GIG BY JACK LUE

"We got a little mellow
song for ya, a little
different; it's a really
sweet song called "My
Michelle" for my friend
Michelle"

AXL

AXL: *Alright, our drummer needs some monitor man. I can use some too.*

DUFF: *We can use a blow job.*

AXL: *We're gonna slow things down for you. This song is called "Don't Cry."*

AXL: *We've got a couple dedications for this song. This is for all the wimp bands.*

AXL: *This one is for everyone that gets on your nerves, you know what this song is? What was it? What is the name of this song? For girls that get on your nerves, alright.*

CROWD: *Back Off Bitch.*

SLASH: *Alright, this is a funky dance tune. This one is called "Rocket Queen."*

Slash was well-lubricated and irritable, taking a long swig of whiskey onstage before Rocket Queen, which featured a slide lead. Jojo, the band's roadie, was trying to put the slide on Slash's finger, but he kept dropping it. Slash angrily pushed Jojo away. A girl came up onstage to dance, and Slash was still irritable. He gave her a dirty look and Jojo escorted her off the stage, helped by a rough push by Slash who was actually angry because the lead was a little out of tune.

DUFF: *This one we wrote about a special kind of wine we drink. It's called "Nightrain."*

AXL: *We've got another mellow song for ya. A little different, it's a really sweet song called "My Michelle," for my friend Michelle.*

They played the song with fog effects.

AXL (as he was trying to unwind the tangled scarfs from the microphone stand): Looks like I'm caught in a little mess here. I wanna thank you people for coming down. It's a nice surprise. This song is where we all wanna go to get a moment of free time. We're going down to "Paradise City." Do you wanna go?

SLASH: Thank you. C'mon man, I wanna hear more than that. Fucking make some noise. Alright, listen, we've got one tune left and then we're gonna split. This is something called "Anything Goes."

*Only public performance of "Good Night Tonight."

A FOG MACHINE WAS USED FOR "MY MICHELLE" AND "MAMA KIN"

DUFF: Alright, goodnight.

DUFF: Goodnight man, you're fucking great.

AXL: Thank you, February 1st at the Timbers, with L.A. Guns, unless you wanna hear one more. The way I understand it, I think we could count on like one hand the people in this room that really don't like Aerosmith. Wanna here some "Mama Kin?" Well, you get what you deserve.

DUFF: This song is about your mama.

AXL: This is for the last two weeks worth of partying at the studio, and all those sweet girls that we asked to see their tits. This is called "Goodnight Tonight."

Duff sang most of the leads for the last song.

SONGWRITING

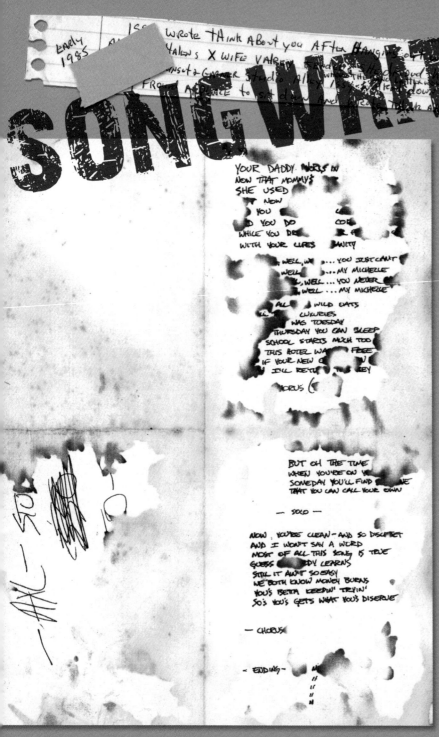

Early 1985 ... wrote THINK ABOUT YOU AFTER HANGING OUT WITH ... HALENS X WIFE VALRY ... Sunset & Gardner Studio Alley ... From ... alley to sit down and wrote the song About you

> Five hearts,
> five souls,
> five attitudes
> that just
> melded
> and formed
> together, just
> the way a rock
> and roll band
> should.
>
> **STEVEN ADLER**

Studio walls, back covers of porno magazines, stained takeout menus and pizza boxes: these were all canvases that captured the lyrics of Guns N' Roses as they were being created.

There was a natural flow to the way songs were written and spontaneity ruled. Steven drummed a beat on an ashtray, Slash took the cue and improvised a melody, Axl jumped in and belted out a verse.

They were an unlikely fellowship -- the warrior, the genius, the thinker, the rebel and the clown -- that came together around a love of music and their desire to conquer the L.A. music scene. Their songs were honest, gritty and raw and were inspired by the ordeals they survived whether it was girlfriends, drugs or the streets of Hollywood.

Izzy wrote "Think About You" after hanging out with Alex Van Halen's ex-wife Valery Kendel. She dropped him off at the Sunset & Gardner Studio Alley. Izzy walked down the alley, found a place to sit down and wrote the song!
MARC CANTER

A tiny studio apartment in Hollywood, on Gardner Street behind the Guitar Center, served as the nerve center for Guns N' Roses. There they rehearsed, slept, fought, partied and wrote music. The close quarters acted like a pressure cooker, forcing their creative collaboration and resulting in explosive music. However far each one of them strayed, they would always end up back at the studio.

DUFF If you tore apart the songs on "Appetite" and asked who wrote what, I think you might get five different stories. You absolutely hear Izzy's influence, you hear Slash's guitar style, you hear the rhythm sections, and Axl coming in on top of it all that with his sort of fuck'em-all mentality. Everybody had their thing that they brought to the song. The writing process wasn't arduous or like pulling teeth, it was just something that happened. It was an extension of the five of us as a collective.

SLASH The song writing process was a little bit more complex than I explain. I might write something with Duff, or I might write something with Axl. There was no set pattern to it. There was never any conscious conversation about song writing or ranging or anything about bridges or the middle-T as they call it or any of that crap! I always had a guitar with me, so I'd write riffs all the time and something would catch Axl's ear. Izzy had a song and he'd have some lyrics that went with it. Izzy was a great songwriter and he would get us started. There were so many different ways things came about. If something sounded good, then we embraced it and started to build on it; here's a riff, somebody else came with their part, someone else had another idea and -- bam -- that was the song. Whenever I got to the bridge section or the lead section, I heard the same thing I heard the first time we wrote the song, and I pretty much played whatever I felt. If I heard something different I might change it at the next gig; maybe a note here or something, or add something altogether that wasn't there when it first got written. But the structure and the melodies were all there from the get-go and that's been the mantra. Guns N' Roses' songs came together as a pretty spontaneous band. And when you think about it, the first record that we did, "Live Like a Suicide," which is the flipside of the "Lies" record, there was a couple original

songs and a couple covers with no real set arrangement.

DANNY BAREL Slash is writing music and Axl is writing lyrics. They just sewed themselves together. We're not talking about the Beatles. I'm talking about really brilliant musicians like Slash trading all of their ideas in this community effort. Slash would just pluck away and come up with these great chords, build a melody out of it and then a song. He recorded it on some simple cassette tapes, gave it to Axl and Axl already had lyrics that he was trying to meld into Slash's melodies.

CHRIS WEBER The song writing process was very organic. I'd come up with a riff and show it to Izzy, or visa versa. We'd create at least two or three parts: verse, chorus, bridge, etc. Then we'd record it on something crude like a tape recorder with a built in condenser microphone and hand the tape over to Axl.

> Izzy was right in the middle between Slash and I. Musically he helped set the balance between punk and hard rock.
>
> **DUFF**

MARC CANTER There were words written on papers everywhere: Izzy would be writing lyrics, Duff would be writing lyrics, Axl would be writing lyrics. Someone picked up a guitar and started playing. Pretty soon there was a new song out of nowhere. And that's why the five guys lived in their studio together. Someone grabbed a guitar, started to play something and said, "Check out this song I wrote." It was typically torn apart in about five seconds by the other guys. So, it wasn't like one particular person was responsible for this, they all kind of put their thing into it. And even though somebody started the backbone of a particular song, it became an entirely different song by the time the band was finished with it. I remember it was either part of "Paradise City" or part of "My Michelle," but Slash just tweaked it a little bit and all of a sudden it became a different song.

DUFF "My Michelle", for example, went through so many different phases as a song. It was all half-time for a while. We would just mess with little transitional parts. Bridges were a big thing for us. The bridge had to sound as good or better than any other part of the song or why have a bridge. We played different versions of songs throughout this time and we got it down pretty quick to the version of the song we wanted. But it wasn't until we played in front of people that we actually knew. One of us would have something in our mind, vocal-wise, and then we'd just go out and play it live. How did that work live to the crowd? Did they like that? All of our songs were really fed by the reaction we got from our audience, playing and trying out stuff during these club days.

SLASH We just started writing because we were living together in this haphazard kind of existence, all five of us. So over time, everyday, there was a new idea of some sort and we'd just start working on it right away. And we'd throw the songs together quickly too. "Paradise City" took all of a couple hours to put together sitting in the back of a van. So everything came together fast, so that in time we had a lot of material as a result of that.

MICHELLE YOUNG At their Gardner studio, Axl did a lot of knee slapping and snapping, hand slapping and singing tunes. He'd come up with something and ask me what I thought. Slash would break out in songs all the time.

PAMELA JACKSON I was in the rehearsal studio with Guns N' Roses when Axl brought in this old tape deck. I remember that rehearsal studio. It was somewhere down near Sunset Blvd. I remember Axl; he pressed this button on an old tape machine and said "you gotta listen to this." He pressed the button and it was a little recording of "Welcome to the Jungle" that he did and he says, "Now we're gonna rehearse it." He made them listen to it for a while and they got up and they rehearsed it.

Axl just sang his head off. I remember seeing his face turn real red when he was singing. I was wondering if he was getting any breath.

He was just giving it his all, which was awesome.

TROUBADOUR

FEBRUARY 28TH 1986

That night they were auspiciously introduced to the packed club. They performed with intense involvement from start to finish.

GUNS N' ROSES SET LI
1. WRECKLESS — SMOKE
2. THEY'RE OUT TO GET ME
3. WELCOME TO THE JUNGLE
4. JUMPIN' JACK FLASH
5. THINK ABOUT YOU — IZZY'S SOL?
6. MOVE TO THE CITY
7. ROCKET QUEEN
8. NIGHT TRAIN — TRAIN EFFECT — SMOKE
9. MY MICHELE —
10. DON'T CRY
11. BACK OFF BITCH
12. ANYTHING GOES
13. PARADISE CITY — STROBE
MA KIN
HEARTBREAK HOTEL

PHOTO BY JACK LUE

This show marked the first public performance of "Out Ta Get Me!"

*SLASH: *"Out Ta Get Me" is Guns N' Roses' big anarchy statement.*

AXL: *Like every time you turn around, someone is trying to screw you over financially, or the cops are banging on your door and you didn't do anything. It's just being railroaded into something and trying to get out from underneath. You know; parents, teachers, and preachers. The last verse, Slash and I put together as a joke because we were talking about how we get in fights and how some people get pissed off that we're drunk. But they're the ones that bought the bottle of whiskey to get you drunk on. Some people say I got a chip on my shoulder.*

SLASH: *There is this big rock star right I know who buys all the fucking booze. You drink it up and he gets fucking irate.*

AXL: *We had that as one of our opening numbers for a while because we were headed to a Roxy show and got pulled over by four cops. They picked up a bag off the street; said we threw it out the window and there were drugs in it. There were no drugs in it and they were just trying to hassle us, saying our advance money in our pockets was drug money. They searched everything, pushed us around, and we were late for a show.* *Reprinted from Geffen Press Kit

YOU LOVE IT·YOU WANT IT·YOU NEED IT.
GUNS N' ROSES

Troubadour FRI. FEB. 28 10:30

For Guns N' Roses Info Send SASE to:
9000 Sunset Blvd. Hollywood, CA 90069
or call: (213) 6__

$2.00 OFF
W/THIS AD

STEVE   IZZY   AXL   DUFF   SLASH

PHOTO: ROBERT JOHN

doug weston's
Troubadour
9081 Santa Monica Blvd at Doheny, West Hollywood, 276-6168
Presents
GUNS N' ROSES

DATE ___ FEB 28 1986
$2.00 DISCOUNT WITH THIS TICKET
TIME ___ 10 P.M.
PM
PARKING ACROSS THE STREET

NO AGE LIMIT
ONE DRINK MINIMUM
ENFORCED AT BOX OFFICE
GENERAL ADMISSION $6.50 $4.50
WITH THIS TICKET

PHOTO BY JACK LUE

RON SCHNEIDER: The greatest rock n' roll band fucking ever man, Guns N' Roses.

AXL: This is a brand new one, I wanna dedicate this to the LAPD, and any young girls that like to fuck around. "Out Ta' Get Me."

SLASH: The fucking Troubadour. What's happening?

AXL: Let me here you fucking scream now. Welcome Desi!

AXL: I'd like to take a minute to thank all you fucking people for showing up. Let me here it for yourselves. Alright.

AXL: How many of you people live out here in Hollywood? This is a song called "Move to the City."

AXL: I wanna dedicate this song, like I always do, to a person who helps me make it through every time it takes to get to another fucking show. Helps keep me alive. This song is for Barbie, it's called "Rocket Queen."

AXL: Alright, it looks like we've got a couple of assholes in the crowd. You know, if you wanna get a really close view of these boots. This is for Michelle, because she is still alive.

AXL: This is for all you people who like to fight amongst your fuckin' selves, this is called "Back off Bitch."

AXL: Time out! I want to kick this fucker out.

With the enthusiastic crowd now displaying some semblance of reasonable behavior, Axl resumed the good-natured give-and-take from the stage.

AXL: Alright, this is our theme song, one of them at least. I think you know this song. What's this song called? You know what this song is called, cause you can do

I'd like to thank
the sweethearts who
fucking bought the
drinks. Alright, thank
you. We needed them,
they don't give a shit
here. **SLASH**

what you fuckin wanna, right? This song is "Anything Goes."

AXL (during "Anything Goes"): *I am going to take time, just in case you don't know everybody here. I'd like to tell you who is hanging out on the stage. On the guitar, to my fucking right, Mr. Izzy Stradlin. On the bass guitar, Mr. Duff McKagen. On the drums, Mr. Steven Adler, and the minute you've been waiting for, he's been dying for, on the guitar, Slash.*

The solidarity between the band and its audience was powerful

SLASH: *Listen, I've got a special announcement. First off there's going to be an after-party, but I don't know the address and I don't know the street so you're gonna have to find it yourself. Anyway, if anybody runs into a couple of guys named Jeff and Allen, feel free to kick their fucking heads in. These are the guys that kicked in our studio door, so if you see them, be my guest.*

AXL: *A couple of real live pussies. This song, is where we all wanna go, this is "Paradise City."*

MC: *Alright. Lets hear it for Gun's N' Roses. You guys wanna here one more. You want more, your going to have to make a hell of a lot more noise than that. Come on.*

Axl and Slash provoked the audience to expressions of frenzied excitement, and asked the crowd if they wanted more thrills.

IZZY: *Would you like to add some zest to this?*

The zest turned out to be dancin' Desi. The atmosphere was electric; the band absolutely owned the place.

After Think About You, Axl thanked everyone in the crowd for turning out to the show and invited them to applaud themselves.The audience wasn't having any of it: One fan who couldn't contain her enthusiasm climbed onstage to ask the crowd...

FAN: *You guys want to see more Guns N' Roses?*

PHOTO BY JACK LUE

She opened her vest, where Guns N' Roses was emblazoned across her chest in lipstick.

SLASH: You guys are fucking beautiful man, we fucking love you. You guys had enough, or do you want more. Come on, lets here it, lets here it.

AXL: I wanna thank everybody here. We'll be playing, on March 21st, with Johnny Thunders down at Fender's ballroom. Opening the show is going to be Jetboy. And we will be playing Timbers with Johnny Thunders the following night. Hope to see your asses there. I think I know what some of you people are waiting on. You heard the last band do some Aerosmith. Did you like that? Well, this song is called "Mama Kin."

AXL: Alright, we'll give you some "Heartbreak Hotel."

AXL: We're Guns N' Roses.
      Thank you, goodnight.

A key night in the history of the band was over. Tom Zutaut, A&R rep for Geffen Records was at this show and he liked what he saw.

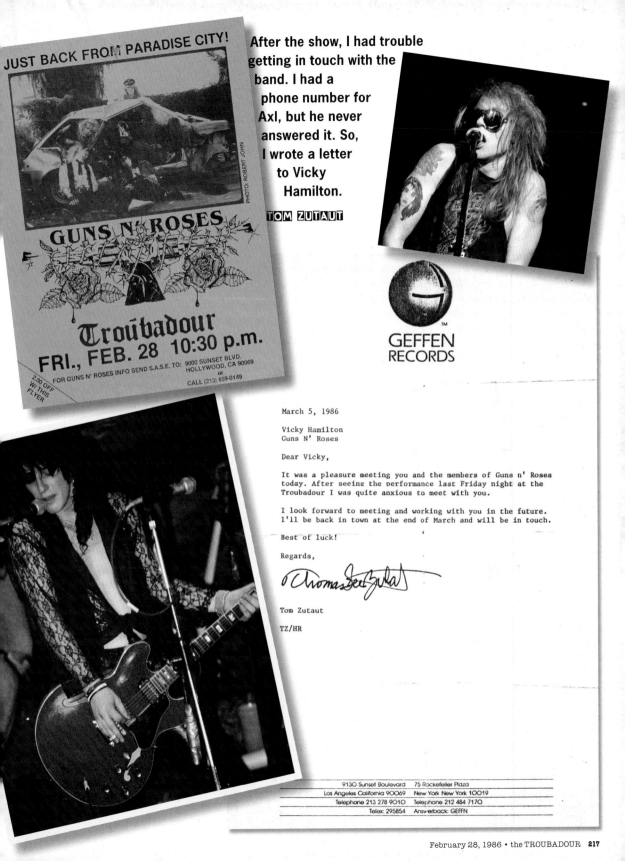

JUST BACK FROM PARADISE CITY!

PHOTO: ROBERT JOHN

GUNS N' ROSES

Troubadour
FRI., FEB. 28 10:30 p.m.

FOR GUNS N' ROSES INFO SEND S.A.S.E. TO: 9000 SUNSET BLVD.
HOLLYWOOD, CA 90069
or
CALL (213) 659-0149

2.00 OFF
W/ THIS
FLYER

After the show, I had trouble getting in touch with the band. I had a phone number for Axl, but he never answered it. So, I wrote a letter to Vicky Hamilton.

TOM ZUTAUT

GEFFEN
RECORDS

March 5, 1986

Vicky Hamilton
Guns N' Roses

Dear Vicky,

It was a pleasure meeting you and the members of Guns n' Roses today. After seeing the performance last Friday night at the Troubadour I was quite anxious to meet with you.

I look forward to meeting and working with you in the future. I'll be back in town at the end of March and will be in touch.

Best of luck!

Regards,

Tom Zutaut

TZ/HR

9130 Sunset Boulevard   75 Rockefeller Plaza
Los Angeles California 90069   New York New York 10019
Telephone 213 278 9010   Telephone 212 484 7170
Telex: 295854   Answerback: GEFFEN

IT'S SO EASY
WHEN EVERYBODY'S TRYN'TO PLEASE ME

As the fan base for GNR grew in Hollywood, it was only a matter of time before record companies would court them. One gig after another saw greater hype and bigger audiences and they were selling-out shows. The buzz was out on the band and Tom Zutaut, an artist and repertoire representative (a.k.a. A&R Rep) at Geffen Records was already on their trail. He was hand picked by David Geffen to bring in the next big thing after signing some very successful bands a few years prior, including Motley Crue. Tom wasn't any ordinary A&R rep, he was intimate with rock n' roll, knew every style that was emerging, educated himself about bands all over the world and most importantly, he knew how to hang. Once A&R reps from other labels got wind that Tom Zutaut was scouting the band, the followed like a flock of birds.

But,the band wouldn't settle for their first suitor. They had achieved the desirable position of courtship and they would play it out as long as they could. Free dinners, thousand dollar bar tabs and a variety of other "favors" were covered by industry suitors. But, when the fun was over, the band had to face serious issues such as creative control and compatibility. They weren't going to hand over their material and hard earned momentum to executives who wanted to bottle their sound and cash it in. They wanted a label that understood what their music was about and respected their demand for control. Whatever the outcome, they knew the balance was finally tipped in their favor and that the first steps toward a contract and a record were about to be taken. Of course, no one really knew what would

happen when everyone was trying to please them.

TOM ZUTAUT This story begins when I was shopping at a record store on Melrose Avenue called the Vinyl Fetish. They had all the cool imports from the

> Geffen said, "This is the band that you think is going to be the biggest rock n' roll band in the world?" and I said, "Absolutely. You gotta find the money." **TOM ZUTAUT**

UK and punk records and homemade records by new bands. The reason I met them, is because they were huge Motley Crue fans, and when I signed Motley Crue they contacted me and said, "we love this band and we want to put them in our window." And I was like, "Really! You guys are the hippest, coolest most underground record store in L.A. and you guys like the Crue." So we became friends after that.

Four or five years after I signed the Crue, I would go in there every couple of weeks and stock up on British imports and underground punk records and stuff. One of the people that worked there said to me, "Hey, there's this new band in L.A. that are better than Motley Crue. You'll love 'em. You need to see 'em." And I said, "What are they called?" and they said "Guns N' Roses." The name

rang to me. I loved the name. There was something about Guns N' Roses together that sounded interesting.

So I was driving down Sunset Boulevard. and I saw one of Slash's hand drawn posters with the pistols and the roses and I thought to myself, "That is fuckin' cool, that is really cool." I stopped my jeep, I got out, and I ripped the poster down -- which probably wasn't good for their press campaign, but what the heck. I took the poster to my office and I looked at my assistant and I said, "You gotta find out when this band is playing and remind me. I really want to see them because the guys at the Vinyl Fetish have been telling me about this band and now there's this really cool poster with a great drawing on it and it just feels like something is going to happen."

She told me later about a ten o'clock gig at the Roxy. I went to the Roxy at 9:30pm and all of a sudden they wont let me in. I was on the Guns N' Roses list, but Guns N' Roses had already played. And I was like, "what do you mean they already played? They're going on at 10!" It turned out that they had traded with the band that was supposed to open for them, so Guns N' Roses went on first. I had to buy my way in and I went backstage to look for Axl. I didn't see him, but I heard he was there somewhere. I found him in a corner and he was sitting by himself. Everyone was afraid to get near him. Here's this mysterious guy and people are afraid of him. So, I went back downstairs and watched this other band get onstage and play.

Then, Axl gets onstage and sings a song with L.A. Guns. After that show he looked a bit more approachable. So I went up to him and I said, "Hey! I came to see you guys you play, but I missed the show and I didn't know you were going on at 8:00pm." He explained to me that they had traded and I asked him when they were playing their next show. And he said, "We're playing the Troubadour in a couple weeks." So, that was my introduction to Guns N' Roses.

I told my secretary, "Look on this day, there is nothing more important than getting to the Troubadour an hour-and-a-half before the show, because I want to talk to the guys before the show." I went to the Troubadour, I went backstage to see Axl and Slash and the guys. I said, "Look, you won't see me after the concert because I won't be here after the show. There are a lot of people here and it's kind of crazy and you have to understand that when I go to a concert like this, lots of people like to watch and see if I like it or not. It gets really crazy. If you see me leave early, that's a good sign. If I hang out for the whole show, then that's probably a bad sign. So you won't see me after the show, but I'll call you."

SLASH Guns basically caused enough mayhem in L.A. to get noticed, for one by Tom Zutaut. It was totally by word-of-mouth that he came down. He was genuinely impressed with the band and he had a background; he knew rock n' roll. He had a good ear for music and that's why he was the top A&R guy over at Geffen.

TOM ZUTAUT I was fed up with all the other A&R people in the industry not using their own ears. Basically, they were watching and following me to see if I got excited about a band and then making competing offers. So with Guns N' Roses, I felt there was something vibing and I hadn't even seen them play. But I saw Axl backstage; he had some kind of star charisma going on and he was unbelievable when he got onstage. I thought this guy could be a huge star, like a Jim Morrison kind of character. I had already felt that from seeing him backstage and then seeing him onstage for one song. I had a feeling about it. So rather than create some crazy situation where ten labels were after the band, I figured my best bet was to go in, make sure the rest of the band was as good

as he is and then split. But I wanted the band to understand that, so they didn't feel disrespected.

I'll never forget it. There were five or six A&R people lined up in the same spot. The band starts the set and people are

looking for cotton and cigarette butts. It was literally the loudest show I had ever seen in an L.A. club. It was unbelievably loud. It was ear splitting. I was definitely feeling some pain in my ears, but I wasn't going to be a wimp and put cigarette butts in my ears or tissue paper or whatever, which a lot of people did. The kids loved it, but it was way too loud for the industry professionals. After about two songs, a bunch of people walked out. They didn't leave, they just were in pain because it was so loud. There were a bunch of A&R people standing by the door sort of half watching and half just being outside so they could spare their ears the decibels. And a guy that worked at Elektra Records at the time, which was my former label where I worked when I signed Motley Crue and Dokken and Metallica, was standing there. He replaced me so it was sort of ironic. As I was leaving, he looked at me and he said, "Tom, you're leaving early!" And I said, "Yeah. It's so friggin' loud in there and they're not that good," and I walked out. I

thought that was pretty funny and I think he actually believed me. Although after I made an offer to the band he came in with a competing offer.

VICKY HAMILTON The Troubadour gig was like a sea of A&R people. It was really funny because most of them were out in front of the Troubadour on the pavement, not inside while the band was still playing, because they said it was so loud. They could really not even hear if the band was good or not. During the show, I remember whipping out the demo and giving it to Tom Zutaut. It was a cassette tape. Tom said, "If they're as good as I think they are, I want to sign them." I gave him the tape and said, "trust me they are, and better." And the next day he was in pursuit of the band. But there were like 13 labels at that show.

RON SCHNEIDER When all these labels were starting to come around, it was weird because there were all these smooth talking record people coming backstage saying, "Oh, you guys were great, we loved you." But we knew they weren't one of us. Every label was in courtship with the band and took them out to eat. That was brilliant when you consider all the times the band was starving to death and eating onions in fields and literally scrounging whatever we could to eat. When these industry guys wanted to meet with them, they'd set up the guidelines saying, "You wanna meet with us, you're gonna meet us at El Compadre and you're gonna buy us dinner." And they'd call me, "Come on Ronnie, we're goin to eat man!" I'd just be like, "yeah!"

SLASH We were wined and dined from that moment on by every record company in town. The tables completely turned in a way that the people we used to turn off and who wouldn't let us in anywhere were now trying to get into our gigs. We used it to our advantage, especially with all of these industry people who we didn't really give a shit about. The band was very opportunistic.

STEVEN ADLER I loved being wined and dined. We were told that we're going to be the biggest thing and they were going to give us this and that. But, nobody was honest. Most of the record people wanted to turn us into something different than we really were. They wanted to change our image and our songs. We knew that wasn't going to happen.

TOM ZUTAUT That next day I went straight to David Geffen and told him that I'd seen the future of rock n' roll and was going to sign the biggest band on his label, probably the biggest band since the Rolling Stones or Zeppelin, and even The Who. And he looked at me like I was crazy, but fortunately he asked, "You believe in that much?" And I said, "yeah."

DUFF We knew right away that Geffen was a company we wanted to work with because it was small. We felt they got the band, but that didn't stop us from meeting with pretty much every other record company. The great thing about that was getting free dinners and free drinks. We milked that as long as we could. I think they got wise to us. It was pretty cool to be sought after by major league labels.

RON SCHNEIDER Tom Zutaut had eventually started to come around. They were talking about signing with Geffen, but Tom was hanging out with us at the stripper's houses, drinking and passing the bottle of Jim Beam around with us. It was almost like an initiation. We thought, "this guy's one of us." I think that was one of the things that helped solidify the deal with Geffen. Tom Zutaut -- he signed Motley Crue, he signed Dokken, so in my book this guy was cool.

SLASH Nobody wanted to work with us in the early days because we were as

notorious as people thought we were. And we made no qualms about it and so we scared a lot of people off upon the first meeting. And there were a lot of people we didn't like who actually wanted to work with us, but we brushed them off pretty quickly. It was a matter of chemistry. That was the most important thing. We had a lot of people that wanted to produce Guns N' Roses who came in with their own ideas and their own agenda. That was an abrupt end to that conversation. We liked Tom a lot, just as a person. We liked what he was about. We knew we were going to sign with Geffen, but we stretched it out for a long time.

STEVEN ADLER Tom Zutaut and Teresa Ensenat encouraged us to be ourselves and that we didn't have to change anything. So we went with Geffen because they let us do what we wanted.

TOM ZUTAUT Axl called me and we had a meeting scheduled. The whole band was on time, but Axl wasn't. I was entertaining the rest of the band, waiting for him to show up, because I didn't really want to get into any serious conversation until the whole band was there. Finally he turned up. I looked at them and said, "look, you guys are the best rock n' roll band I've seen in my fucking life, and that was the fucking loudest concert I've been too. Forget stadium, arena, club -- it doesn't matter." They laughed about it being so loud and said, "yeah, we saw people putting cigarette butts in their ears and we saw a bunch of people leave after the first couple of songs." And I said, "yeah, I stuck through at least four songs, even though I only needed to see the first song," which was "Nightrain." It was a pretty ferocious opening and I saw how great the rest of the band was and Axl was every bit as good as I had imagined from seeing him backstage at the Roxy doing that one song with L.A. Guns.

So they are sitting in my office and we had a great meeting. Axl looked at me and said, "Ok, here's the deal, we'll sign with you but we need $75,000 in cash by Friday," and this on a Tuesday or Wednesday. I was working under the big Warner Brothers corporate umbrella and there really wasn't any way to get cash that quickly. These corporations don't move that fast. So I went to David Geffen

and I said, "look, whatever you have to do, I need $75,000 in cash by Friday at 6:00pm and we'll have the band signed." Geffen said, "This is the band that you think is going to be the biggest rock n' roll band in the world?" and I said, "Absolutely. You gotta find the money."

I called the head of business affairs at Warner and he said there was no way to get a deal memo done and that it wasn't going to happen. I called David Geffen back and I said, "look, I'm really serious. These Warner Brothers people are telling me its going to take at least two weeks to do some kind of a deal memo draft and I need $75,000 for these guys in two days." And David said, "what's the rush?" I said, "by the time they play their next show and meet with five other record companies, it's going to cost us ten times as much money and the more people they meet, the more their heads will get twisted into pretzels and they might not sign with us." And David said, "Ok I'll sort it out." So Warner Brothers assigned a guy just to get this deal done and they got it done in two days. They couldn't give me a briefcase full of cash, so they got a cashier's check. I called Axl just to make sure that he would take a certified cashier's check, which I explained can be taken to the Bank of America where it was drawn and cashed, money put into a briefcase right on the spot. He said, "yeah, that's fine as long as it's the same as cash and when I go to the bank it actually turns into money." And I said, "it will, for sure."

Axl calls me back later that day and he says, "Tom, I'm really sorry, but we may have to sign to Chrysalis." I said, "What?" And he said, "We had this meeting at Chrysalis and there was this really cool British chick and she liked us, but her boss was an idiot." And I said, "well, why would you want to sign there?" And he said, "we thought this chick was really cool and it was really funny that her boss didn't know who Steven Tyler was. After the meeting we told her that her boss was an idiot, but if she walked naked from her office, down to Tower Records on Sunset, we'd sign with her." So here I am, all day Friday, with my shades open watching this office down the street to see if this woman walks by naked because that was going to cost me the band. And, of course, she never had the courage to do it, but can you imagine if she had done it; what it would have meant to her career. Her name was Susan Collins and her brother was the famous British record producer Peter Collins. I'm sure when she looks back on that she might wish that she had walked naked from her office to Tower even if she got arrested, because

"Ok, here's the deal, we'll sign with you but we need $75,000 in cash by Friday,"
AXL TO TOM ZUTAUT

what she would have done for her career by having Guns N' Roses would've been extraordinary.

VICKY HAMILTON We were at the apartment and we were supposed to meet everyone at Geffen at 6:00pm. Axl couldn't find his contact lenses. So he got very upset, and he says "I am not going down there until I find my contacts," and he went storming out of the house. So Slash and I were standing there thinking, "Ok, what do we now? We're supposed to be down there right now." So we started going through Axl's clothes and we found the contact lenses inside a pair of pants that he'd had on a couple days prior. By then, we couldn't find Axl. Meanwhile, time is elapsing. we're supposed to be there and I think it was Steven that grabbed me and was said, "Oh my God, come look." And I went outside and looked and there was Axl sitting yogic on top of the Whisky A-Go-Go.

TOM ZUTAUT It's Friday at 6:00pm and this attorney from Warner Brothers is there and he's got the certified check and once the band puts their signatures on this deal memo they get the check and they're signed. Now, it's like 8:00pm and he still hasn't shown up. The rest of the band were there and they're starting to get drunk, and we're waiting. The guy from Warner Brothers is like, "Dude, I got a life, this guys not even going to turn up." And I said, "no, he's always late but he'll get here. We've got to wait." So now I'm trying to keep the band entertained and they're getting more and more drunk as time's wearing on and this guy from Warner Brothers wants to get home for his weekend.

VICKY HAMILTON So we got Axl to come down and then we went down to Geffen to sign the contracts. We were like two hours late and all the executives were just sitting there waiting.

TOM ZUTAUT Finally, at 8:45pm, Axl rolls in, he says, "you got the money?" And I said, "yeah I got it." And he's like, "ok." The band signs the contract, done deal.

DANNY BIRAL They negotiated a stellar deal. It was crazy. They got a big advance plus six albums, plus tour support. I remember when Geffen himself came into the office and wasn't really specific.

PHOTO BY JACK LUE

He was like, "Hi. How are you? Looking forward to working with you." It was that kind of mush. I do remember when Tom Zutaut sort of stated the deal they wanted. Geffen frowned, he thought for a little bit and said something. To me, that was the pivotal point, when I knew that Geffen was going to go for it. I knew it even if the guys didn't know. He saw something and he was going to go for it one way or another. It was a negotiation, but Axl perceived it kind of like a war and in the end he was right. His inexperience and his "I want the world and I'm not taking no for an answer" approach to those negotiations worked. It's kind of amazing how that happened because he was playing without a real strong poker hand.

SLASH We finally signed with Geffen, which was ironic for me because David Geffen was friends with my parents when I was a kid and he had no idea that I was the same little boy that was sitting in front of him in an office at Geffen Records where he was offering us $75,000 for a record deal. That was pretty funny, I figured that was definitely fate.

VICKY HAMILTON I remember when they got their advance check from Geffen Records, Axl went to get a bank account

> **He was walking around with $7,500 dollars in his boots!**
> — **RON SCHNEIDER**

and they wouldn't let him open a bank account under Axl Rose. So he took all his money in cash and kept it in a sock underneath the couch that he slept on in the front room of my apartment. One day, I was trying to straighten up -- my place was a complete disaster at all times, McDonalds cartons all over the place and French fries, and amps and just crap everywhere -- and I found that sock under the couch just full of money. Axl was like, "Are you trying to steal my money?" I said, "You should probably open up a bank account with this kind of money in a sock," but he wasn't going to open one until he could get a bank account under Axl Rose.

RON SCHNEIDER When the band got signed and they got an advance, everybody got about $7,500 for the first installment. Axl had his share stuck in his boots. He was walking around with $7,500 in his boots!

> **After that, they had the world by the balls. And they spent a lot of money on new tattoos.**
> — **VICKY HAMILTON**

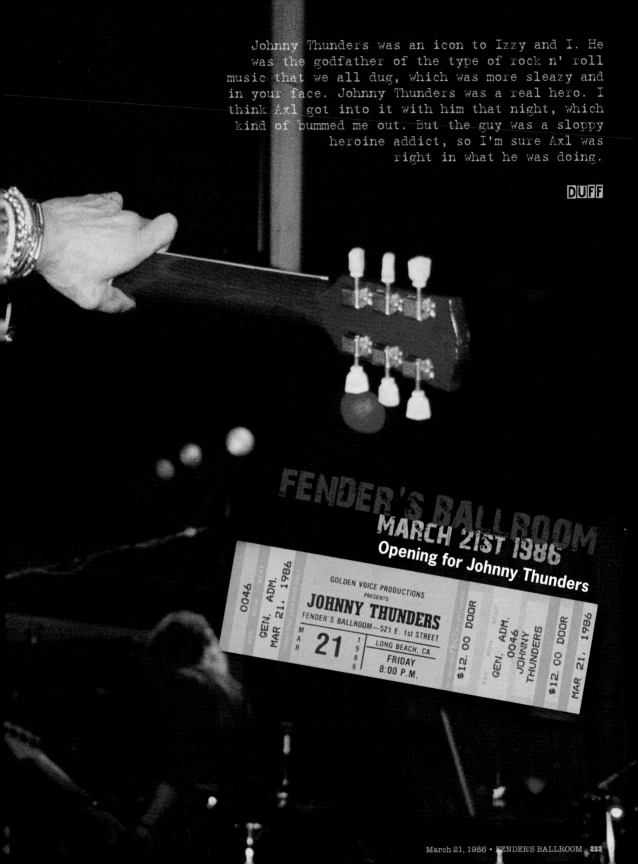

Johnny Thunders was an icon to Izzy and I. He was the godfather of the type of rock n' roll music that we all dug, which was more sleazy and in your face. Johnny Thunders was a real hero. I think Axl got into it with him that night, which kind of bummed me out. But the guy was a sloppy heroine addict, so I'm sure Axl was right in what he was doing.

DUFF

FENDER'S BALLROOM

MARCH 21ST 1986

Opening for Johnny Thunders

GOLDEN VOICE PRODUCTIONS
PRESENTS
JOHNNY THUNDERS
FENDER'S BALLROOM—521 E. 1st STREET
MAR
21
1986
LONG BEACH, CA.
FRIDAY
8:00 P.M.

0046
GEN. ADM.
MAR 21, 1986

$12.00 DOOR

GEN. ADM.
0046
JOHNNY THUNDERS

$12.00 DOOR
MAR 21, 1986

Out Ta Get Me
Welcome to the Jungle
Nightrain
My Michelle
Rocket Queen
Don't Cry
Back Off Bitch
Nice Boys
Mama Kin

Axl expressed his gratification at the large turnout and shared information about the imbibing he had been indulging in and its influence on his performance, dedicating a song to "a particular bottle of vintage wine called Nightrain. It's the cheapest way to get knocked on your ass."

SLASH: Long Beach, what's happening?

AXL: Are you people ready to forget why you do what the fuck they tell you to? This is called "They're Out to Get Me."

AXL: "Welcome to the Fucking Jungle." We're Guns N' Roses, remember that.

AXL: I like this, a lot of fucking people here. We've got a song here, we dedicate this song to a particular bottle of vintage wine called Nightrain. It's the cheapest

GUNS N' ROSES

PHOTO: ROBERT JOHN

The spirit of the New York Dolls must have moved westward, because so many bands in Los Angeles have picked up on their trashy, tacky, and tattered personas. While a lot of these glam-cum-metal bands seem to equate quality with how many bandanas they can wrap around their various body parts, **Guns N' Roses** haven't forgotten that nothing — not even the baddest pout this side of David Johannsen — is a substitute for a killer hook. "Anything Goes" sounds like vintage 1974-styled Aerosmith though it's a bit histrionic in the vocal department. Sure, they can be as sexist as the next leather n' studs guy, as in "Back Off," but that sort of thing comes with the territory. After all, you don't even *think* about going to see a band like Guns N' Roses if you want your consciousness raised.

— CD

Guns N' Roses appear with Johnny Thunders at Fenders in Long Beach March 21 and play two shows at the Roxy on March 28.

way to get knocked on your ass. This song is called "Nightrain."

AXL: *You have to excuse me, I haven't been asleep in about 48 hours. I think I am coming down on my fuckin' dope. So this next song, is about getting too fucking high. This song is called "My Michelle."*

With this show Axl had started singing the first few verses of "My Michelle" in a high pitched voice, and the lyrics were now completed.

AXL: *We'd like to thank everybody for coming down. We'd like to thank Jetboy. I hope your looking forward to some Johnny Thunders. We've got a show coming up, two shows, Friday the 28th at the Roxy. This song is called "Rocket Queen."*

The mood of the audience and the band turned somewhat edgy. After "Don't Cry," someone in the crowd said something.

IZZY: *Fuck you.*

AXL: *This song is for all the posers tonight. (addressing someone in the audience) Get out of my face. We're gonna slow things down, this song is called "Don't Cry."*

It wasn't only the audience that irritated the artists; the technical crew came in for some biting comments as well.

AXL: *We're gonna take a moment to tune the guitars, and I'd like to thank the sound man for fucking with me. Asshole.*

SLASH: *Do me a favor, try not to kill each other. Alright, so we're in tune. This is something dedicated to all the pain in the ass girls that we've met throughout the years. I know all of you motherfuckers know who you are because you're all here tonight. Because you always comeback, this is dedicated to you. This is called "Back off Bitch."*

AXL: *You got a song that you wanna hear*

that we play. Let me hear something. You wanna hear some nice boys. We're gonna play you some nice boys.

AXL: It's a long time coming motherfucker.

IZZY: Get off your asses and come on.

AXL (before "Mama Kin"): This is our last song. I think you know what this is. This is an old cover tune. Let me hear what you think. Do you wanna hear it or not?

Axl imposed some needed discipline on the unruly band before "Mama Kin," the last song of the set.

AXL: Quit fucking around and play it.

SLASH: Izzy Stradlin on the guitar motherfuckers.

Axl thanked the sound man, whom he addressed as "asshole" for "fucking with me."

AXL: We're Guns N' Roses.

Thank you, goodnight.

THE BAND BACKSTAGE MOMENTS AFTER
LEAVING THE STAGE. RON SCHNEIDER
THE BAND'S ROADIE AND FORMER BANDMATE
OF SLASH FROM THE TIDUS SLOAN AND
ROADCREW DAYS, APPEARS IN THE CENTER
WITH SAILOR HAT.

THE ROXY
10PM
MARCH 28TH 1986

These shows were originally planned as a showcase for all the record companies, but as it turned out, Geffen had already snagged them two days earlier.

ALL PHOTOS THIS SHOW BY JACK LUE

GUNS N' ROSES ROXY FRI., MARCH 28TH

Axl showed up at sound check sporting a brand-new tattoo reading "Victory or Death." The band had bought a lot of new equipment and clothes with their advance money from the record deal. Axl kept his money, about $7,000, stashed in his boots while performing that night.

Slash greeted the less-than-full house that had turned out for the first show with bitter irony.

SLASH: *Full house tonight, right?*

Guns N' Roses fans wouldn't come out to early shows if there was a late show the same night, so the audience wasn't just sparse – it consisted mostly of record industry types --who didn't make for the kind of crowd enthusiasm and rowdiness the band thrived on.

AXL: *Hello. Everybody nice and relaxed?*

DUFF: *Welcome to our first show. Right when we got here -- we were a little bit late --We got pulled over by four fucking cop cars looking for drugs. This song is called "They're Out Ta' Get Me."*

DUFF: *Welcome to the Roxy, Thanks for coming.*

AXL: *We're gonna tune these guitars. We've got a show next weekend at the Whisky-a-Go-Go, and it's been a long time since we've been there. We're gonna be playing with some good friends of ours. Opening the show is gonna be a band called Faster Pussycat with Taeme, and the second band is called Shanghai. I want y'all to come down for that.*

SLASH: *Alright, this is something about a drink we all know and love. This is a song dedicated to the band. It's called "Nightrain."*

AXL (before "My Michelle"): *This song is for Tommy Zutaut.*

AXL: *Get rid of the feedback.*

AXL: *Can you help us with that feedback*

GUNS N' ROSES
9000 Sunset Blvd., Ste. 405
Hollywood, CA 90069

EVENT: GUNS N' ROSES

WHERE: ROXY THEATRE
9009 Sunset Blvd.,
W. Hollywood

WHEN: Fri. March 28th

HOW: 2 shows
8:00 Carrera   10:00 Lions & Ghosts

WHY: Because we need the money

R.S.V.P.: Vicky Hamilton (213) 659-0149

To: Circus Magazine
115 East 55th
NY, NY 10022

ATTENTION
Gerald Rothberg

DANCE YOUR ASS OFF, DRINK YOUR FACE OFF
GET YOUR ROCKS OFF

GUNS N' ROSES

2 SHOWS!
FRI., MARCH 28th 8 & 10 p.m.

ROXY THEATRE
1ST SHOW   2ND SHOW
CARRERA   Lions & Ghosts

FOR GUNS N' ROSES TICKET INFO
SEND S.A.S.E. TO: 9000 SUNSET BLVD.,
HOLLYWOOD, CA 90066 or CALL 659-0149

TICKETS AVAILABLE AT TICKETMASTER

Out To Get Me
Welcome to the Jungle
Think About You
Rocket Queen
Nightrain
My Michelle
Don't Cry
Back Off Bitch
Paradise City

up here somebody. It's ringing like a motherfucker.

SLASH: *So Roxy, what's happening? I know this place is empty, but I've heard louder than that man. Fuck.*

AXL: *This song, means a lot to me. This song is called "Don't Cry."*

AXL: *This song is for the Music Connection. It's called "Back off Bitch."*

SLASH: *Alright, we're gonna leave you with one last tune. This is something about a little trip we took. I don't think anybody else has ever been there, so it's our song. This is called "Paradise City."*

This show was the first time "Paradise City" was enhanced by a strobe effect.

SLASH: Goodnight.

This is was an advance on a $1.6 million dollar, six record contract!

VICKY HAMILTON: *The funny thing about the check is that it says Stash instead of Slash.*

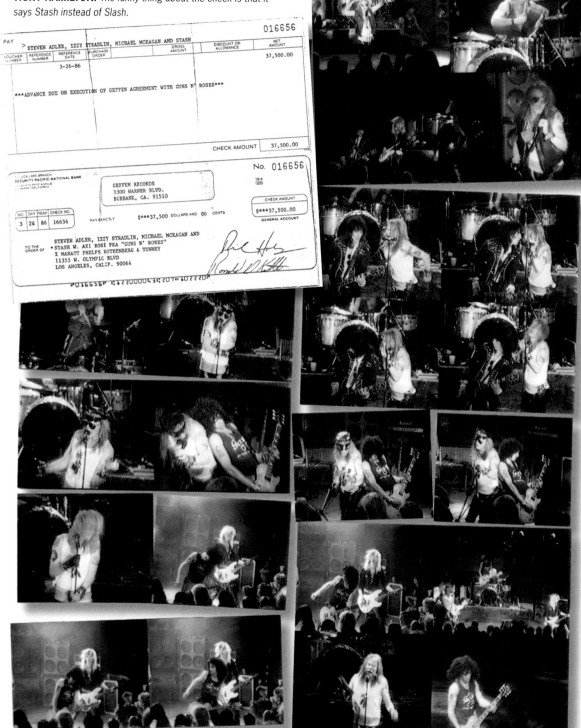

VIDEO PRINTS FROM FOOTAGE BY MARC CANTER

GUNS N' ROSES

CARRERA

LIONS & GHOSTS

TWO SHOWS

FRI. MAR. 28

ROXY

Tickets Available At TICKETMASTER

THE ROXY
12AM
MARCH 28TH 1986

ALL PHOTOS THIS SHOW BY JACK LUE

Axl shared some of his criticism of the local press near the outset of this rowdy set:

AXL: We'd like to thank everybody for showing up here tonight. Alright, I don't know if there is anybody here from the L.A. Weekly tonight. Did anybody read their choices of ten bands, and the comment about the thrash, glam and heavy metal? You know, they called us New York Dolls and labeled us jaded posers.

You know, I may have my differences with other bands, but I don't think Gun's N' Roses here, L.A. Guns, or Poison deserve that shit from a fucking moron who has probably never even seen a fucking show or knows how to rock n' roll. This is the "fuck L.A. Weekly" show. This song is called "Back off Bitch."

During "Back Off Bitch," Axl popped open a bottle of champagne and poured some on his chest.

DUFF: I'd like to thank A.W.S for the champagne.

SLASH: Alright, this is a new tune dedicated to the bottle. It's called "Nightrain."

Slash displayed a similarly festive manner: He hoisted a bottle of Jack Daniels and took a healthy swig.

AXL: This song, is called "My Michelle," about a very good friend of mine named Michelle. This goes out to her and the man of the hour to me, Tommy Zutaut.

AXL: I wanna take a minute here to tell everybody about the show next weekend.

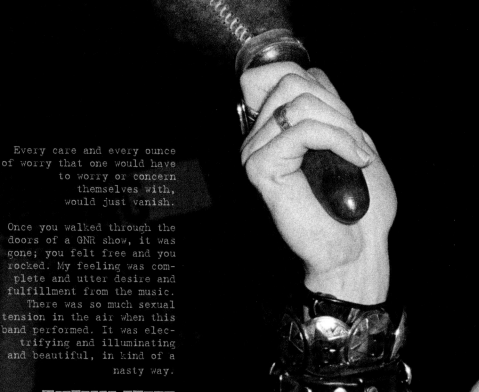

Every care and every ounce of worry that one would have to worry or concern themselves with, would just vanish.

Once you walked through the doors of a GNR show, it was gone; you felt free and you rocked. My feeling was complete and utter desire and fulfillment from the music. There was so much sexual tension in the air when this band performed. It was electrifying and illuminating and beautiful, in kind of a nasty way.

MICHELLE YOUNG

When's the last time you've been to the Whisky to see a rock band? Has it been a long fucking time? Is it about fucking time for the Whisky-A-Go-Go. Next Saturday night, we're playing the Whisky. We've got Faster Pussycat opening the show, we've got our good friends and bitchin' band Shanghai that a lot of you haven't seen. Check 'em out. They'll kick your ass. Then we'll wanna shut that fucking place down and I need your help.

SLASH: The first and last time it's going to be open.

AXL: You wanna have a good time? This song is called "Paradise City."

AXL: This song I wanna dedicate to Vicky Hamilton, for putting up with me being a really weird fuck. I am just a pain in the ass. This song is called "Mama Kin."

AXL: We've got some funk rock for you. It's about a badass woman called the Rocket Queen.

Slash used his B.C. Rich Mockingbird for "Rocket Queen" having broken a string on his Les Paul during "Mama Kin." This was the last time he played the Mockingbird before pawning it to raise quick cash. To his regret, he never retrieved that guitar – the first he ever owned – from the pawnshop.

DUFF: I wanna thank you guys all for coming down to the Roxy tonight. Are you guys having a good time? Thank you.

SLASH: C'mon, you can make more noise than that. Tear the fucking house down.

AXL: This is a song that we left out of the set earlier. This song is called "Reckless Life."

AXL (in a high pitch voice): Goodnight ladies and gentlemen.

SLASH: See you next weekend.

Axl said good night and exited. Pam Manning, a stripper friend of the band,

came out on stage. Despite her best efforts – she wriggled cheerfully in a very small outfit – the audience remained subdued.

PAMELA MANNING: *Hey you guys, you want some more? Let me hear it, cmon. Wake up.*

STEVEN ADLER: *Lets hear the fucking noise. C'mon.*

DUFF: *Yo, yo Roxy, c'mon.*

Axl returned to the stage and surveying the blasé audience.

AXL: *I think you guys have been eating Quaaludes. This song lets you do whatever the fuck you want. This song is called "Anything Goes."*

DUFF: *Alright you mother fuckers, lets go!*

During "Anything Goes," Slash tripped while running back and forth on stage, somehow executing a perfect backward somersault without missing a single note.

AXL: *I wanna take a minute to introduce the members of the band here. The man over there on guitar, is Mr. Izzy Stradlin. The man here on the bass is Mr. Duff McKagan. The man on the drums, Mr. Steven Adler. And the man sitting on his fucking ass, falling all over himself…*

SLASH: *Drunk dumb fuck.*

AXL: *…is Slash. And he has been waiting for this all night.*

SLASH: *That's it. Goodnight. We've got one more.*

During "Heartbreak Hotel" Slash's top hat migrated to the top of Axl's head.

AXL: *Thank you. The Whisky on April 5th. Ok, lets close the fucking place down.*

SLASH: *This was a benefit for Belleview.*

AXL: And fuck BAM Magazine.

This show was prime Guns N' Roses: raunchy, rowdy and raucous. It began with a pre-show bikini contest featuring a grand prize of five dollars. Of the five young women who entered, four ended up topless.

THE WHISKY
APRIL 5TH 1986

The band was beginning to carve out its place in the music industry. That night, Tim Collins, manager of Aerosmith, came out to see them and there had been some talk around this time of Tim taking Guns N' Roses under his wing. Axl's parents had flown out from Indiana to see their boy's band, and Axl dedicated "Welcome to the Jungle to them."

AXL: I'm dedicating this one to my parents. "Welcome to the Jungle," everybody.

AXL: We'd like to thank everybody for coming on this rock n' roll re-opening of the Whisky. Are you having fun so far? Are you drinking a drink? We wanna give a special thanks to Tom Zutaut from Geffen records. The guy has been so much help to us. It's amazing. It's nice to find someone like that. We're ready to rock.

A musical associate of the band supplied some tasty saxophone licks to this gig, as well as a number of Dilaudid suppositories for post-show experiment in recreational substance abuse that Axl chose not to repeat. Slash took part in the experiment as well, and Axl's conclusion was that his bandmate hadn't been favorably impressed by the results either. Slash thought the crowd could be a little livelier.

SLASH: Make some fucking noise. I mean you guys are so fucking quite. This ain't no fucking wedding man. C'mon man. Let's here the fucking balcony.

AXL: This song is for fifteen-year-old girls who move out here and don't have any idea what the fuck to do. It's called "Move to the City."

The necessary supplies of whisky were provided to set the proper tone.

SLASH: I'd like to take this moment to request to our roadies that I really need that bottle of whisky on stage now.

AXL: This is a distance song

AXL: It would be good if we could clear out the feedback from the vocals. I don't know where it is coming from.

SLASH: Listen, I wanna take this time out to thank this girl we know for supplying us with the whisky tonight. A gift from the gods above, thank you. So in her honor, we're going to do a tune now, it's called "Nightrain." To alcoholism!

The contributions of the local press were noted by Axl.

AXL: This song is for all of you, and for the Whisky, because we know that you know where the real rock n' roll is. And I would like the L.A. Weekly, and the Music Connection, and Band Magazine, and the Reader, to feel this one right between the legs.

SLASH: Alright motherfuckers. Man, this is the fucking Whisky. C'mon man.

Out Ta Get Me
Welcome to the Jungle
Think About You
Move to the City
Rocket Queen
Nightrain
My Michelle
Don't Cry
Back Off Bitch
Anything Goes
Paradise City
Mama Kin
Heartbreak Hotel
Nice Boys
Jumpin' Jack Flash

The musicians also displayed their tender and romantic sides.

AXL: *This next song, is for anybody who ever fell in love, and don't fucking lie to me. This song is called "Don't Cry."*

DUFF: *This song is for all the girls out there.*

Desi came out and danced to "Anything Goes." Before Slash's guitar lead in the jam in Anything Goes, Axl introduced him as Dr. Doom, the Hollywood thug, Slash." Dr. Doom took a swig from a bottle of whisky he was handed by someone in the crowd, which he pronounced "one cool brand, baby." The song was also graced by a few bluesy improvised verses sung by Axl during the scorching saxophone lead.

SLASH: *Wake the fuck up man. So, how is everybody? Hey, listen, thanks everybody for coming down, man. It's good to see all your fucking faces.*

DUFF: *This one we wrote on a little road trip, it's called…*

AXL: *Whoever stole a red jacket and some car keys, it would be really nice if like they gave it back. Especially if I find out who the fuck you are, and I ain't joking. This shit ain't cool.*

DUFF: *It ain't cool. This one's called "Paradise City."*

There was some verbal tussling between Axl and Slash.

AXL: *Thank you, goodnight. (To Slash) Do you wanna have a party instead? Do you wanna cut this leaving the stage bullshit?*

Now we're gonna play for ourselves. I got some "Mama Kin" for ya.

STEVEN: *This one's for my mom.*

AXL: *Play some guitar Slash.*

SLASH: *Free leather jacket. Who wants it? You fuckers, I paid ten bucks for this.*

Slash tossed his vest out into the crowd.

AXL: *We got accused for doing too many covers. I think there are some people here who like these songs. That's all we're doing.*

SLASH: It's time for a drum solo. Let's do "Nice Boys."

AXL: *This song is called "Nice Boys Don't Play Rock N' Roll.*

The crowd-pleasing party banter continued into the close of the show.

AXL: *(during "Heartbreak Hotel") You want to hear that one more time?"*

AXL: *We ain't going to be seeing you people for a little while, so this is our last fuckin' chance to get it out of our system. Without you, we would be fuckin' nowhere.*

The festive finale featured three of the bikini contest hopefuls dancing enthusiastically and quite effectively -- they were, after all, professional strippers -- to "Jumpin' Jack Flash."

AXL: *We'd like to bring up some of the entries, and the winner, of the bikini contest. For this song, "Jumping Jack Flash."*

AXL: *This is for Michelle.*

AXL: *Thank you, and good fucking night. We'd like to thank our lovely dancers, Pam, Christina and Melissa.*

At the end of the show, Steven announced, "Party's at Vicky's, c'mon." Viky Hamilton was still managing the band at that time and lived right across the street from the Whisky. Most of the band members were staying at her place because Axl was hiding from the vice squad. A young woman had accused Axl and Slash of attempted rape, and because of his previous run-ins with the cops he was convinced they wouldn't believe he was innocent. The charges were eventually dropped. The band meanwhile, had to leave their live-in studio behind the Guitar Center by Gardner Street and Sunset Boulevard were they lived the gritty Hollywood life chronicled in their songs.

DEL JAMES If the party didn't start at the studio, it ended there. It was naked girls, the perpetual smell of weed and blow, and booze and more booze and guitars. It was our feeble attempt at being like "Exile on Main Street!"

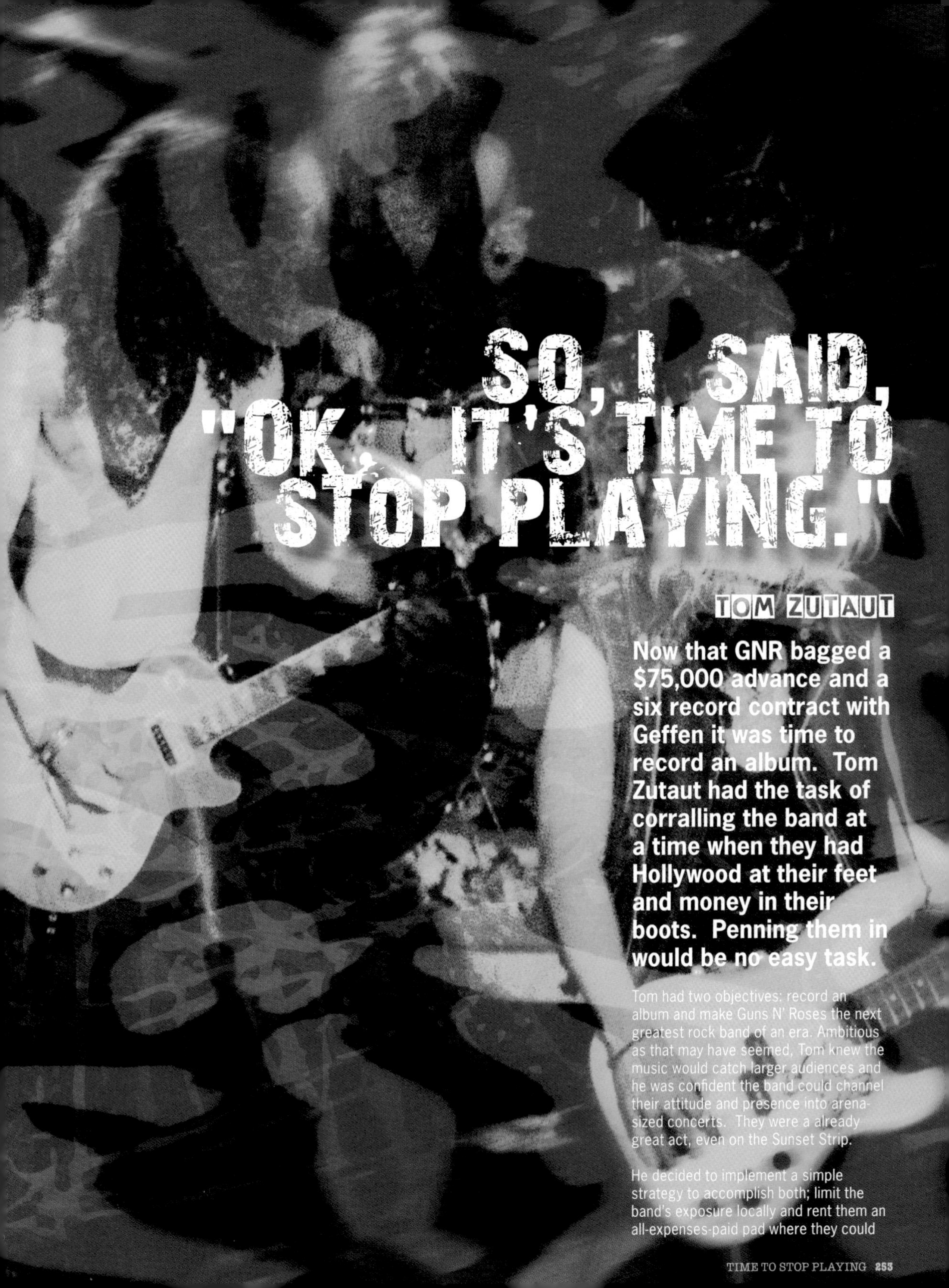

SO, I SAID, "OK, IT'S TIME TO STOP PLAYING."

TOM ZUTAUT

Now that GNR bagged a $75,000 advance and a six record contract with Geffen it was time to record an album. Tom Zutaut had the task of corralling the band at a time when they had Hollywood at their feet and money in their boots. Penning them in would be no easy task.

Tom had two objectives: record an album and make Guns N' Roses the next greatest rock band of an era. Ambitious as that may have seemed, Tom knew the music would catch larger audiences and he was confident the band could channel their attitude and presence into arena-sized concerts. They were a already great act, even on the Sunset Strip.

He decided to implement a simple strategy to accomplish both; limit the band's exposure locally and rent them an all-expenses-paid pad where they could

write a few new songs to round out the album. Tom directed the band to only play one or two gigs a month, which, according to his theory, would make them more desirable when they did play. He got them out of their transient lifestyle and into a clean, air-conditioned apartment so that they could write in peace.

What Tom didn't consider was the inherent nature of Guns N' Roses. They were animals on the hunt, not creatures of comfort and he took away the only two things that kept the band sane: performing on stage and hard living. Tom's strategy was disastrous.

With the keys to the city and cash to burn, the $75,000 advance that was meant to sustain them through the recording of an album was gone within weeks. They developed an insatiable appetite for drugs, tattoos and new clothing until

their funds dried out and their creative discipline diminished. No new songs had been written.

PARADISE CITY

Geffen was concerned. Where was their money? Where was their record? Tom Zutaut created another plan while the band got back on stage, sometimes billed as Guns N' Roses and other times under the alias "Fargin Bastydges." They simply could not stop performing. Tom found more money and pushed them to compose new material. The band stalled -- they didn't like being told what to do

-- and the growing tension almost derailed the deal. Tom knew he couldn't baby sit the band forever and something had to change.

TOM ZUTAUT I said, "Ok, it's time to stop playing." I felt like they needed to let the mystery build. There was this big buzz on the band and I've always subscribed to the theory that less is more. If you think back to Led Zeppelin, when I was a teenager, they never did interviews. If Jimmy Page or Robert Plant did an interview, I was at the newsstand waiting for it to come out because it meant something. And it was going to tell me something important. The one quality I had seen with Motley Crue was that they were readily available, twenty-four seven and it eliminated the mystique. When you have a charismatic draw, it's better to have a little more mystique about you.

To me, what's the point of thrashing out the same old songs a dozen or a hundred more times? On one hand, I felt that it was good to build up the mystique, but on the other it was, "guys, we need to write new songs and get enough material to make a debut album that just blows everybody away. Let's kill two birds with one stone here. People are going to get hungrier for you than if you hit the Troubadour once a month instead of once a week. If you're not there all the time, then people are going to turn up and create pandemonium when you do play." So it was a combination of building mystique and getting them to focus on writing new material. The idea was that when they did play, each performance was more special and they can debut new material before a crowd. That was my reasoning at the time.

SLASH After we were signed, our label didn't want us playing locally. They said, "We want you to lay low, we're going to get you a manager." Time off meant trouble. I had $7,500 and that was exciting. Unfortunately, that was eaten up by a drug habit that I had at the time. That's what we did -- not everyone -- but a couple of us just spent the rest of that time in and out of trouble.

DANNY BIRAL My addiction became so severe that it became a point of issue when they got signed with Geffen. Their new manager essentially said that whatever they do, it would have to be without me because from his point of view, I was an extremely bad influence on them.

DESI CRAFT The thing that sucked was when they got signed, Geffen Records warned Izzy that I wasn't of age and that it wouldn't be profitable for him to continue seeing me. They warned against him that my mother could press charges. We worked really, really hard to get the band in this position, but it was his time, so I had to accept it and let it go.

TOM ZUTAUT They were getting bored and restless and it seemed like they didn't have all the songs they needed to really go in and record. They just weren't quite ready and even though there was this ferocious live show that could pack out the clubs in L.A., they weren't quite ready for the big stage yet. I was trying to encourage them to rehearse and write songs and come up with twelve phenomenal songs to make a debut album that would set the world on fire. Of course, the band and I would have differing opinions about when that time was. Every time I would go to a rehearsal and they would play through their songs,

I would say, "You know, you're still two-thirds songs short." They would rebel and make trouble. At one point, they tried to fire me as their A&R guy because I wouldn't let them record, but we patched it up.

ROBERT JOHN I was hanging out with those guys during pre-production and they were getting pretty pissed off. Tom Zutaut had them in pre-production for a long time to tighten up the band before they went in to record "Appetite," and I know they were gettin a little sick of that. In the end, it was probably the best thing.

SLASH The record company was freaking out because it didn't look like anything was going to happen and, unbeknownst to us, we were looking at

These doors were opening up to the band and we had to figure out what was through them.

DUFF

being dropped from the label if we didn't get something happening. I remember one or two meetings with Tom where he sat us all down and said, "look, man, you guys look like shit. I keep hearing stories about what you are doing out there, and you really need to get your shit together. We have a record to do." A couple of us were in really bad shape. We'd come walking in to a meeting at the office and you'd think they just pulled us out of the gutter on Hollywood Boulevard. It was hard living.

DUFF Success happened and none of us knew how to deal with it.

TOM ZUTAUT The hardest part was finding a place for them to live, because we put them in this apartment on Fountain and Crescent Heights and they burned through that $75,000 pretty damn fast. All of a sudden they don't have any money and they don't have a place to live and I knew I needed to sort it out. So I told them, "We're not going to give you any more cash, but we will cover your rent." We gave them a monthly subsidy for food, a place to live and a rehearsal space so they could write songs and create.

STEVEN ADLER We got a pad in the Hollywood Hills and we never stopped.

We had strippers and drug dealers and everybody up there. We were playing and we were living the life.

TOM ZUTAUT There was one particular night where I was almost ready to throw in the towel. They burnt through the first money and they burnt through another $100,000 in monthly expenses. I know the money didn't go in their pocket because they weren't actually getting any cash from us, they were just getting living support. I don't know where they got the drug money unless it was their stripper girlfriends.

Anyway, I went over to the house and they were all strung out on junk. On one hand it was really quiet, but on the other hand it was really scary. There were a couple of girls strung out with them and they were just watching MTV, nodding in and out. A couple of them said to me, "we're really hungry." And I said, "well, what do you want?" And they told me, "cookies and milk." I went to the store on Santa Monica Boulevard. It was a Mrs. Fields cookie store -- back when there were Mrs. Fields -- and I got a bunch of bags of cookies.

Then I went to 7-11 and got some cartons of milk and I came back. I'm there not longer than ten minutes and the door knocks. I go to the door to answer it since everybody else is incapacitated, and it's the cops! I don't want to open the door too much, and I asked, "can I help you?" And they're like, "We've got a disturbing the peace complaint about loud noise coming from this apartment" I looked at them and said, "I don't know what you're talking about." And they asked, "Can we come in?" I'm thinking to myself, "Well, they're just sitting there eating cookies and drinking milk and I suppose if I say no, that's going to make more trouble." So I took the gamble and I let the cops in. They came in and they saw some crazy, long-haired rock dudes, which, let's face it, the sheriffs in West Hollywood saw that all the time in those days. They come in and see all these guys watching MTV, drinking milk and eating cookies and they said, "Sorry to disturb you, can you turn the TV down a little maybe?" The landlord is there and she's screaming at the cops, "They're making noise!" and the cops are looking at this lady like, "We're really sorry lady, but they're just watching TV. There's nothing against the law here." So she then threw them out as soon as she could.

After that, I was desperately trying to find the band a manager.

SHARK ISLAND WITH AXL ROSE
APRIL 26TH 1986

Axl and Tracii from L.A. Guns (Axl's old bandmate) joined Shark Island. They were a local band and Axl was friends with the singer Richard Black.

He considered Richard a great performer and they ripped through a version of Led Zeppelin's "Rock N' Roll."

Move to the City
Don't Cry
Jumpin' Jack Flash

They were asked at the last minute to play a fifteen-minute set at this special acoustic show.

The backdrop shows a "no amps" icon; they jumped the gun on MTV's Unplugged. As I was setting up my camera equipment, the PA informed me I couldn't make a video. I told Axl about this setback. Axl loyally said the band wouldn't play unless I could tape.

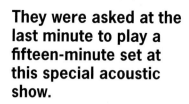

CENTRAL UNPLUGGED
MAY 1ST 1986

AXL: Can you guys hear these guitars?

SLASH: Can you hear the guitars or what?

AXL: This next song, is called "Don't Cry." This will be the first time acoustically. Can you make it a little bit darker in here?

AXL: Thank you. This next song, is called "Jumpin' Jack Flash."

AXL: (after Jumpin' Jack Flash) Thank you.

RAJI'S UNDER THE NAME
FARGIN BASTYDGES
MAY 13TH 1986

tle Kings and the inner-Hollywood crew. Dobbs tells us that **Paul Stanley** (**Kiss**), looking a little worse for those years of pore-clogging makeup and in holey jeans, showed up for the recent Raji's **Guns and Roses** show. Rumors raging about Raji's have it that the Kiss-er may be producing the glam-boys' upcoming LP.

SAT. MAY 31
Y · PHILLIPS
SPECIAL ADDED GUESTS
FARGIN BASTYDGES
(GUESS WHO)

METAL MEETS FUSION
U.F. ⇌ H₂ + H₂ = He

Stegler

The version of
"You're Crazy"
that appears on
"Appetite" is
performed here
for the
first time.

Around this time, they sometimes liked to play casual, often last-minute gigs around town under the name Fargin Bastydges. They came up with the name – spelled differently every time – after watching a character in the movie "Johnny Dangerously" who has a speech impediment; everything he said came out garbled.

There was a girl in the audience by the stage who kept spraying beer in Axl's face – she was evidently profoundly drunk herself – which caused the singer to be shocked repeatedly by the electrical equipment. Near the end of the first song she threw her bottle at him and Axl pushed her away with his mic stand, yelling at the top of his lungs…

I threw up between every
song at this gig.

SLASH

AXL: *Somebody get this stupid bitch out of here.*

Axl spilled the open secret that Guns N' Roses, bored at taking a hiatus from live performing as they readied their album, were actually the Fargin Bastydges.

AXL: *I wanna thank everybody for coming down here tonight. You know us, those Fargin Bastydges. Be on the lookout for another Fargin Bastydges show. Of all places, on the 31st, at Gazzarri's at 1:00 am. We get fucking bored. We have to have something to do.*

DUFF: *Isn't it free beers for the band or something like that?*

AXL: *I wanna dedicate this next song to all the girls who spent some time fixing themselves up, decided they look bitchin, and came down here on the prowl. This song is called "Rocket Queen."*

AXL: *Thank you, give us a moment here. This is a brand new song and this will be the first time I ever, well wait…I sang it kind of back there with the band a little bit. And I'm gonna make this up as we go. This song is called "You're Fucking Crazy."*

AXL: *Wasn't that kind of fun? We're gonna slow things down a bit here. I think a lot of you might know what this song is. What was the name of this song? "Don't Cry"*

AXL: *This song is for anybody here that does too many drugs, but really doesn't give a fuck. This song is called "My Michelle."*

AXL: *Alright this is our last song. We're gonna take you down to a place we like to go. It's called "Paradise City."*

AXL: *Thank you, May 31st, The Fargin Bastydges.*

PA: *Guns N' Roses.*

Immediately after the show a girl from the audience approached Axl to say that the girl he had hit with the mic stand wanted to apologize to him. Axl said, "not right now." She persisted and Axl repeated, "not right now – please let go of my fuckin' arm." About twenty minutes later the boyfriend of the girl who had been hit showed up. He was Bob Forrest, the lead singer from the band Thelonious Monster. A serious fight ensued immediately; even

up. During the fight, Forrest picked up a heavy drum stand, swinging it furiously at Axl's head. His eyes were bulging out of his head and he appeared to be under the influence of drugs. Axl charged, knocking him down and kicking the side of his body with his boot for about thirty seconds. Then friends of both parties stepped in and managed to separate them. On the way out, Forrest uttered threatening words to Axl. Axl threw his hands up and made a face as if to say, "You started it." Fierce as this encounter had been, later relations between the two were okay, and their bands even played on the same bill together quite amicably.

*IZZY: *No. It's called "You're Fucking Crazy."*

SLASH: *It's called "You're Crazy" on the record.*

AXL: *Yeah, it's called "You're Crazy" because I didn't want some asshole picking up on it and say, "They put fuck on here," and then not even give it a chance. It was written on an acoustic about another girl we know who was crazy.*

*Reprinted from the Geffen Press Kit

UNDER THE NAME
FARGIN
BASTYDGES
MAY 31st 1986

One of the roadies had to hold Steven's bass drum down throughout the set because of a broken part.

AXL: I hope you know where you are. I hope you know what you need. "Welcome to the Jungle," baby.

Axl followed Welcome to the Jungle with a declaration of how happy they were to be performing during a period of "laying really low" while getting their album done.

AXL: We've been laying really low from all the bullshit we seem to get into, getting ready for this album. And we can't stay the fuck away. We need to play. This song is for everybody here. This is called, "Think About You."

```
Out Ta Get M
Welcome to the Jungle
Think About You
Move to the City
Rocket Queen
Nightrain
My Michelle
Jumpin' Jack Flash
Don't Cry
You're Crazy
Paradise City
Mama Kin
```

AXL: This next song is about coming down here to L.A. like everyone in this band. There are no fucking natives here. This song is called "Move to the City."

AXL: We'd like to thank our friends, for coming down.

Duff's brother Matt and his two friends joined them on stage with their horns. Matt played the trombone for an extra-long version of the "Move to the City" with a jam at the end.

DUFF: My brother Matt, on the trombone.

AXL: This is basic instruction on how to be a bitch and get away with it in style. This is called "Rocket Queen."

SLASH: Will one of you fucking chics out there buy me a fucking drink.

SLASH: Alright, this is dedicated to any one person out here that will fork out the bucks to buy me a drink. This is called "Nightrain."

AXL: To remind you, the bar is over there. You got fifteen minutes.

AXL: Anyone here had a night this week where they took it a little too far, next fucking day you couldn't move. This song is for you. ("My Michelle")

AXL: I'd like to introduce a friend of mine. This is all kind of makeshift; thrown together at the spur of the moment. Richard, are you out here anywhere? I'd like to introduce Richard Black, the singer of the band Shark Island.

RICHARD: Good evening folks. How are you doing tonight?

AXL: We're gonna do a little song together, verse by verse, called "Jumping Jack Flash."

RICHARD: There is a lot of people here tonight, isn't there?

AXL: Thank you, we'd like to thank Richard from Shark Island. June 15th, right,

LiveAction
Chart

The **Live Action Chart** reports on the three top-drawing acts at various Los Angeles Area clubs. The clubs range from small 100–150 seaters to 1,000 seaters. We rotate the selected clubs each issue in order to give the widest possible range of information. Each club's top three is reported to us by the individual responsible for the bookings.

Reporting Dates
May 27–June 9

Blue Lagune Saloon
Marina del Rey

1. Rebel Rockers
2. Zulu Spear
3. Bonedaddys

Manhattan Jazz
Manhattan Beach

1. Doug McDonald Trio
2. Luther Hughes
3. Billy Childs

Hiatt on Sunset
Hollywood

1. Matt Dennis
2. Mal Waldron
3. Bill Holman

Palomino
North Hollywood

1. Paul Butterfield
2. Rave-Ups
3. Buffalo Springfield Revisited

Madame Wong's West
Santa Monica

1. D.B. Knight
2. Secret Life
3. Ice Teaze

FM Station
North Hollywood

1. Avalon
2. Silent Son
3. Edge

Country Club
Reseda

1. Joshua
2. Alrisha
3. Mary Poppinz

Gazzarri's
West Hollywood

1. Hurricane
2. Fargin Bastydgis (a.k.a. Guns N' Roses)
3. Crossbow

McCabe's
West Los Angeles

1. David Lindley
2. Leaders featuring Chico Freeman
3. John Doe w/Gene Taylor & Bill Bateman

Safari Sam's
Huntington Beach

Thurs., June 5 — **Bevvy, Reindance, Hardchoir.**
GAZZARRI'S, 9039 Sunset Blvd., W. Hlywd. The self-proclaimed "godfather of rock & roll," club proprietor Bill Gazzarri, lords over his part of the Strip more like God the Father. Outside, this temple of hard rock features a 15-foot likeness of his grace, while inside, a concert-hall-size stage dominates what's left of the club; a full bar, some gold records on the wall and the faithful crowded in between. Services held Fri.-Sat. 8:30 p.m., new amateur bands Sun., 7 p.m.; 18 & over, cover $7.50. Call (213) 273-6606.

Fri., May 30 — Rockwest Productions presents **Bitten, James' Band, Temporary Insanity, Riser.**
Sat., May 31 — **Stegler, Y, Phillips,** and a band with a "rosy" future, if they don't get shot, **Fargin Bastrydges.**
Thurs., June 5 — High Times Events presents the Thursday KNAC Rockfights, the best of L.A.'s unsigned hard-rock bands.

at the Whisky. We wanna slow things down again. I think you know this song. It's for everybody here who needs some one. "Don't Cry."

AXL: This is our last song people. This song, I wanna take you somewhere. We're going down to "Paradise City."

SLASH: Good fucking night. You guys are fucking great man. Thanks a lot Gazzarri's, you surprised me.

DUFF: Alright, alright, alright.

SLASH: Do you wanna hear about your mama?

AXL: Where's my fucking water.

AXL: We're Guns N' Roses. Thank you, good fucking night.

PA: It's now 2:20. Please leave as quickly as possible. Watch out for the sheriffs and thanks a hell of a lot for coming down here tonight.

GUNS & ROSES

FRIDAY JULY 11th TROUB.

JULY 11 1986

They were invited by the club to play this gig, for which they were paid $2,500 and played for ninty minutes. This was the last time they played the Troubadour and their longest show to date.

AXL: *(before "Welcome to the Jungle")*
Thank you for coming down. You're the only thing that makes it happen.

Out Ta Get Me
Welcome to the Jungle
Rocket Queen
Think About You
Move to the City
Nightrain
My Michelle
Don't Cry
You're Crazy
Back Off Bitch
Anything Goes
Mama Kin
Paradise City
Nice Boys
Heartbreak Hotel
Shadow of Your Love
Jumpin' Jack Flash

Not long after this show, Slash did the unthinkable. He pawned his Les Paul for drug money.

MARC

AXL: *I wanna take a minute to tell you about something we're doing. We wanna tell you about this Geffen thing. We wanna thank you for making that happen. But, it's gonna be a long time before we are able to put this album out. We haven't been able to really give anybody here a god damn thing, so we're putting out our own album before the Geffen Album. It's gonna be on our own label, Uzi Suicide records. It's gonna have a few originals and a lot of the covers that we do, since they might not be on a later project. So some of you could get your hands on it. It's gonna be a limited edition, but I thought you might like to know that. This next song, is for the same person that I always dedicate it to. This one is for Barbie for helping me save my life two more times this week. This is "Rocket Queen."*

Duff's brother and his friend joined them on the horns for "Move to the City" and a short jam.

DUFF (before "Move to the City"): *Alright, we wanna bring out some horn players right now.*

AXL: *Some people have been yelling for me to turn up.*

SLASH: *Neil, we love you.*

AXL: *This is something that we all done did. I'm sure a lot of you have too. Hit it boys.*

AXL: *This next song is about some bad ass cheap shit that will knock you on your ass. I drank a big bottle of this stuff and I came down here, and, I'm told, that I got in a fight with like the whole place. You got to be real careful on this shit. And we wanna dedicate it to Stewart, out in the bar, for making a bad ass drink. This song is called "Nightrain."*

The attitude Axl expressed about the local press was a departure from his usual petulance:

AXL: *I would like to thank -- you've heard about fuck BAM Magazine, and fuck the Music Connection and shit like that out of us. We'd like to take the time to thank some people. We'd like to thank the L.A. Weekly now, Scott Marrow, and some other people. Thank you, and thank you KNAC. This is for those of you who like cocaine. This song is called "Michelle."*

DUFF: *If anybody has some beer…*

SLASH: *Hey Neil, we're having some trouble with the guitar mics down here.*

AXL: We're gonna slow things way down. This is for all of the girls here tonight. This is "Don't Cry."

DUFF: Alright c'mon, whew.

AXL: Did I hear someone say the word bitch.

The band displayed a sense that they had been thinking about their rowdy reputation – and decided it was just fine.

SLASH: Alright motherfuckers, we've been catching a lot of flack around town about the way we act. That's why all you turned up tonight because you don't fucking give a shit. Right?

AXL: This is for those who don't like it, this is called "Back of Bitch."

AXL: (before "Anything Goes") This is the last song.

AXL: Thank you, goodnight.

During the first encore featuring "Mama Kin" and "Paradise City," a bunch of people jumped up on stage and started slamdancing at the end. This inspired the band to play two more encores: "Nice Boys" and "Heartbreak Hotel" was the second and "Shadow of Your Love" and "Jumpin' Jack Flash" was the third.

AXL: I here you're mama calling.

DUFF: Hello, Hello, what's this song called?

AXL: This song is called "Paradise City."

SLASH: Hey man, have a good time, but don't tear this fucking place down, alright.

AXL: We've got a slam song for you. Do you feel like slamming? This song, you

got it, what's the name of this song? This song is called "Nice Boys Don't Play Rock N' Roll."

AXL: Thank you and goodnight.

DUFF: Alright, you guys have been fucking great.

AXL: You guys want some more? We've got just what the doctor ordered up here. We've got some Elvis here for you.

AXL: Do you wanna hear some "Shadow of Your Love." This song is for our road crew. The whole fucking lot of them, especially Ronnie!

AXL: This song is called "Jumping Jack Flash."

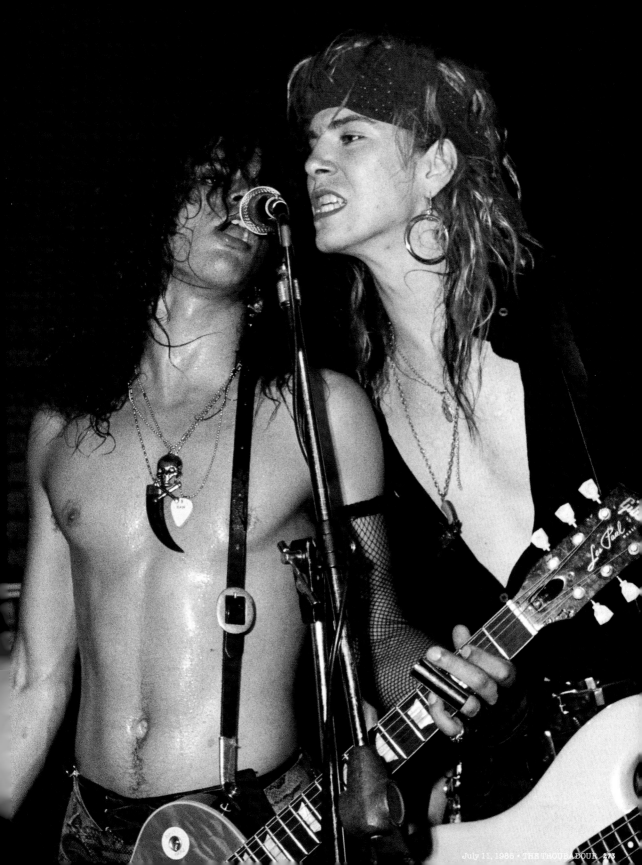

L.A. BEAT

GUNS & ROSES: BAD BOYS GIVE IT THEIR BEST SHOT

By JEFF SPURRIER

Four days after the five members of Guns & Roses got together in Silver Lake and decided to form a band, they left on a West Coast tour. On the way to Seattle, their car broke down in Fresno and the musicians spilled out onto the road with their gear and hitchhiked for the next 40 hours.

When they arrived in the Northwest, they found out the rest of the tour had been canceled and they were only getting $50 for the show, not the $250 they were promised. They played their set on borrowed gear and then turned around and hitched back to Los Angeles, broke and tired.

That was June, 1985. A year later, the band was getting ready to depart for Britain to record its debut LP for Geffen Records, and despite a hefty advance, Guns & Roses remains a decidedly street-oriented, living-on-the-edge Hollywood rock band. The perennial bad boys are even getting evicted from the West Hollywood apartment they share.

Clearly, success has not spoiled Guns & Roses. If anything, it's made them wilder.

"We're just a band," said guitarist Slash, 20. "We don't have to be the 'cool' thing or the 'in' thing. It's

real important we get out there and express ourselves and play. (Kiss bassist) Paul Stanley came down to one of our shows and hung out where we hang out. I'm looking at this guy watching what we do. He's a nice guy, but he didn't have a clue as to what we were doing. Everyone gets the basic idea: They're a rock 'n' roll band. But they don't get the formula."

The formula mixes influences such as AC/DC, Alice Cooper, Aerosmith, Led Zeppelin and the Sex Pistols with a large dose of a street-born, get-stuffed attitude, an ear-shattering decibel level, four-letter lyrics and an appreciation for, in Slash's words, the "extremities of violence and sex." It's a combination that's not likely to win Guns & Roses any fans in the Parents Music Resource Center.

"(Our first video) is going to be realistic and it might show a lot of violence so it might get banned," said lead singer and lyricist W. Axl Rose, 24. "There's a lot of violence in the world. That's the environment we live in and we like to show what we live in rather than hide it and act like everything is nice and sugary.

"Everybody likes to paint their pretty pictures, but that just ain't how it is. It just seems easier to know the rougher side (of life) than the more pleasant side just because it's more readily accessible."

Rose moved to Los Angeles from Indiana in the early '80s with his childhood buddy, guitarist Izzy Stradlin. After bouncing around in a variety of bands (Rose, Hollywood Rose, L.A. Guns), he and Izzy

teamed up with two other regulars on the Hollywood club circuit—Slash and drummer Steve Adler. Bassist Duff McKagan completed the lineup. Guns & Roses quickly attracted attention, especially at the Troubadour, where the group built a following despite its lack of in-crowd connections.

"It seems like when you come to this town unless you are part of the mommy's-boy-daddy's-money poseur rock scene they try to puke you right out," said Rose. "You fight for your place. I remember two years of standing at the Troubadour and talking to no one, not knowing what to do, and everybody thinking they're so cool. Eventually we did our own thing, made new friends, and brought a new crowd to the Troubadour."

While Guns & Roses was wowing audiences at the Troubadour (where they'll play a thank-you-and-farewell show Friday) and eliciting label interest, the band

was based in a squalid one-room Hollywood apartment, living. Just as a record-company bidding war was heating up last winter, two rape charges were filed against Slash and Rose.

"Everyone was trying to hide it from the record company," said Rose. "'Rape charge? What rape charge?' The charges were dropped eventually, but for a while we had to go into hiding. We had undercover cops and the vice squad looking for us. They were talking a mandatory five years. It kind of settled my hormones for a while."

While the band's recent signing may have propelled it out of the club circuit, the group strives to maintain friendships formed during its years of hanging out. Rose in particular enjoys introducing Guns & Roses audiences to new bands.

"If you don't support your own scene your trip is not going to happen," says bassist McKagan, 22. "You've got to support your friends. It's a family. You can't go out there and say, 'We're the best. Screw you all.' You've got to say, 'Look. These guys are good, too.'"

Recently, however, it's been difficult to dedicate as much time as

before to the blossoming hard-rock scene in Los Angeles.

"We've been very busy with a lot of new pressures we've never experienced before," said Rose. "We've got to go have a meeting with some guy that's a millionaire. I don't have a cent in my pocket and I have to act like I'm more in charge than he is. That's really strange.

"You have to come down from the pressures of that to talking with a friend, and sometimes the transition is rough. We've been neglecting some of our friendships recently but once we get some management hopefully we'll be able to get back into that and deal with just being people again."

First, though, the group has a job to do: Record a debut album that will justify Geffen's faith in the band. And even if Guns & Roses doesn't hit the bull's-eye, Rose will be satisfied as long as he gives it his best shot.

"I have something I want to do with Guns & Roses and this is part of me that I want to get out and take as far as I can," he said. "That can be a long career or it can be a short explosive career—as long as it gets out and it gets out in a big way." □

Guns & Roses—Steve Adler, left, Slash, W. Axl Rose, Izzy Stradlin, Duff McKagan—stuff a booth.

With the band having a hundred percent creative control, there were a lot of issues with producers saying, "I can't to do my job."

TOM ZUTAUT

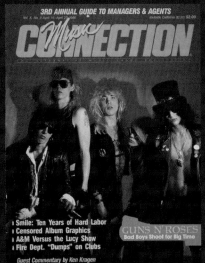

Whoever Tom Zutaut hired to produce "Appetite" had to have nerves of steel and the humility of Buddha.

Creative control was non-negotiable and the band's tolerance for "professionals" with an agenda to shape their music was less than zero. Suggestions to cut songs in order to make them more tangible for broader audiences or pop friendly radio were tossed out along with the producers who brought it up. Shooting the messenger was common practice and Tom Zutaut had trouble finding the right fit.

In the meantime, Tom hired his long time associate Alan Niven to manage – i.e. control -- the day-to-day details of the band while they searched for a new producer. Like a chameleon; Alan could hang with the guys, then shape-shift into a straight-laced rep for the press or to get the band out of any trouble. He kept the band away from bad influences, organized their schedules and managed the growing concerns of the record company. Although his role was more oriented toward management, he was in tune with the sound and feel Guns N' Roses wanted to accomplish on the album and wasn't afraid to voice his opinion. The band trusted him.

Producers were brought in who had a history of making records that Axl and Tom appreciated and which provide a sort of blueprint for the sound they wanted to achieve with "Appetite." Axl was a huge Nazareth fan and Manny Charton, the guitarist and co-producer of Nazareth, was flown in from Scotland to record over two dozen tracks with the band, known as the Sound City Demos. Their work was productive, but Manny returned to Scotland after three days. He never heard from the band or Tom again and realized they better off working an engineer, not a producer. Once prospective producers got wind of the band being too

difficult or controlling, or recognized the clear direction they had internally, the engagement period quickly ended. As the revolving door of producers continued to spin, Tom decided to end the search and produce the album himself, seeking out an engineer to lay down the master tracks.

The road to record "Appetite for Destruction" continued with Spencer

> **Steven:** They couldn't hear for two, three days.
> **Izzy:** Loud is a way of life.
>
> ## THE MUSIC CONNECTION TOUR
>
> **Slash:** Why do we deserve the cover of this magazine? To tell you the truth, I have no idea. Ask our manager. [*Laughs*]
> **Izzy:** Ask your boss. He should know.
> **Slash:** 'Cause we've created so much noise that we deserve to be on the cover of *Music Connection*.
> **Izzy:** The magazine is out for two weeks, right? It's going to be a 14-day adventure—like a *Music Connection* tour. We're going to play every 7-11 there is.
>
> ## THINKING BIG FOR THE FUTURE
>
> **Izzy:** We'll get richer.
> **Slash:** I'll have more pairs of shoes to choose from.
> **Steven:** I'll have my own place to live.
> **Axel:** All the socks we can buy.
>
> * * *
>
> Guns N' Roses signed a record deal with Geffen on March 26, 1986. I hear tell that the band received a cool 37 thou as *part* of their advance. All five members were unavailable the next day. Their manager reported that the boys were out shopping, but this time for a deal of a *different* kind—on new equipment. My final word: Hey, if you guys have any dough left, how 'bout forkin' over 40 bucks for a new tape recorder? If not, fuck *you* and your *band*. (Just kidding, I think.) ∎

Proffer, who Geffen Records hired for his talent at fashioning a great sound and taking acts mainstream through his bold marketing tactics, as he did for Quiet Riot just a few years prior. The band cut several songs at Pasha Studios in Hollywood and Spencer adjusted to their idiosyncrasies when it came to showing up late for call times or intoxicated recording sessions. Spencer attributes their sudden end to a confrontational moment with Axl, but for the band, Spencer's treatment of their material

wasn't to their liking. They completed the Pasha demos and Tom was again on the hunt for a new producer.

Again Axl and Tom brought up names based on albums they admired and singled out "Stranger in the Night" by the English seventies group UFO. It was a live album that had just the right balance Guns N' Roses wanted to capture for "Appetite" and they invited Mike Clink, the co-producer and engineer of that album, to cut a demo. In their first meeting, Mike immediately understood the direction they wanted to take "Appetite" and subscribed to the band's need for creative control. He cut a demo, just like all the other prospects before him and Axl and Tom were pleased with the results. The only question remaining, was if Mike had the personality to tolerate the absurdities and discipline the band.

SLASH When we wrote the songs and put the songs together we never allowed any outside influences. It seemed like we had to make compromises or sacrifices to work with a producer that we didn't want to work with. Every manager or producer that they tried to hook us up with either couldn't deal with us or we didn't like them.

STEVE ADLER All the other records companies and producers wanted to change us. And we're like, "fuck that! We're not going to change." Either you liked it or you didn't.

TOM ZUTAUT I would play the demo for producers, who would listen and be intrigued. Then they would sort of back off and say no. Axl was very picky and this made it difficult to find a producer, because when I talked to him about a bunch of different producers, he would say, "Yeah, but he made this record," or "That record was crap and I don't think I can work with him because I don't respect the fact that he made that record." You know Axl had a definite opinion on almost anyone that I brought up.

cont.

SMOKING GUNS: Guns N' Roses recently finished recording some 27 songs as a demo project for their label, Geffen Records. The demo sessions, produced by Manny Charlton (late of Nazareth), were recorded at Sound City Studios. The band also announced that they will be playing their "Farewell to Hollywood" concert on July 11th at the Troubadour, after which they leave for England to begin recording their debut album, scheduled for a fall release. Meanwhile, Geffen will release some of the demo material as an "authorized bootleg." That oughta hold you for a while.

THE SOUND CITY DEMOS

Out Ta Get Me
Rocket Queen, (take 1)
Rocket Queen, (take 2)
Nightrain
My Michelle
You're Fuckin' Crazy
Paradise City
Move to the City, (take 1)
Move to the City, (take 2)
November Rain, (acoustic)
November Rain, piano
Shadow of Your Love
Reckless Life
Think About You
Welcome to the Jungle
Don't Cry
Nice Boys, (take 3)
Back Off Bitch
Anything Goes
Mama Kin
Heartbreak Hotel, (take 2)
Ain't Going Down, no lyrics
Jumpin' Jack Flash, (take 2)
Jumpin' Jack Flash, (acoustic)
Move to the City, (acoustic)
(Untitled song in progress)
You're Crazy, (acoustic)
The Plague
Cornshucker Stomp

TOM ZUTAUT One of the things that Axl responded pretty positively to was that he and I were both huge Nazareth fans. Manny Charlton, who was the guitar player for Nazareth, produced some of the records and his name came up. Axl said, "yeah, lets do a session with him." So I flew to Scotland, found this guy in the middle of nowhere in Edinburgh and played him the demos. We talked about the band and then Manny said, "yeah, I'll come to L.A. and do a session with them."

MANNY CHARLTON Tom Zutaut came over to Scotland and asked me if I was interested in producing the band. At the time I was recording an album with Nazareth called "Cinema," so I had commitments with my own band and the schedule was kind of tight. He asked me to come to L.A. and meet the band anyway. The board mixes that Tom brought with him weren't very good. I couldn't hear the vocals properly. I said to Tom, "let's get to the bottom of this. Let's go into the studio, cut their set live, straight to two-track and then I can listen to the songs and get a handle on this."

When I arrived in Los Angeles, I was supposed to see them the next day for rehearsals. Tom picked me up to go to the rehearsal space and there was nobody there. None of them showed up. We hung around for a while and I looked at him and asked, "Are you sure you know what you're doing here?" To me, that was not very professional to have a guy travel 6,000 miles to see a rehearsal and none of them even showed up.

We went into the studio for three days and we got on pretty good. I remember going into the studio and seeing racks of new Les Pauls and Mesa Boogie amps, so I knew Tom was taking care of them. I asked them to cut their set; everything that they were doing at the time. We just cut it live off the floor of the studio. Axl was stuck between two studio doors, with a little window watching the band and he gave it his all. He didn't bitch about it, there were no tantrums about not being able perform. He just got on with it. The band set up and they played. That went straight down to two-track because there were no multiple-tracks involved. There was no overdubbing either. I just set them up and got a really good balance and they played their asses off. They worked well together and they had their arrangements down. It was really good stuff.

TOM ZUTAUT It was mixed down to two-track tape -- there were never multi-tracks at that time. It went really, really well. Bootlegs are probably still floating around out there.

MANNY CHARLTON They weren't just some bar band. They were a band with a capital "B." An important band is always greater than the sum of their parts. You take one part away and the chemistry is shot and it's never the same. The five guys worked together and produced something that was great as a whole. The word is chemistry. That's what they had. They had great chemistry and they were a great band. As soon as you took one cog out of the wheel, one link out of the chain, that was it. I thought the stand-out songs were "Welcome to the Jungle" and November Rain." Axl was playing the piano and Izzy was doing a little bit of

background vocals and it was fantastic. That's when I went, "wow, there's proper songwriting skills here," and I thought that I would really like to produce them.

TOM ZUTAUT But for whatever reason, after Manny did those two days, he thought it was a little crazy. Then there was some dissension in the band about whether or not Manny would be the right guy. So we did the session with him and he disappeared. It was back to the drawing boards.

MANNY CHARLTON I didn't disappear; I went home. I told Tom about my commitments with Nazareth. What happened was I never heard a thing from them at all after our sessions and then "Appetite" came out. If there was dissent from within the band, I knew nothing about it. I got the feeling that Slash wasn't particularly impressed. I don't think he was as big a Nazareth fan as Axl was. Maybe he wasn't impressed with me as a guitar player. The only positive thing I heard was from Izzy. He said, "Manny's really cool." I wasn't socially integrated with them. I didn't get a chance to get to know them, personally. I wasn't in L.A., I was in Scotland and I had never heard of them before. So I was at a little bit of a disadvantage. I didn't know anything about the L.A. scene with all the other bands that were going on at the time. I guess they must have looked at me like I was some kind of alien with my Scottish accent and being a father, but they respected me for what I had done with Nazareth's "Hair of the Dog." But there wasn't really a chance for us to hit it off.

Ultimately, I think they wanted somebody who wasn't going to interfere with what they were trying to do and who would get a great performance out of them. They didn't want to be disciplined by anyone. They had their own internal discipline and they didn't want anybody coming in from the outside and tell them what to do. What would I have done as producer? All I would have done was make sure they were comfortable and that they sounded great. As far as I'm concerned, a good producer gets the best performance out of the artists and I could have done that with Guns N' Roses. In the end, I thought the album was not that far away what we did in the studio. *cont.*

These songs were recorded in just a couple of days on a simple two-track system; nevertheless, they really captured the band – the blazing intensity and the sheer raw energy just jump right out.

I had a chance to give the tapes a good long listen soon after they were made one night when Slash ended up in jail. He had been a passenger in a car that was pulled over by the Sheriff's department for a broken taillight. Danny Biral, a roadie for the band, was driving. The sheriff's deputies found a hypodermic needle in the car, and somehow Slash ended up getting arrested. This wasn't the first time the band had been in trouble with the Sheriff's Department, and it wouldn't be the last.

Axl and I went down to the West Hollywood Sheriff's Department to bail Slash out. By the time we arrived, Slash had already been shipped off to the L.A. County jail. So we headed downtown. On the way we picked up some Tommyburgers and listened to the demos. When we arrived at the jail to post Slash's $178 bail, one of the officers noticed the medallion in the shape of a tiny gun hanging around Axl's neck. Evidently alarmed at the threat posed by Axl's necklace, the officer threw him up against the wall and frisked him. Finding no additional threatening objects, he let Axl go, and we went back to my car and waited about five hours for Slash to be released. During the long wait we listened to the demos over and over.

Some of the songs from these demo tapes can be heard in the background of the making of "Don't Cry' and "November Rain" videotapes. They were used as fuller music between interviews.

MARC CANTER

MARC CANTER Spencer Proffer was also working with the band at the time. He produced a demo of as a test to see if the band would want him to work on their album.

SPENCER PROFFER I was the only guy that actually got further than the audition phase to where we actually had a contract and I made a deal to produce the whole album. Randy Philips and Arthur Stevac who went on to become very reputed and integral managers in the music community, were managing Guns N' Roses at the time. They were really smart, good managers. They were doing all the right things; they were getting gigs, they were helping get the momentum going and they were attracting media attention. I got introduced to the band and started hanging out with the guys. I thought the music was cool. It had great attitude, it had great spirit, it had great energy and I smelled that it would make a major socio-cultural impact based on the fresh approach of taking the metal genre and infusing it with a lot of unique lyrical and musical elements. They had the shit that makes great rockn' roll. Axl is a great performer; Slash is a first-rate guitar player. They could have used a little guidance and blueprinting and that's the reason Randy plugged me in there. He thought I could help them and keep the raw energy.

We went into Pasha Studios, worked on pre-production for about a month and we started making the record. We zeroed in on four or five songs that we started arranging. I worked with them in a rehearsal studio on constructing the arrangements, the breakdowns and the vocal approaches. Randy was waiting for the results of our work so he could quarterback the rest of their touring and the next chapter of their career.

About the time that we were in the studio doing overdubs on the tracks, after we had the arrangements laid out, my wife at the time was expecting our first child. The baby was late and we set up a Caesarean section at the hospital on a specific day. The band would come to the studio everyday late, drunk, stoned or somehow fucked up, one way or another. I called a band meeting a couple of days early, knowing that there would be a Caesarean and that I wanted to be at the hospital spending the time with my family. I didn't want to abrogate my responsibility to work with the band, so I said to them, "would you, on the day of the birth, show up on time? Come to the studio at noon and I'll work with you for five hours, then I'm leaving to go the hospital to spend the evening with my newborn son." They, of course, swore that they would. On that day, the hours passed and they didn't show. Close to five o'clock, they show up collectively. Slash came in and he couldn't wait to get to the bathroom, so he took his stick out and pissed on the wall of the studio. Axl went into the control room and he threw up on the control board and asked if I wanted to go party with him. When I refused, he told me to get fucked, forget fatherhood, and that if I left, I was an asshole. He said either work with Guns N' Roses and rock, or be a dad, but I couldn't do both. I told him

to get fucked. I told them to never show up at my studio again, I walked out and called the Geffen people the next morning and told them I was out. That was the end of my involvement. I sold the tapes back for next to nothing because I didn't want these people in my life, karmically, ethically or otherwise. I thought they were the scum of the earth. I left a lot of money on the table after however many millions of albums sold, but I don't regret it because I have my integrity.

SLASH I just don't recall any of that. We recorded "Sweet Child O' Mine," we recorded "Nightrain" and a couple of other things during that time at Pasha. We did all the live stuff for "Live Like A ?!*@ Suicide." We did finish the arrangement of "Welcome to the Jungle" out of those sessions over at his place. The songs didn't sound better than demo quality, so we didn't achieve record quality status yet. We were trying to check him out and get a certain sound out of him and we moved on because we thought he didn't capture it. We didn't think that the stuff that we recorded was album quality. If he thinks he fired us, I think that's bullshit. Or else, I didn't know about it and Tom didn't tell us. That's a possibility.

TOM ZUTAUT Then I introduced the band to Paul Stanley and Gene Simmons from KISS, because we were thinking about working with them, but one of them told the band that they'd have to rearrange "Welcome to the Jungle," and the band was like "fuck that guy." The band walked out and that was the end of it. They would say, "no one is going to rearrange 'Welcome to the Jungle.' We've played it for our fans, and we're not going to change anything." And that stood true, even when the record finally came out and there were people at the label that wanted to edit the song. The band would always have creative control and would not change the song. And, you know, they were right, because it's a classic. With the band having a hundred percent creative control, there were a lot of issues with producers saying, "I can't to do my job." At the same time, I was desperately trying to find the band a manager and everyone was turning them down because they had this reputation of making trouble.

SLASH Alan Niven was the first guy that could deal with us at face value as we presented ourselves. Without getting squeamish or bullshitting us, he could deal with Izzy and I being strung out. He could deal with Steven being Steven. Duff was always on the even-keel and then there were Axl's idiosyncrasies. Axl already had a major rock star persona and was a little bit unpredictable and Alan handled all of that with a shrug of the shoulders. It was no big deal to him. So we felt comfortable and at ease with him, not feeling like we had to impress him or try and bullshit him into thinking we were something we were not. So that worked great. And he had good ideas and we looked at where he was coming from and how it related to the band and how it all worked. All things considered, he was just the right guy at the right time. He understood the sensationalism of the whole thing. In other words, he knew that a band like this; a reckless sort of live-by-the-moment hardcore rock n' roll band, was actually entertaining and he knew how to market that. He came from a Sex Pistols background. I think the only time we ever changed the arrangement of anything was "Welcome to the Jungle," because of Alan. There's a breakdown section in the song that we did twice instead of once, and Alan said, "Well, what if you just take that section out, it would cut like a minute of the song," and we thought, "No. We don't want to." Eventually we ended up trying it and that was that. That was the only arrangement change that we ever made.

MARC CANTER Alan Niven was the boss. He ran things like a CEO; he knew how to get things done. He took the band under his wing and fought hard for them.

RON SCHNEIDER Alan was like the Peter Grant of our generation; he was large and in charge.

TOM ZUTAUT One day, I realized that I was going to have to find an engineer and produce the record myself. That was going to be the only way the band would get what they wanted without stepping on someone's ego. I started going through the list of people who I thought were great engineers who I thought could capture lighting in a bottle for Guns N' Roses. And a couple of the names that came up were Bill Price, because of his great engineering from Roxy Music to the Sex Pistols, and Mike Clink. Mike Clink had engineered some of the great UFO records. Axl, Slash and I had a conversation about how great these UFO records were, especially the live record, "Strangers in the Night." I contacted Mike Clink, talked to him and then I introduced him to the band. Mike was looking to step out of an engineering role and move into more of a production role. He subscribed to the theory of the band having creative control. The band would basically be co-producing and I would be heavily involved as an A&R person riding shotgun over the whole thing.

MIKE CLINK I got a call from my manager Teri Lipman that I had a meeting set up at Geffen Records. I went to Tom Zutaut's office. Tom, Alan Niven, and Axl were there and they played some records that I worked on. They said, "We like this record, we don't like that record." The records that they liked the most that I had worked on were the UFO records, especially "Strangers In The Night." That's the record they really loved. They also played me some failed attempts at some previous recordings that the band had made that no one was happy with. The recordings weren't right and they didn't represent the angst and the energy that the band had. It was a little too processed, which was the sound in that day. People tended to make things very processed sounding, very slick, and they were looking for something a little more raw. So they were looking for someone to come in, fix it, facilitate it and capture the Guns N' Roses sound.

SLASH Luckily, Tom found Mike Clink and there was a perfect chemistry there. Whatever producer we ended up working with, there had to be mutual respect. The way that things sounded reflected how the producer gelled with the band. If it didn't sound right, then we probably didn't really like the person as a result. And if it sounded great, then that would give us an idea as to the character of the person. When we first met Mike, we really liked his energy. We liked hanging out with him. He was very low key and quite. He is simple guy without a lot of airs. He was amiable and didn't try to act a certain way to hang out with us. He just seemed very in control. We were eager to go in and do the demo of "Shadow of Your Love" and when we got it and it sounded great, we struck up a great relationship that was very well-rounded from that point on. Although Mike was labeled as a producer of the band, what he really did was capture the band live and be able to put it on tape properly. We tried a number of different producers who just didn't know how do that.

MIKE CLINK What they wanted me to do was go in the studio with them and record one song and see how it turned out. So we went in the studio and I recorded "Shadow Your Love." During the process it was a matter of getting the band to trust me and understand that I had their best interests at heart.

TOM ZUTAUT Mike is probably on a scale of nice people who you meet in life who are really talented at what they do; he's a ten. You know you just meet him and he makes you smile. You needed someone with the patience of Job to be in a session with these guys and Mike is one of the nicest, most patient guys you'll ever meet.

STEVEN ADLER It took a while, but we lucked out with Mike Clink.

MIKE CLINK After I had finished doing a mix of the song and had given it to everybody, **my phone rings at about four o'clock in the morning. It was Axl. He said, "This is great. I love it. Let's start tomorrow."**

BOGART'S JULY 21ST 1986

Slash and Izzy showed up very late to this

gig. Bogart's, now closed, was in an uninspiring suburban mall, but it was actually a very comfortable club that presented a good cross-section of local bands.

IZZY: *You guys ready or what?*

AXL: *Hey, this place ain't so bad.*

DUFF: *This one's called "They're Out to Get Me."*

AXL: *Welcome to Bogart's, and "Welcome to the Jungle."*

AXL: *This is about coming to Long Beach. This is called "Move to the City."*

AXL: *This next song is for all the women here who are out to dress to impress. This song is called "Rocket Queen."*

AXL: *How many people here have been drinking tonight? I think we've got some liars. This next song is about a bottle of cheap wine that knocks you on your ass. This song is called "Nightrain."*

AXL (Before "My Michelle"): *This is for those of you who like cocaine.*

AXL: *Thank you very much. We're gonna slow things down a bit. It's getting hot in here.*

SLASH: *What's happening? So this is the Long Beach crowd; quite and sedated.*

AXL: *Any of you girls know some other girl that just won't leave your fucking boyfriend alone. Any of you guys got some girl that just won't stay off your back. This is called "Back Off Bitch."*

AXL: *Thank you very much. This is our last song. We're Guns N' Roses and this is "Paradise City." I wanna dedicate this to the dopes.*

AXL: Good fucking night.

BOGARTS
LONG BEACH   (213) 594-8976
IN CONCERT
July 21
GUNS & ROSES
& MARSHES OF GLENNY
July 22
JACK MACK & the HEART ATTACK
July 28
THE CALL
July 29
FISHBONE
August 4
LORDS OF THE NEW CHURCH
August 11
TOWER OF POWER
CALL FOR INFO
TICKETS AT ALL TICKETRON OFFICES

PHOTOS THIS SHOW BY LEONARD MCCARDIE

CLUB LINGERIE
UNDER THE NAME
FARGIN BASTYDGES
JULY 24TH 1986

Thursday, July 24
FARGIN BASTYGENZ Strikes Again!
RASZEBRAE
THE PRODIGAL SONS

Friday, July 25
FAITH NO MORE
GANG GREEN from Boston
CELEBRITY SKIN

Saturday, July 26
CHUCK E. WEISS & HIS GODDAMN LIARS
THE BLACK SEDANS
THE KEEN ONES

Sunday, July 27
THE LAWLESS
THE TRADE
THE SPECTORS

Monday, July 28
RUNAMUK
THE RETURN

Tuesday, July 29
MAGGIE MAYALL & THE CADILLACS
JUDY RUDIN
PETER FAHEY & THE TRUST
THE BARNBURNERS

Wednesday, July 30
...CORMICK & THE UNINVITED

Axl quit the band that afternoon and was fired too, for good measure. Nevertheless, the band regrouped by show time. Axl joined the opening band, the Prodigal Sons, for the song "Forty Days."

SLASH Axl and I had a fight and we were just about to break up and the only reason we did this show was because Tom Zutaut managed to get us all on stage. I stood facing my amp the whole time. I don't know how Tom managed to coral us back together to do this gig.

_____

AXL: *We'll bare with this equipment shit. We get shocked every time we touch it. This is "Think About You."*

AXL: *We'd like to thank everybody for coming down here. A friend of mine is a keyboardist in a band called Johnny and the Jaguars and got in a car wreck and smashed his fucking hand. We want to dedicate this next song to him, because he is our bro. This song is called "Nightrain." This is for you Dizzy.*

AXL: *This song is dedicated to Tom Zutaut for helping me get through the fucking day.*

Billy, the singer from Prodigal Sons, came up and sang back ups on a "Paradise City."

AXL: *This one is called "Paradise City."*

SLASH: *This is really important. Someone, I need a beer and a fucking cigarette. I aint' got no cigarettes, I aint' got no beer.*

DUFF (in Spanish): *"Dos, dos!"*

SLASH: *All right, someone was nice enough to get me a cigarette. Now would someone please get me a beer?*

AXL: *Could you tell me what song that is? What's the name of that tune? This one's called "Mama Kin."*

AXL: *Thank you goodnight. You wanna hear some "Rocket Queen." We're gonna change that. We've got some "Nice Boys" for ya.*

AXL: *Thank you Goodnight.*

CLUB
Lingerie
FULL BAR • MUST BE 21 W/ VALID I.D. • LARGE DANCE FLOOR
6507 SUNSET BL. HOLLYWOOD 466-8557

PHOTOS THIS PAGE BY LEONARD McCARDIE

```
  Out Ta Get Me
Welcome to the Jungle
  Think About You
     Nightrain
    My Michelle
  Move to the City
     Don't Cry
   Paradise City
     Mama Kin
     Nice Boys
```

Not a stellar night for the band. Axl showed up late. The house told the band if they didn't play they wouldn't get paid, so they went on without Axl.

Lacking a vocalist, they improvised on "Anything Goes," including a protracted guitar solo. Axl showed up at the end of the song. Because "Anything Goes" was always played near the end of the show, he assumed that the band had already gone through most of the set.

AXL: (before "Rocket Queen") I'm sorry about being late. I was told 11:00 and turn this shit up.

STEVEN: How are y'all fucking feeling?

Someone in the crowd made a remark

AXL: It ain't my fault!

IZZY: If you don't like it leave.

AXL: "Mama Kin." Turn these vocals up.

DUFF: Thanks a lot you guys. Sorry for the lateness.

TIMBER'S
JULY 31ST 1986

THE LORDS
OF THE NEW CHURCH

GUNS & ROSES

The Flamethrowers

last LA show !

thurs.
JULY
31st
830pm
Timbers
Ballroom
1920 E. Alosta, Glendora
818-335-2673

BASTIAN
RESENTS

THE SCREAM AUGUST 15TH 1986

Robert John took the photo of the band backstage at a late-night gig I mIssed at the Scream, which appears on the cover of L.A. Rocks, a tabloid put out by Ruben Blue. The band had been scheduled to play a show with True Sounds of Liberty (TSOL) the next night down in Orange County, but cancelled at the last minute because the gig was so far away.

Guns & Roses at the Scream

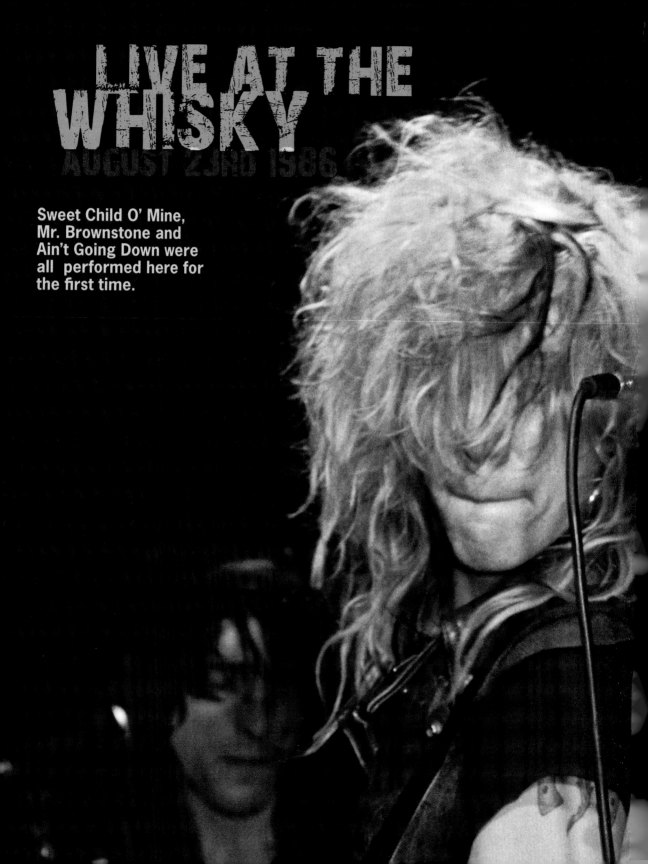

LIVE AT THE WHISKY

AUGUST 23RD 1986

Sweet Child O' Mine,
Mr. Brownstone and
Ain't Going Down were
all performed here for
the first time.

"Ain't Going Down" ended up being an outtake from the "Use Your Illusion" albums. It ended up on the Guns N' Roses pinball machine that came out in 1994. At sound check that day, the band did some final arranging on all three new songs.

AXL: *This is a new one. This one's called "I Ain't Going Down."*

AXL: *We'd like to thank everybody for coming down here tonight. This is an absolutely fucking outrageous crowd. So give yourselves a fucking hand. This next song is a brand new one And I think it goes with a little word of warning. I've seen a lot of my close friends, and I've seen a lot of other people I know, get really fucked up when they discovered this drug called heroin. The next thing you know, your life is fucked because you are just too fucking cool. This song is called Mr. Brownstone. And I think you should stay the fuck away from that bad shit.*

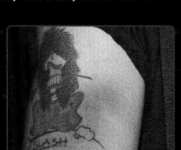

GROUP SHOTS BY MARC CANTER

SLASH This is the show when I first wore a top hat and I'll never forget it. I got the top hat that day. I was really high and the hat was great because it could help me balance.

DESI CRAFT I remember I drove Slash on my motorcycle to a retail store on Melrose and bought his first top hat with him. I just felt it in my bones; that was definitely it for Slash.

SLASH: So what's happening? Man, the Whisky's fucking cooking man. Fuck.

AXL: I've seen some pretty fine looking ladies here tonight. This song is called "Rocket Queen."

AXL: You came here for some heavy shit and you wanna kick some ass. This is a song called "Nightrain."

"Nightrain" included a drum roll and a different beginning at this show.

AXL: Had a few drinks, done a few lines. When you get done, you're gonna do some more. This is called "Michelle," for those of you that need your cocaine.

STEVEN: So what's happening?

SLASH: Alright, this one's a new one. This is one of our newer ballads, this is something called "Sweet Child O' Mine."

DUFF: Alright, thank you very much.

The lead in "Sweet Child O' Mine" was just as it would appear on the record.

AXL: In case we put you to sleep, I wanna remind you next weekend, we will be playing at the Santa Monica Civic with none other than Ted Nugent. We'll be going on real fucking early. Can't help that. This is to wake everybody up in here and this is what we're all about. This song is called "You're Fucking Crazy."

AXL: "Welcome to the Fucking Jungle" baby, I think you know this one. This is for you.

AXL: I'd like to thank Kelly for the interview in L.A. Rocks. I'd like to thank L.A. Rocks and Ruben Blue for all their support. Lets here it for fucking KNAC while we're at it. And this is for our dancer who got a busted leg, got hit by a car, wrecked on her motorcycle. This one's called "Anything Goes."

Before "Paradise City," Axl shared some of his reflections on the band's reputation and its possible ramifications for their career now that they landed a record deal and seemed poised for stardom.

AXL: This is our last song. If life gets to be a bitch for you -- it does for us. You know a lot of people think we're fucking rockstars because we got signed. We ain't put no album out yet. We ain't even got shit, you know. It's like we've got to prove

our fucking selves. I wanna thank all of you. This song is called "Paradise City."

AXL: (singing) Thank you. Next Saturday night with Ted Nugent. We're Guns N' Roses, good fucking night.

DUFF: Alright, thanks a lot you guys.

SLASH: Thanks a lot. You're beautiful. Thank you. You wanna hear another one. Wanna hear a tune about your mama? Wanna hear a tune about your fucking mother. Alright then, this one is for the Whisky. Hey, wait a second.

AXL: Where's them party ninjas? This one is called "Mama Kin." If you don't wanna hear it, it's alright, we won't play it. I mean we don't want to piss you off.

AXL: (before Jumpin' Jack Flash) Tell me if you know this song. Ladies and Gentlemen, this is Izzy Stradlin. Take it away boys.

DUFF: Thanks a lot, goodnight you guys.

_____

DESI CRAFT One time, Slash came to our place on Orchid with a lump of Mexican tar heroin and he wanted to cook it all up. Izzy and I told him to just do a little bit because there was this death tar going around. He said it was okay and shot up. Well, he pretty much went rigor mortis in the chair and we got him on the floor. I gave him mouth-to-mouth and I remember him going "Is this death or is this an angel I'm seeing," because he was so out of it. Right after that, we wrote **"Mr. Brownstone"** and I wrote that with them. I was really upset that I never got credit for that. But why dwell on the past. That's how that song came about.

_____

*AXL When we moved out of our place on Fountain and La Cienega, I was the last one to leave, and found this piece of yellow paper wadded up in the corner where Izzy's and Steven's room was. It had the lyrics to "Mr. Brownstone" on it. I read it and went, "This is great." They said they had music for it and we ended up starting to rehearse this thing.

SLASH A lot of people have a misconception about this song. They think it's about drugs. It's not so much a statement about our drug habits; it's more a statement about other people's drug habits. It's a good little ditty that people can listen to and maybe think about what they're doing and try and get themselves into perspective. I know one thing, a lot of people who are doing a lot of fucking drugs all the time don't have any kind of focus. A band can keep you together. Like we can all go through all kinds of shit, but the band keeps us together. But if you don't have a band, don't have a job, don't have anything you're trying to do, then somehow drugs can take over.

IZZY It can mean a million different things to a million different people. It's like when you listen to a Zeppelin song, what do you think? I have all kinds of fucking wild ideas about what "Custard Pie" is about.

_____

*AXL "Sweet Child O' Mine" is a true song about my girlfriend at this time.

IZZY That's a real love song.

AXI I had written this poem; reached a dead-end with it and put it on the shelf. Then Slash and Izzy got working together on songs and I came in. Izzy hit a rhythm, and all of sudden this poem popped into my head. It just all came together. A lot of rock bands are too fucking wimpy to have any sentiment or any emotion in any of their stuff unless they're in pain. It's the first positive love song I've ever written. I never had anyone to write anything that positive about.

DUFF It was probably the hardest song for me and Steve to record, just because you have to keep a steadiness and also keep the emotion in it.

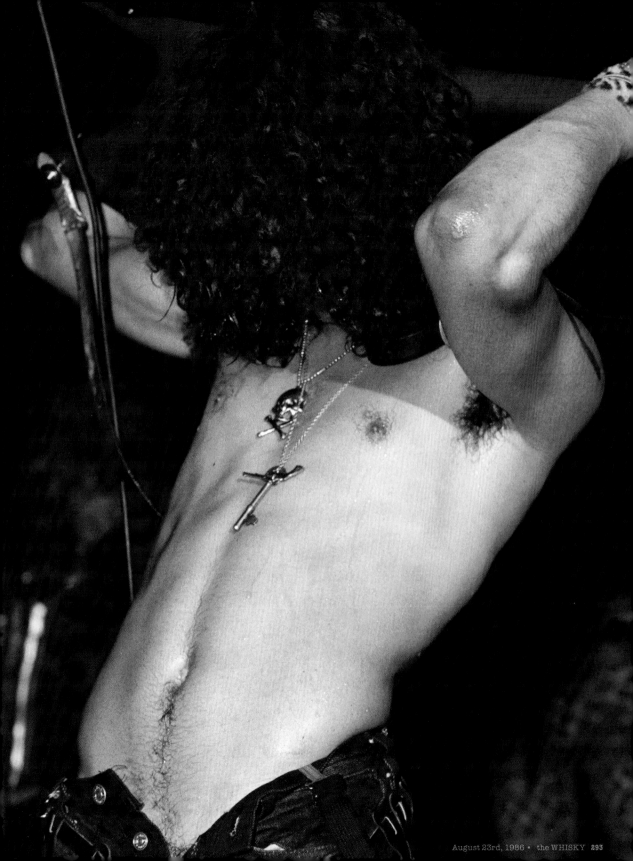

UNWINDING BACKSTAGE AFTER THEIR STUNNING SET; THE
BAND MEMBERS SURROUND A&R GOD TOM ZUTAUT AND A&R
GODDESS TERESA ENSENAT.

OPENING FOR TED NUGENT

AUGUST 30TH 1986 SANTA MONICA CIVIC AUDITORIUM

tastic songs and has a ton of energy, doncha think? I really liked their set, especially "Nasty, Nasty" (I think that's the title of their forthcoming album), "Does She or Doesn't She?" (great backing vocals), "Without Love," and a tune I *think* was called "Running Out." These guys should really go far. But I guess we'll just have to wait 'N see (hee-hee).

Guns N' Roses went over well, although I missed most of their set 'cause my ticket said 8 p.m. and they went on at 7:30. They sounded real bluesy, Aerosmithy, and nasty, and Axl's cool outfits and hats were an added bonus.

That's all for now, Ted. Sorry I had to split after eleven songs—my friends were kinda bored, and I had to agree with 'em. Maybe I'll catch ya next time around.

Love,
—Katherine Turman

Antonio Carlos Jobim

The Greek Theatre
Los Angeles

Way, *way* south of the border, Brazilian composer and pianist Antonio Carlos Jobim has been a superstar of the bossa nova for years. And while those seductive, swaying rhythms may not rank up there with hard rock or electro-funk in the popularity stakes on this side of the border, a packed house at the Greek quickly proved that the performer's Los Angeles debut was long overdue.

The setting was perfect as Jobim sat behind the piano and eased his way through a long and entertaining set of his songs, many of which—"The Girl From Ipanema," "Desafinado," "One Note Samba," and the haunting "Quiet Nights of Quiet Stars"—have since become standards. All were delivered in the deceptively low-key, charming style that has become his trademark, and what Jobim lacks in pure vocal ability, he more than makes up for with style and grace. Singing in a mixture of Portuguese and English, Jobim's breathy and understated phrasing acted as the ideal anchor to the shifting, expressive tempos that propel all his compositions.

He was backed by a superb five-piece band that featured his unusual lineup of cello, bass, drums, flute, and guitar (played by his son, Paulo Jobim). The family affair also extended to his five female singers, his wife and daughter among them. Jobim cannily made use of all the possibilities inherent in such a gathering, at times allowing the vocal ensemble to scat-sing and showcase their impeccable harmonic and rhythmic sense, at other times allowing the flute or cello to sit centerstage and carry the music.

It's hard to believe that this was the legendary performer's first-ever local concert. After such a successful (if belated) beginning, let's hope he returns again soon.—*Iain Blair*

Ted Nugent/ Black 'N Blue/ Guns N' Roses

Santa Monica Civic
Santa Monica

Dear Ted:

Sorry I couldn't stay for your entire show the other night. You looked great in your baby-blue, chest-baring jumpsuit, and you still had your great wild-man attitude, but yer set just didn't click. I know, the sound at the Civic *was* kinda high-endy and too loud, but something more was wrong. "Free for All" was well-received, but too choppy and sloppy. Other older tunes, like "Great White Buffalo," were simply boring (and long), though you and your band seemed to be having fun. Your voice *did* sound great on "Painkiller," and your guitarist/vocalist Dave Amato was good, if somewhat rigid. I thought your new tune, "Angry Young Man," was okay, as were "Hey, Baby" and "Talk Too Much," but the show was *not* riveting. I *wanted* to love ya, Ted, but the vibes just weren't there.

Your choice for openers, the two "N" bands, was interesting, though. Black 'N Blue writes fan-

MUSIC CONNECTION, SEPTEMBER 29—OCTOBER 12

MARC CANTER Slash and Izzy had been in San Francisco for a gig with Jetboy and they were delayed in getting back to L.A. as they were obtaining some necessary personal supplies. When they got to town they headed right for the Santa Monica Civic and immediately hit the stage.

Because my name had been left off the guest list, I almost didn't make it into the show and had to sneak in with Slash and Izzy. I wasn't able to get all my equipment in, so I couldn't videotape the show. I did manage to bring my camera to take still photos.

SLASH We came back from a trip to San Francisco, got back to our apartment and we couldn't get any dope. Danny Biral stole all my smack, but he didn't tell us and so we searched the house. We tore it to pieces looking for it, then we got really sick and our dealer wouldn't call us back. We were freaking out. So, we're getting sicker and sicker and finally one of Desi's girlfriends found some smack. She drove us down to Izzy's old apartment where this girl was staying, and we waited around until the smack showed up. We do it really quick, jump in this car and fly across town. We get to the gig and my zipper broke as we were jumping over the fence to get into the

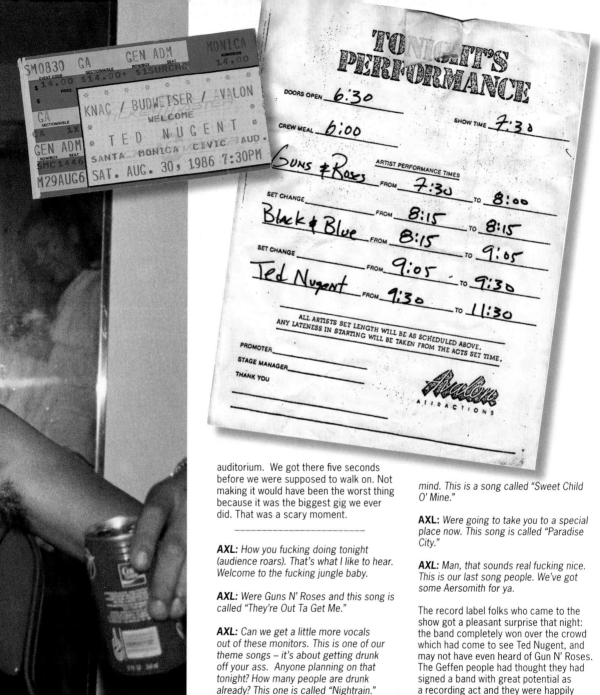

auditorium. We got there five seconds before we were supposed to walk on. Not making it would have been the worst thing because it was the biggest gig we ever did. That was a scary moment.

———————————————

AXL: How you fucking doing tonight (audience roars). That's what I like to hear. Welcome to the fucking jungle baby.

AXL: Were Guns N' Roses and this song is called "They're Out Ta Get Me."

AXL: Can we get a little more vocals out of these monitors. This is one of our theme songs – it's about getting drunk off your ass. Anyone planning on that tonight? How many people are drunk already? This one is called "Nightrain."

AXL: This is for those of you out there who like to partake in a special drug called cocaine. This song is called "My Michelle."

IZZY: I smell some reefer in here.

AXL: It smells nice.

AXL: We're going to slow things down a little bit. But I don't think your going to

mind. This is a song called "Sweet Child O' Mine."

AXL: Were going to take you to a special place now. This song is called "Paradise City."

AXL: Man, that sounds real fucking nice. This is our last song people. We've got some Aersomith for ya.

The record label folks who came to the show got a pleasant surprise that night: the band completely won over the crowd which had come to see Ted Nugent, and may not have even heard of Gun N' Roses. The Geffen people had thought they had signed a band with great potential as a recording act and they were happily astonished to find they actually had a powerfully commanding arena-ready act on their hands. In Axl, they saw a front person who could electrify, not just a club-size audience, but a stadium-size crowd. Axl recalled that Ted Nugent tried to have the sound turned down on them because they were rocking so hard and had the crowd eating out of their hands.

He also remembers Nugent hitting on his girlfriend, Erin, backstage.

MUSIC MACHINE
SEPTEMBER 13TH 1986
Motley Crue's management turned up at this show to check out the band!

AXL: Get this fucking curtain out of the fucking way. Ladies and gentlemen, we're Guns N' Roses. This song is called "Welcome to the Fucking Jungle."

AXL: We'd like to thank the Unforgiven. This is a song called "Think About You."

AXL: Jason, can you fix that thing for me? This is a song about taking things a little too far, doing a little too much. It's called "Mr. Brownstone" and lets see if you can figure out what it's about. Hey Dizzy.

STEVEN: What's happening motherfuckers.

AXL: We wanna apologize for our technical difficulties. This is a song about getting drunk. We dedicate this to Dizzy and his hand. This is a song called "Nightrain."

AXL: We're gonna slow things down a little. Take a little fucking break. This is a song called "Sweet Child O' Mine."

AXL: Thank you. This is a song, it's called "Paradise City."

AXL: Do you wanna hear a song about your fucking mother? Do you know the name of this song? We'll give you some "Mama Kin."

AXL: Thank you, and good fucking night.

MC: Yeah! L.A.'s own Guns N' Roses.

AXL: In honor of our fucking technical difficulties, we're gonna get some of our frustration out of our systems now, I hope you can live with it. This is a song called Nice Boys Don't Play Rock N' Roll.

DUFF: C'mon you motherfuckers.

AXL: God damn!

PHOTO BY JACK LUE

PHOTO BY JACK LUE

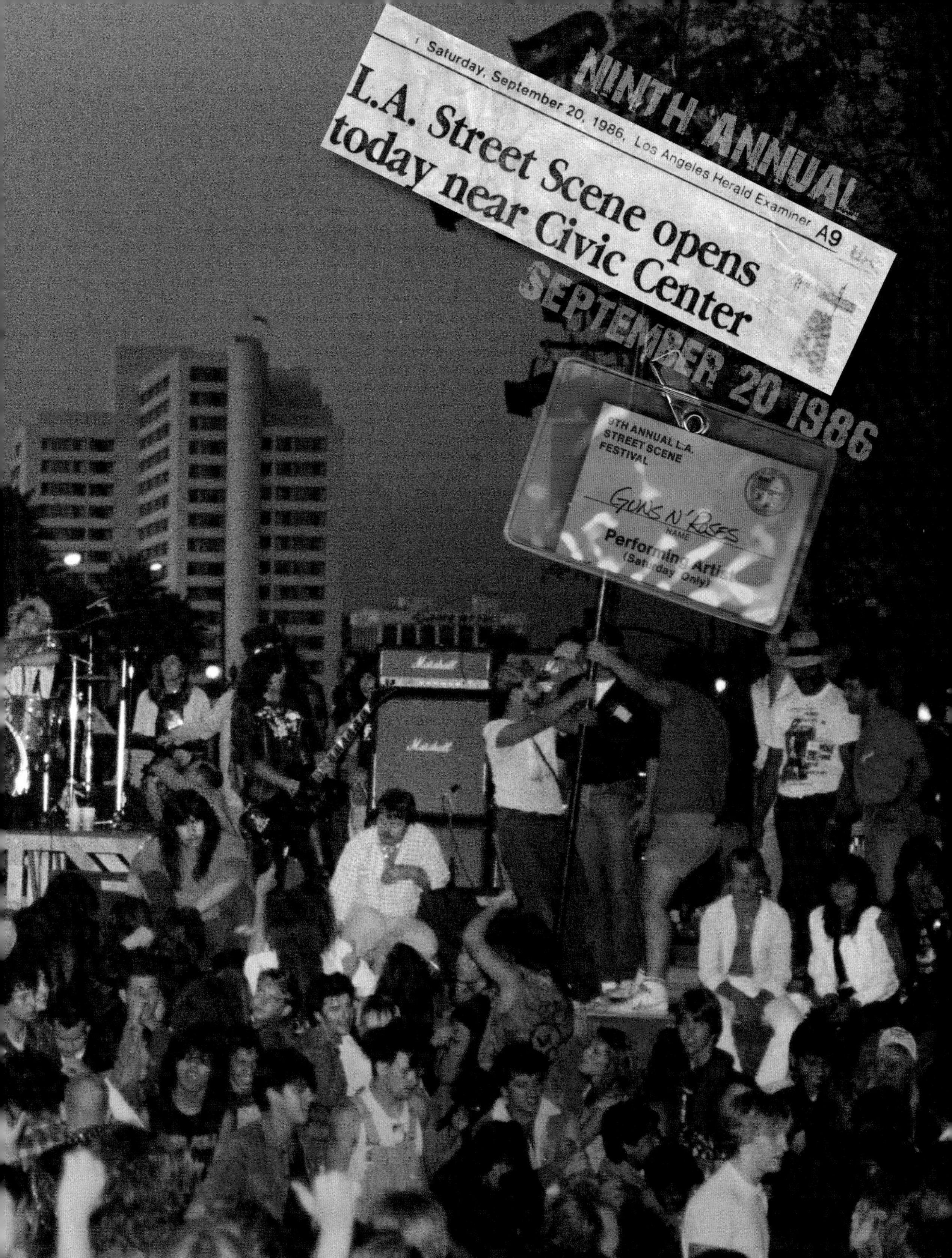
1 Saturday, September 20, 1986, Los Angeles Herald Examiner A9
L.A. Street Scene opens today near Civic Center
NINTH ANNUAL
SEPTEMBER 20 1986
9TH ANNUAL L.A. STREET SCENE FESTIVAL
GUNS N' ROSES
NAME
Performing Artist
(Saturday Only)
Marshall
Marshall

For a band who had yet to release an album, it was some scary, big time rock n' roll shit with no parental guidance, no common sense, and nobody giving direction on where or how to set up the gear. It was just this clusterfuck of drinking vodka on stage and the attitude was like, "Whatever's gonna happen is gonna happen." It was fun. **DEL JAMES**

An early rock star moment for Slash.

They were announced to the crowd of between five and seven thousand by a ten year old boy who had been hanging around backstage.

BOY: From the back streets of Hollywood, the sleaziest band in L.A.: Geffen recording artists Guns N' Roses! People from the crowd kept climbing up on stage. There were all kinds of security guys making sure they were removed right away. The crowed proved difficult to control.

AXL: How you fucking people doing tonight? God damn! "Welcome to the Fucking Jungle."

AXL: (before "Out Ta' Get Me") They told me to tell you people... hey! Don't fuck up my microphone. Hey! I lost my monitors now. They'll shut it off. Their gonna shut the show off unless we fuckin... I mean I wanna get as crazy as you but... Let me hear it for KNAC. This is a song about the fucking cops around here.

AXL: Thank you. Looks like we have a fucking rowdy turnout. This next song, is a song about doing too much heroin. I know that sometimes things go a little too far. This song is called dancing with "Mr. Brownstone."

After "Mr. Brownstone," someone threw a bottle at Axl.

AXL: Alright, we've got some assholes out here. Alright, I just got hit with a fucking bottle.

DUFF: Whoever threw the fucking bottle is a god damn sissy.

The band's security guard whispered something in Axl's ear and Axl said over the P. A.:

AXL: Alright, hey. Thanks guys. You just... I'd like to thank the people in the front row that got a little crazy with the water. You dumped water on the electrical cables. The show is over, and you (he made an empathetic gesture of annoyance at one particular person in the crowd)...fuck you!

It was then officially announced that the Guns N' Roses set was over because the crowd was too rowdy, and Poison would be on next if people mellowed out.

SLASH: Just try not to tear the fuckin' place down, you know. Have a great time, but just don't break everybody's fuckin' necks, man. You're beautiful.

SLASH: Before we split...wait...those people over at KNAC were nice enough to do me a favor and they gave me a bunch of these buttons to give to you fuckers.

OPENING FOR ALICE COOPER
AT THE ARLINGTON THEATER
OCTOBER 23 1986

The band did this show without Axl.
It was their first show with Alan Niven as their manager.
Axl showed up late, during the middle of the set, but his
name wasn't on the list and he wasn't allowed in.

Shadow of Your Love
It's So Easy
Mr. Brownstone
Nightrain
Think About You
(Blues in E
Whole Lot of Rosie

...he band did their best to carry on without their
...inger. Izzy did the vocals, except for those on
..."It's So Easy," which was Duff's song.

...DUFF: "It's So Easy" is a song West Arkken and I wrote. It's an account of a time that
...of us were going through, We didn't have money, but we had a lot of hangers on and
...rls that we could basically live off of. Things were just too easy. There was
...emptiness; it's so easy.

...ASH There's a lot to say for that period of time
...hen you start to lose the excitement of chasing
...hicks. You start going after really
...zarre girls, like librarians and stuff,
...st to catch them and say I finally
...ent out and caught a girl that
...ouldn't be my normal date.
...ecause everything else
...as starting to get – it's
...o easy.

...XL I got the great-
...t picture. I cut this
...d out of magazine.
...s this girl bent
...ver so her ass
...up in the air
...d it says, "It's
...o easy." It was
...n ad for Easy
...ates. I sang in a
...w voice cause
...at fit the attitude
...that song better. It
...asn't something I really
...ought about, I just started
...ping it. I just sing whatever the song
...eserves. And that song deserved to be sung different
...an the other material. It's a hard, tight, simple, punk rock song.

eprinted from Geffen press release

Izzy was making up lyrics on the spot, for example, "elephant dick under my arms" in "Nightrain," instead of "rattlesnake suitcase" and "I want to tell you a story about this fat bitch I know when it comes to blow jobs she makes me go, in "Whole Lot of Rosie."

IZZY: What's happening? Come up here and tell me all about it.

SLASH: Hey fuckers!

IZZY: Alright, alright, alright.

IZZY: This is about smack. it's called "Brownstown."

IZZY: This is called "Nightrain."

SLASH: Anyway, this is a back to roots gig for us. Where is my fucking tequila? Vodka? Alright this is one of those nights.

right? This is something dedicated to Santa Barbara. This is something called "Think About You."

Before the band jammed on Blues in E, Slash asked the audience if they could help them out:

SLASH: Alright, we wanna ask a basic question. Where is our long lost singer? You didn't think we were fucking serious. Did you? You fucking suckers. Anyways, we wanna find out if there is anyone out there who knows how to sing and wants to do a cover version of "Whole Lot of Rosie."

DUFF: Does anybody know all the words to "Whole Lot of Rosie."

SLASH: Fucking pussies. I bet there are about three hundred of you out there that know the words. You got fucking

songbooks at home, I betcha. Alright, well while we're waiting for a singer to come up and do a version of "Whole Lot of Rosie," we're gonna do some blues in E for Alice Cooper, who's been away for so long.

Slash took a long swig from his bottle, then let loose with some passionately soulful blues. He improvised some blues lines on the spot about not having a singer.

IZZY: C'mon. You want a whole lot of what?

SLASH: C'mon up, we've got room for you up here. Alright, we're gonna do it without a singer, this is "Whole Lot of Rosie."

IZZY: Steve Adler on drums.

The band left the stage so Steven could do some kind of drum solo to kill some time. It lasted only about fifteen seconds because Steven wasn't prepared to do a solo, and when he finished, someone in the crowd booed him.

SLASH: Boo? I heard that, you fuck! C'mon up. We got room for you here. All right, we're going to do it without a singer.

After the show the band trashed the dressing room and broke all the mirrors. Later on in the parking lot the band bumped into Axl. **Axl asked Slash, "How much did we make?" Slash answered "the band made $500. You didn't make anything." Axl grinned and said, "That's cool."**

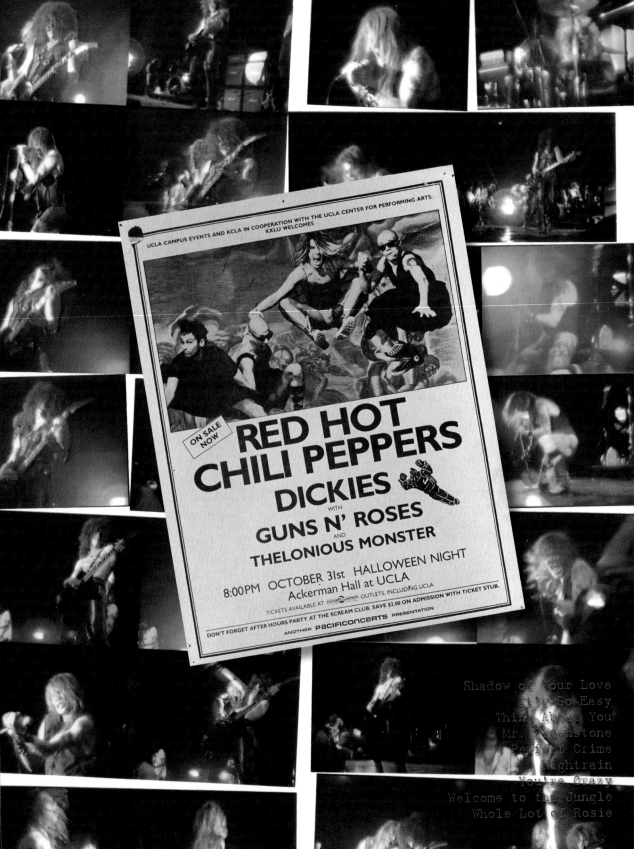

OPENING FOR RED HOT CHILI PEPPERS OCTOBER 31ST

"Perfect Crime" was performed publicly for the first time at this show. I"t's So Easy" and "Whole Lot of Rosie" were performed by the complete band here for the first time.

Thelonious Monster was also on the bill. Even though Axl had gotten into a knock-down drag-out brawl (described earlier) with lead singer Bob Forrest. There was no tension between the bands that night.

AXL: How ya'll doing?

MC: I was gonna introduce these guys from Whittier, but they're not from Whittier. They're from here, Los Angeles. The fabulous, beautiful, Guns N' Roses.

AXL: This is for Paul.

AXL: This is a brand new one, written by Duff Mckagan., called "It's So Easy."

AXL: Good evening. It's good to see so many people here. We're Guns N' Roses. This is a song called "Mr. Brownstone." It's about taking things too far, dancing with the devil.

AXL: I'd like to apologize if there is anybody here that heard the shit with the Alice Cooper show. We just fucked up. That's what happened. But I'd like to tell you guys that this fucking thing that we keep promising you guys, this EP, we just had it mastered today. The artwork is done. We got to print it and package it. It will be out in a couple of weeks.

Axl was evidently talking about how the band had trashed the dressing room. They were aware that Geffen was worried about their reputation. The label was concerned about whether anyone would want to work with them in the future if they persisted with their rowdy antics.

AXL: Alright, this is a new one, by Mr. Izzy Stradlin, this one is called "Perfect Fucking Crime."

AXL: Welcome to the fucking jungle people.

AXL: This is our last song. This is a cover tune. We don't have a whole lot to say. **We're just gonna end this one with some kick ass rock n' roll.**

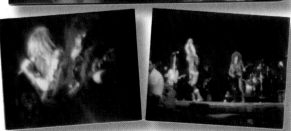

VIDEO SCREEN CAPTURES FROM THE SHOW

FENDER'S BALLROOM
OPENING FOR
CHEAP TRICK
DECEMBER 21 1986

Intro: music from Scarface
Reckless
Mr. Brownstone
Move to the City
Welcome to the Jungle
It's So Easy
Perfect Crime
Don't Cry
Nice Boys
Shadow of Your Love
Think About You
Mama Kin

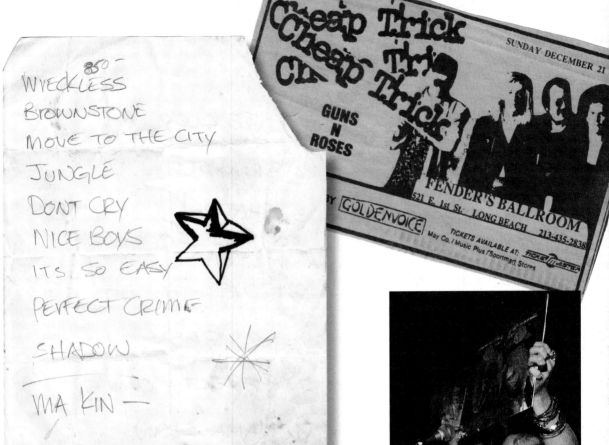

WYCKLESS
BROWNSTONE
MOVE TO THE CITY
JUNGLE
DON'T CRY
NICE BOYS
ITS SO EASY
PEFFECT CRIME
SHADOW
MA KIN —

850—

Cheap Trick
Cheap Trick
Cheap Trick

GUNS
N
ROSES

SUNDAY DECEMBER 21

FENDER'S BALLROOM
521 E. 1st St · LONG BEACH   213-435-2838
BY GOLDENVOICE
TICKETS AVAILABLE AT:
May Co. / Music Plus / Sportmart Stores   TICKETMASTER

SLASH'S HANDWRITTEN SET LIST DIFFERS FROM THE SONGS ACTUALLY PLAYED.

AXL: I wanna thank you all for coming out. This is called "Move to the City."

AXL: This is a new one. It was written by Duff Rose McKagan and our friend, Mr. Smith and Wesson, Wes Arkeen. This is the first time he's ever seen it live. I wanna tell you about something, let me have that record. This is something that we've finally got out. It's called "Live Like a Suicide." Look around in the stores for it. This is called "It's So Easy" and god dammit it is.

IZZY: What's that fucking noise coming out of the PA? We're gonna pull this one like bread out of the fucking water. It's another brand new song. This is called "Perfect Crime."

SLASH: What's happening? So let's hear what the Long Beach crowd really fucking sounds like.

AXL: This is an old one. We haven't really played it in a while. This is called "Don't Cry." Let me have my jacket.

Facing a large crowd that had come out to see Cheap Trick, Axl informed them of the availability of the self-produced Guns N' Roses EP.

AXL: I'd like to tell everybody about a party that we're having, it's on a Tuesday night. Riki and Taime's world famous Cathouse, on La Cienega Boulevard, at the Osko Disco from nine to eleven. It's free, and with special acoustic performances by Jetboy, L.A. Guns and Yours Truly. Tuesday night, from nine to three. The Riki and Taime's Cathouse, you be there.

IZZY: I know you wanna hear another one, right?

Some people in the crowd replied by chanting, "Cheap Trick!, Cheap Trick!"

SLASH: What was that? cheap dick?

AXL: Yeah, well this ain't Cheap Trick, and this ain't really Guns N' Roses. This is some fucking Aerosmith for ya. You want some "Mama Kin?"

Cheap Trick fans continued to demand the headliners.

AXL HOLDING UP THE EP "LIVE LIKE A SUICIDE."

IZZY: They're coming up soon.

AXL: Thank you, we're Guns N' Roses, Tuesday night. Our record party at the Cathouse in Hollywood. Good fucking night.

LIVE LIKE A SUICIDE
EP RELEASE PARTY

DECEMBER 23 1986

ALIBI ARTISTS
&
GUNS 'N ROSES
INVITE YOU TONIGHT TO
PARTY *!•#$ Like A Suicide
AFTER CONCERT PARTY
FEATURING
D.J. JOSEPH FROM CATHOUSE
AT THE
ROSE GARDEN
320 S. LA BREA (BETWEEN 3RD & 6TH)
NO AGE LIMIT   BEER, WINE, SAKI
ANOTHER ALIBI EXCLUSIVE
$5 COVER CHARGE

ABOVE IS A REPRODUCTION OF THE INVITATION TO THE ALBUM RELEASE
PARTY WHICH FEATURED THE BAND UNPLUGGED.
LIVE LIKE A SUICIDE CAME OUT DECEMBER 16 1986.

Guns N' Roses
Live?! Like a Suicide
Uzi Suicide

Though it'll be some time before these guys officially debut on Geffen Records with a full-length album, this enticing four-song live set will just have to do for now. In a nutshell, Guns N' Roses play unadulterated, balls-to-the-wall rock. The only problem here is that the four songs on this record seem to degenerate in both originality and creativity as the EP progresses. Clearly, the inventive "Reckless Life" and "Nice Boys" are the tunes that best highlight the band's musicality. It wouldn't be a bad idea to re-record them and put them on the "official" album, guys. Lead singer Axl Rose is loose as a goose as he displays some very special vocal abilities and a definite flare for improvising. I do take exception, however, to his intro preceding the final track. Shouting "This is a song about your fuckin' mother" hardly gives you any insight into the song itself, but the kids will love it merely for the cursing. Since nobody is sure about an exact release date for the LP, you might wanna snatch this one up right now. If you're into rock, very few bands do it better.

—Kenny Kerner

MUSIC CONNECTION, FEBRUARY 9 — FEI

APPETITE FOR DESTRUCTION

WHY IS "APPETITE FOR DESTRUCTION" ONE OF THE BEST RECORDS EVER MADE? BECAUSE IT CAPTURED GUNS N' ROSES WHEN THEY WERE IN THE SPIRIT OF MIND TO BE CAPTURED!

TOM ZUTAUT

LEFT TO RIGHT — VICTOR DEGLIO, SLASH, STEVE THOMPSON, IZZY, AXL.
PHOTO TAKEN BY MIKE BARBIERO.

With Tom Zutaut's backing and Mike Clink as producer, Guns N' Roses went into Rumbo Recorders in Van Nuys, California to record "Appetite for Destruction." The goal was to record an album with a sound and feel that reproduced the raw and energetic qualities of their live shows. They wanted nothing to do with the trend in rock and pop music at the time; using synthetic elements ad nasueum and compensating for poor songwriting with over-produced orchestration.

Mike's style suited the band. He had an easy going personality that disarmed the band when it came to creative collaboration, but he also played the disciplanarian; demanding that the band show up for their scheduled recording sessions on time. The band responded well to both; their days were long and productive.

But the hooligans of Hollywood didn't allow the marathon days with Mike affect their nights out. Guns N' Roses carried on the usual debachary and Mike became acostumed to the variety of explanations for broken bones, missing equipment and run-ins with the cops.

Just because the band had achieved the status of Geffen artists and were recording their first album didn't change their state of affairs on the street. They were still living hand-to-mouth, bumming off of friends for food and a place to sleep. Izzy was kicked out of his girlfriend's apartment and slept in the utility closet at Rumbo studios when Mike allowed him. Slash had nowhere to live and also set up camp in the studio.

Overall, the environment was highly collaborative and full of energy. Mike Clink and the band delivered the goods. Once the track recordings were complete,

Tom engaged the mixing services of Mike Barbiero and Steve Thompson in New York City who were producing another Geffen artist Tesla. Slash, Axl and Izzy flew to New York and mixed the album to perfection with their new team. Among the small entourage from Los Angeles that followed the three Guns to New York was Adriana Durgan, Steven Adler's girlfriend and a Sunset Bouleveard stripper. Axl propositioned her to record some last-minute "enviornmental" sounds for "Rocket Queen" and she reluctantly agreed, but not without a guilty conscience.

At the end of the mix, everyone involved knew they had gold, even though no one predicted the success that would follow. "Appetite for Destruction" was ready to launch and it was up to Tom Zutaut to get airplay, sell millions of records and create the next chapter of rock n' roll history. What he didn't know was that no one in mainstream radio would touch the band.

TOM ZUTAUT It wasn't until I heard "Sweet Child O' Mine" that I believed they finally were ready because now they had a record. They had all these great raw, punky, thrasher songs from their early days, but now they also had "Welcome to the Jungle" and they had "Sweet Child O' Mine" and they had a bunch of other songs to flush out what became "Appetite for Destruction."

MIKE CLINK In that initial meeting in Tom Zutaut's office, they showed me some of the pop records that I worked on that they didn't like. But I was pulling from some of those experiences and bringing it to Guns N' Roses, not blatantly, but just to help tailor the sound for what they were doing. When you hire a producer, what you're doing is you're hiring them for all the experience they've had working on different records. So I was taking all of those experiences and brining it together with the blueprint being the Aerosmith records. I fashioned the sound of Guns N' Roses, with that two-guitar sound playing off of each other in a sexy, slinky and

powerful way. The Aerosmith correlation was just a blueprint of where I was going, and I pulled elements from a lot of records I had worked on previously.

ROBERT JOHN What's interesting about them going into the studio to record "Appetite" is that I didn't really notice a change in the band. It was almost like everything was just a natural process for these guys. When they went in there, it was just so natural. They'd go in, start recording and I didn't see anybody hyped up about it. Other bands would get hyped up and pumped up, like, "Yeah, we get to record." I didn't see that with these guys. They said, "Okay, we have to do this." They lived for their music.

GUNS N' ROSES ROLLED TAPE WHEN THEY WERE READY TO ROLL TAPE!

TOM ZUTAUT

TOM ZUTAUT Guns N' Roses might have worked consistently for one week, and the next week they didn't turn up. It was pretty erratic, probably because of the drug use and stuff. When Axl was in the frame of mind to work, he might work for two or three days straight and then not turn up for a week or he might come everyday during an eight-hour period. I can't even imagine this scenario happening as corporate as music companies have become today. We thought it was corporate back then. It was hard enough to get people into the concept of, "Here is a band and they're real and you roll tape when they're in the mood, alright."

MIKE CLINK So many people come to me and say, "Those guys knocked it out in one take, didn't they?" No, they didn't. If that were the case, we probably would have been done with the record in two weeks. It didn't happen that way. When Slash played his parts, none of the other guys were there. They wanted to be partying when they didn't have to be there. I always said one of the hardest things about recording that record was getting five people in the same room doing the same thing at the same time. That was not an easy chore because everyone was off doing their things.

SLASH We did the whole album by getting it on the second or third take. That's where the spontaneity comes from. If you don't get it by then you've lost the feel of it.

TOM ZUTAUT I found myself saying to a potential engineer, "I don't know if this is going to be a nine-to-five kind of a job, or a six-to-midnight kind of a job. When the band is in the mood to roll tape, I've got to call you and we've got to roll tape." This presented problems even with Warner Brothers, because again you know they're very corporate. They would tell me, "I have to issue a purchase order and it has to go through this approval procedure." I

had to get David Geffen to call Warner Brothers and give me a book of P. O.'s, so I could issue my own at two o' clock in the morning. So that's another reason why that record was good, because there wasn't necessarily a regular schedule. It rolled when the band was in the space to roll. Mike Clink was perfect for GNR because he could sit in that studio and sit out all shenanigans. And honestly there were a lot of them.

MIKE CLINK I ran a pretty tight ship when I was there. I had set hours that I started and everybody was pretty good about being there. Once we found the hours we were going to work, it was all great. Call time was around eleven in the morning out at Rumbo Studios to cut the basic tracks. Everyone showed up around noon and by one o'clock we were pretty much rolling. They were pretty good about showing up on time and being there. I started with Slash around noon and we worked up until eight at night. Axl was scheduled to come in around nine. What happened was nine became ten and ten became eleven. And then we started working around the clock. Axl was typically late. However, I wasn't sitting around waiting for them to get something done. Use Your Illusion was a whole other story. But while they were in the studio, they were very focused and we got a lot accomplished every single day. "Appetite for Destruction" did not happen by accident. We really worked hard to make that record. It was a labor of love. I put a lot of love into that record.

MICHELLE YOUNG I think that Mike was probably somebody they really needed and they knew that he wasn't messing around. He wouldn't let them get away with stuff. He was kind of like a father figure and none of them really had

that. I actually worked with Mike's wife when he was working with them at an advertising agency. Mike was very stern with them. He didn't mess around. He said, "You've got to be here, and if you're not going to be here then I'm not going to do this." They got busy and they worked.

MIKE CLINK In the studio, we got work done. We worked solid. We worked hard. Outside of the studio it was total chaos. Duff would show up at the door one afternoon when we were doing guitar dubs and his arm was in a sling. I think he might have had a black eye and he was limping. When I asked what happened, he said, "Well, you know, we were stair diving." He was trying to jump from the top stairs of someone's apartment, all the way to the bottom without hitting a step. In the studio lounge it was going haywire. I remember sitting there when we were cutting basic tracks and all of the sudden I heard this raucous. It sounded like an earthquake. Steven was upset about something and was trashing the lounge; knocking over the sofa, the tables, and the refrigerator. There was definitely chaos going on around me, but I rarely left the studio. I was always in the studio working, pulling the guys in, getting something accomplished no matter what happened fifteen or twenty feet away from me.

SLASH The process of recording "Appetite" was a lot simpler and quicker and basically lackluster then the album turned out to be. I was in at 12:00pm, made a Jack [Daniels] and coffee and recorded a song a day. That's how I put all the guitar tracks on. Izzy's tracks were from the basic track recordings and I just stood in the control room with the speakers blasting and just put all my guitars on. And then at 10:00pm we'd be done and then I'd go into Hollywood and just stir up a lot of shit and then somehow make it back the next day at 12:00pm. That was the making of "Appetite" for me -- at least the recording part.

TOM ZUTAUT Why is "Appetite for Destruction" one of the best records ever made? Because it captured Guns N' Roses when they were in the spirit of mind to

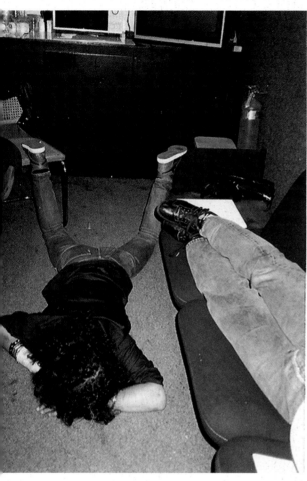

be captured. When they were ready to roll, we rolled whenever that time was. It took a guy like Mike Clink with that kind of patience to be willing to put up with that. I mean most people need a schedule.

MIKE CLINK I always said that they were a gang. When we would go out at night, if one person got in a fight, everyone got in a fight. They were a tight knit group. I had never experienced a band that basically lived on the street. They were streetwise kids and I wasn't used to it. But, I caught up to it and it was a lot of fun.

STEVEN ADLER In the studio, I would always say that I wanted the drums to sound like drums. I didn't want them to

sound like machines. I want the snare to sound like a real snare drum, the bass like a bass drum; no effects.

RON SCHNEIDER There were some days that Slash was kind of nervous. Nobody was in the room at the time because he just needed some time to flow on his own without any distractions. Everybody had to go. In fact, at that time, Slash had broken up with his girlfriend and had two green garbage bags full of clothes and all of his other personal effects and was living at the studio. Whenever they had this one room that wasn't being used, that was Slash's little room. When he was hanging out, that's where he camped out and was calling home for a little bit.

MIKE CLINK Izzy wanted to live at the studio. For insurance reasons he couldn't actually do it. But during the day we let him stay there. So he actually lived in a closet at the studio and had all his things there. But at night when we would lock up, he would go out with the guys. But he would always come back, and would have a little bed in the closet and had all his possessions. They didn't own that much stuff so it was easy. They could basically pick it up with a couple suitcases and take it.

MICHELLE YOUNG I went to the studio and listened to some of the tracks and

I was just blown away by what I was hearing. It was just genius being put out for the world to hear and the magic in the studio was great. At that point, they were so carefree and they didn't have all these anger issues or money issues or life issues or whatever they began to have later. They had a strong bond and lots of energy and were willing to just take it and run with it at that time.

MIKE CLINK I knew the record was going to be a success. I really did. In fact, when Tom Zutaut came down to listen to the playback of the rough mixes that I had done, he said to me, "what do you think the records going to sell?" And I said, "I think it's going to sell two million records." I really had a gut feeling that this was something unusual and exciting and interesting and Tom said, "No you're wrong. It's going to sell 5 million.

SLASH After the studio recordings with Mike, Axl and Izzy and I went out to New York to mix the record with Steve Thompson and Mike Barbiero.

STEVE THOMPSON Tom Zutaut sent me the Guns demos and I really liked the band. I remember getting demo after demo and thinking, "Holy shit, this stuff is great." And I think the songs don't deviate much from the demos. The band had the essence of "Appetite" on those demos. Tom asked us to produce it and we had so much work we were doing at the time, we just couldn't get it in there. It sucked, because I really loved what I was hearing. We told him that we couldn't produce it, but we'd love to mix it. I remember when we started working on "Appetite," I felt that that's where rock needed to be. Nothing was really jumping out and kickin' you in the ass. And Guns was just the perfect band, the perfect attitude, just the perfect vibe for what was going on then. I felt if that record didn't make it then I should get out of the business. I really believed that.

MIKE BARBIERO Tom Zutaut originally asked Steve and I to produce the first Guns N' Roses LP, "Appetite for

There was no computer used.

That was one of the last mixes Steve and I did that was not computer assisted. I think we blew about six sets of Yamaha speakers. Generally, I set up the overall sound of the mix, and Steve would push the rhythm guitars and solos for dynamics, while I rode the vocals. Victor Deglio, my assistant, provided an occasional third set of hands and used to trip extra vocal effects I might not be able to get to, like delays that might require a buss to be pushed on a certain beat somewhere.

"Appetite" was mixed at Mediasound Studios' studio B, in New York City, on a Neve 8068 console that had been modified to include twelve or sixteen 1081 channels of EQ in addition to the standard three band channels of EQ included with the console. We used a great many Pultec EQP1A equalizers outboard, as well as compression on individual tracks. I do recall running the kick drum through an LA2A with the meter barely moving, just to get the sound of the tubes on the kick. The stereo bus for the mix was not compressed or EQ'd, but we hit the tape pretty hard to get a little of that saturated sound overdriven tape gets in the top end.

In those days a lot of rock was cookie-cutter stuff; very sampled and artificial sounding. All bands were sounding a lot like one another. We decided we liked a more organic thing; big room sound, no sampling, natural drums.

MIKE BARBIERO

Destruction". My recollection is that he liked the work we had done earlier on the Phantom, Rocker and Slick albums we had done for Capitol, but we wound up passing on the production of "Appetite" because we were involved in something else. That decision definately turned out to be a bad move in retrospect. Fortunately, Zutaut came back to us with the mix of the album after he heard what we'd done with Tesla's first album, which was also for Geffen. Tom was a big supporter of our work in those days, and we owe him a debt of gratitude for keeping us involved in many of his signings.

STEVE THOMPSON We worked at Media Sound in NYC on a vintage sound board. This was before Pro Tools and computers and everything was manually mixed. You could tell that there was a very angst, humanist way they approached music. I'm one of the die-hards. I remember in the late 1980's when we were mixing the album, drum sounds were very ambient; big chamber snare drums. The cool part was that this music was a lot drier and less processed sounding then the style of songs that were going on. Matt Sorum is a good friend of mine and I have total respect for him, but I kind of like Adler's style better because it was looser. Matt would be more of a clinical type drummer. Adler had a swagger to him. And that's what was cool about the band. I don't think the music was over-analyzed. It was a gut instinct. Which a lot of bands today and at that point would overanalyze everything and make everything perfect. I felt it had everything music was lacking at that point, because everything was just being cookie cutter with all the so-called glam bands at that point with the teased up hair and the spandex. They were nothing like that. They were just in your face. To me, it was refreshing to hear a band like Guns N' Roses. I don't think there was anything you could compare it to.

MIKE BARBIERO The guys in the band were great. There were no ego problems of any kind and everybody was really in sync. Most of the time the guys would hang out down the hall with Tom while Steve and I put the mixes together. When we were ready, we'd call them in to listen. Most of the time they'd just go, "That's great!" and we'd be done. I do remember

that for "Paradise City" they wanted the end to be a bit more raucous than we originally had it. Axl and Slash described it as more of "a fist fight between the guitar and vocal, where nobody wins." So they went out, while Steve and I did it. When they came back, I was editing the new piece in and made two marks where I thought the cut would work. We got into telling stories, and when I went to replace the end, I cut the insert in late, repeating a whole section of the song. I was horrified, but before I could move to fix it, the band said, "that's killer! Leave it that way." So the mistake stayed in and they began playing it that way live.

STEVE THOMPSON The people in the mix were Axl, Slash and Izzy. Each day they would come in to explain a little bit about the tracks and then we'd go off and do our thing. Then, when we felt we were ready for their ears, we would have them come in. I remember when we were mixing "Paradise City," I goofed this one part during the breakdown before "take me home." I basically copied that part of the song and duplicated it. Axl heard it and loved it and said to keep it in there. Back in those days, if you wanted to do experimenting, it was tape editing. What I liked about mixing that record was that you weren't being over anal, which a lot of people in music and films do today. They just overanalyze everything and that's when you tend to screw things up. We went for a vibe and the gut, song by song. We worked closely with Tom Zutaut. He was there every day and I'd have to say Tom has an amazing ear and I really liked his perspective on things. I think he was right on the money on everything in terms of the approach on the mixing of the record. Just keeping it raw and keeping it in your face. You can credit Tom Zutaut with a lot cause he camped out for a long time. He got in the trenches with them. Tom had the passion and to me, that's everything. That's what makes something successful.

MIKE BARBIERO Tom Zutaut was very specific in his instructions for what he wanted the album to sound like. He had a cassette tape of rough mixes that Mike Clink had done which he played for us. He actually did an A-B of each mix against that tape on a beat box that he had brought from L.A. to make sure the mixes had the sonic elements he wanted. He said he wanted the sound of that rough mix, but bigger. So that's what I went for.

STEVE THOMPSON Izzy woud get on the console every now and then and check things out. Slash would come around. I remember we were working with "Rocket Queen" and Axl said it was missing something. He said "I want to get some sex noises on this." So obviously you could go into your porn collection and record some stuff, but he said, "No I want something real."

*AXL There was also something I tried to work out with various people -- a recorded sex act. It was somewhat spontaneous but premeditated; something I wanted to put on the record. It was a sexual song and it was a wild night in the studio. This girl we know was dancing; everyone was getting really excited. The night could have gotten really explosive, lots of trouble for everyone, and I thought wait a minute, how can we make this productive.

*Reprinted from Geffen Press Kit

ADRIANA DURGAN Slash invited me to go to New York where they were finishing the recording of "Appetite." I used to live there, so I had friends I could visit and a place to stay. So I went out at same time as the band and I ended up hanging out at the recording studio the entire time. One night I got drunk in the studio and Axl propositioned me to have sex in the recording studio. Axl was having a hard time finding anyone to do it. I know that he'd asked several women to do it, including his girlfriend and they wouldn't. He said, "No one will do this for me; Erin wouldn't, no one will." Alan Niven got me a big bottle of Jack Daniels for me and Slash if I did it. That was that deal, I would do it for a bottle of liquor for me and Slash because we were drinking buddies. This was something that Axl wanted and I absolutely adored Axl and I fully trusted him. I said to myself, "Right on for the band, I'll do it for the band."

RON SCHNEIDER Let me tell you about the girl you hear in the background, moaning and groaning. That is the real deal. That is a stripper, an ex-stripper, a very good friend of ours. Her name is Adriana Smith. Axl threw a blanket on the floor in the recording studio, they set up a mic, dimmed the lights and Axl proceeded to fuck this girl right there. She's getting nailed right there and it's for real. Adriana Smith was originally Steven's girlfriend but her and Axl went at it for a while.

MIKE BARBIERO The truth is that I didn't want any part of what I perceived at the time to be a betrayal of a member of the band. I guess one could argue that it was all in the spirit of rock n' roll,

but I didn't really dig the vibe, though a lot of folks at the session were eating it up. I left the recording of that bit to my assistant, Vic, hence his credit, "Vic *the fuckin' engineer* Deglio."

STEVE ADLER I love Adrianna Smith. She is amazing. She did what she did. We were going out and she did what she did on "Rocket Queen." It was cool. It was all right. It didn't matter. We weren't married or anything, we were just close. We were naked skydivers from hell.

STEVE THOMPSON We had to mic her up and Axl did his thing and it was recorded and that's basically what happened on the session.

ADRIANA DURGAN The process was pretty mechanical. We went into the recording studio. Axl and I were in the vocal booth where the singers go and I was ready to go. There was a bunch of people that wanted to be in the studio and I didn't want that. I said the only people that can be in the recording studio area -- that could see the vocal booth -- were Tom Zutaut and maybe one or two other people. I kicked everybody else out because I would be having sex in front of them. There was wood paneling and we'd laid on the floor, put our headphones on and began to have sex for about two hours and it all got recorded on a reel to reel. I don't care how screwed up or drunk you are, some people would never do that. But I totally trusted the process. I trusted those guys and I trusted Axl, who guided me through the whole thing. There was a lot of, "Adriana shut up, quit fucking around," on the recording because we listened to it later on. But there's over two hours of us doing stuff. I'm sure they could've used more on the album because they only used a little piece and it's like muted down way low.

STEVE THOMPSON If it's blatantly in your face, I don't think it has as much of an impact. I thought it was done very well.

PHOTO TAKEN OF ADRIANA BY AXL DIRECTLY AFTER RECORDING THEIR PART FOR "ROCKET QUEEN."

I've talked to people who have listened to "Rocket Queen' before and didn't even know there was sex noises on there. Until you told them and they go, "Holy shit!" That to me works better than just having it up in your face and everything like that. I thought it created the right mood for the song.

ADRIANA DURGAN After the whole ordeal, Axl took me upstairs to his hotel room where we were staying and he played me November Rain for the first time on a piano. He told me that it was something that he wrote when he was fifteen. And it was the most beautiful thing I had ever heard. It was awesome. The next day I woke up in the hotel room. I was all alone and Slash called me and said, "You need to come down to the studio right now." And I was like, "Oh fuck, what did I do? Oh my God." I was incredibly embarrassed and I realized there might be repercussions to my current relationship with Steven [Adler], which was a rocky relationship anyway. Instead of being happy about what I did, I got a lot of crap about it because Axl was seeing Erin and I was seeing Steven, so I was now this big slut. I said I wanted the tape destroyed, but too late; Axl was overwhelmingly happy. He was stoked! This was just what he wanted. He was happy as pie.

```
It's kind of cool that
I actually did that.
I'm the Rocket Queen!
```

GUNS & ROSES

LIVE IN CONCERT 2 LETHAL NIGHTS

Monday, March 16th
with Elektra Recording Artist

JETBOY

Sunday, March 29th
with Elektra Recording Artist

TICKETS GO ON SALE FRIDAY, 13TH
Special After Parties To Be Announced At Event
Doors open at 8:00

WHISKY
MARCH 16TH 1987

Riki Rachtman introduced them to the packed club as hometown heroes.

They omitted the jam and guitar solo from "Anything Goes" and performed it publicly for the first time with the new lyrics. They played all the songs from **"Appetite for Destruction."** This show sounded just like the record because they had just finished recording it. Steven soundchecked his own drums before the show in front of the crowd.

Axl was jubilant.

*DUFF "Anything Goes" used to be a twelve and a half minute song.

AXL Izzy and I and Chris Weber wrote it a long time ago. It's had different verses at different times. Every time I'd do it live, people liked it. But it just depressed the shit of me on stage.

IZZY Used to be speed metal too.

AXL Yeah. We did it so fast. Then we wrote another version about our times at the old studio and we kept that for a while. But then, when we came down to record it, we didn't want to, but Tom Zutaut was very adamant about wanting that song recorded, so we figured 'we're going to have to rewrite it. In preproduction, we came up with something we liked a lot better, but the verses weren't written until the night we recorded the song. Basically I just wanted to get that song across as an anything-goes-in-sex type of song.

AXL: I'd say it's been about a million years, wouldn't you? In other words it's been a real long fucking time. I wanna thank everybody for coming down. I wanna thank Riki Rachtman for making this possible. And this is about those same god damn people who are always on your ass, the fucking LAPD, and this is called "They're Out Ta Get Me."

AXL: Hey, I can't hear shit in these monitors.

AXL: Can we do something, Colin, about the monitors because I can't hear shit. And a lot of other people can't either.

Axl noted that Anything Goes had been polished over many years and that what they would play was virtually a brand-new version.

AXL: This is a song that's been changed over the years many times, this is a brand new version of "Anything Goes."

AXL: This is a brand new one and this is for our man, one of our main men, and one of the co-writers of this song. This is for Wes Arkeen. And this motherfucker's called "It's So Easy."

AXL: (before "Rocket Queen") I'd like to take this moment to say a couple words about The Scream club. I don't know who's responsible necessarily, but they seem to try to fuck up a lot of people's gigs. They don't like to pay their bands worth of shit. So basically in general, fuck The Scream. And right-on to Alibi Artists with Riki Rachtman. We've got a show coming up on the 29th, another Alibi Artist Riki Rachtman show. It will be on the 29th at The Roxy with Faster Pussycat. And if you could turn this up a bit...that means the monitor's down. I'm game. It ain't my fault the PA sucks, man. Back off.

AXL: Now, a lot of people call us junkies. This is a song called "Mr. Brownstone."

AXL: Thank you. There's gonna be a Guns N' Roses Alibi Artists party after this, and it's gonna be at 320 South La Brea. That's between 3rd and 6th Street. There is no age limit; beer, wine and Saki. It's at the Rose Garden at 320 South La Brea and the DJ will be Joseph from Vinyl Fetish and The Cathouse. Gonna drink you under the table! We're gonna slow things down now with a song called "Sweet Child," and we'll do that for all the ladies present tonight.

SLASH: This is for the very few out there who can tolerate me when I'm really fucked up and bouncing off the walls. So this is a little something for you guys. This is called "Nightrain."

The energy on stage during that song was so intense that Axl ended getting a fat lip during an onstage collision with Slash.

AXL: Thank you. God damn.

AXL: Fat lip. I wanna dedicate this song to my ex-girlfriend, this is to Erin, this is called "Your Fucking Crazy."

AXL: (before "Paradise City") Hey, if any of you pick up any of these magazines -- all very nice magazines -- just remember; don't believe everything you read and that we say half of that shit. You know we wanna thank all the magazines for helping us out as much as possible. Alright boys, lets go. This is a place we all like to be. Duff would like me to dedicate this song to Adriana Barbeau.

AXL: Thank you, goodnight.

AXL: (during encore) You people ever listen to KNAC? We'd like to thank them and this is a song called "Move to the City."

AXL: (before "Mama Kin") This is a song about your fucking mother.

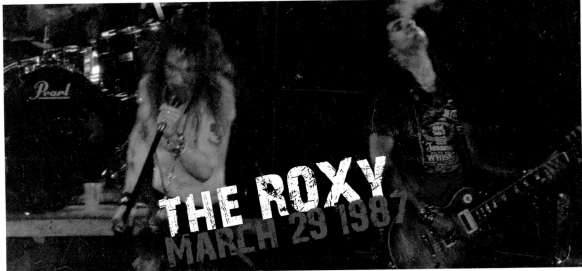

THE ROXY
MARCH 29 1987

At sound check they played "Anything Goes," "Paradise City," "Nightrain," "My Michelle," and "Mr. Brownstone." Axl attended sound check to try to solve the monitor problems they had been having.

RIKI RACHTMAN: *It's going to be a long time before we see these guys in a club this size. They've been in a couple of magazines and they got a record coming out real soon on Geffen Records.*

SLASH: *Hey fuckers, suck on Guns N' fucking Roses.*

AXL: *Welcome to The Roxy and welcome to the fucking jungle baby.*

AXL: *Alright, I wanna thank all of you for this great turnout. I'd like to dedicate this to all the overly active women in the crowd. This is a little chauvinistic song called "It's So Easy."*

AXL: *This album you've been waiting on, for ourselves here, we just got done recording it Friday. It's gonna be out in a couple of*

months due to all of the artwork and shit like that, but the motherfucker's done. Maybe this is the reason why it took so long to get off the ground. This is called "Mr. Brownstone."

DUFF: *The dancing girls are here.*

SLASH: *So lets order a drink for the girls.*

DUFF: *This song's called "Anything Goes."*

SLASH: *So how many totally fucking wasted fuckers do we have out here tonight? That's it, this is Hollywood man, speak up. I know there is more of you.*

After "My Michelle", Axl noted that he was having problems with his cordless mic.

AXL: *This is a song called "Sweet Child O' Mine."*

DUFF: *We've got a special present tonight.*

AXL: *Alright this is for anybody out there*

who has a fucking problem with us. This is called "You're Fucking Crazy."

AXL: *This is our last song people. And we're gonna take you somewhere, were we all wanna go. We're going down to the "Paradise City."*

SLASH: *We're having a party tonight – if you don't have a fuckin' pass, it's a dollar at the door; it's at Imperial Gardens, where the Glam Slam used to be.*

DUFF: *The after-party is free if you show your fucking tits. This one is for fucking Del.*

SLASH: *Do you guys ever listen to KNAC?*

AXL (before "Mama Kin"): *We're gonna leave you with your fucking mama.*

SLASH: Goodnight fuckers.

The Drunk Fux was a side project with some of their musician friends.

DRUNK FUX
MAY 10 - JULY 21 1987

The purpose of Drunk Fux was to rotate the band's lineup in order to get free drinks. They played a sloppy drunken set of cover tunes at the Coconut Teaszer on May 10. Del James was on vocals, West Arkeen on guitar, Duff on guitar and Todd Crew, formerly of Jetboy on bass. And then there was Steven on drums. West had co-written "It's So Easy" and a couple of songs that appeared on the "Use Your Illusion" albums. Del James was Duff's roommate at the time and later became Axl's right hand man.

He co-wrote "The Garden" which appeared on "Use Your Illusion One." Axl, Slash and Izzy weren't part of the gig because they had to go to New York at the last minute to help with the mixing of "Appetite.' The song lineup included punk covers, jumping the gun on the "Spaghetti Incident," and several songs penned by Duff and Del James.

Todd Crew died unexpectedly a few weeks later and his friends put on another Drunk Fux show in his memory

on July 21st at the Coconut Teaszer. All the members of Guns N' Roses, as well as a number of their musician friends took part. The songs played that night included a cover of Dylan's **"Knockin' on Heaven's Door,"** dedicated to Todd.

DEL JAMES You had to be a drunk fuck to be in the Drunk Fux! It was like a silly little side bar of Guns N' Roses' folklore!

SLASH'S FLYERS BELOW SHOW THE LATEST INCARNATION OF THE OLD ROADCREW MASCOT BABE!

LA'S PREMIERE OF —
IN THEIR NEVER ENDING BATTLE AGAINST SOBRIETY..

DRUNK FUX

(FEAT. MEMBERS OF GUNS N' ROSES)
...AND OTHER NOTORIOUS DRUNKX!

NIGHT TRAIN

SUNDAY MAY 10th 5612 SUNSET BLVD.

DEL JAMES AND TODD CREW
PHOTO COURTESY OF ADRIANA DURGAN

THE REST I

At the core of producing "Appetite for Destruction" was the collective belief that the music Guns N' Roses had created was inherently powerful and fiercely original.

Not one remix or rewrite would be made to appeal to the mainstream or to sell more records. The integrity of the music, as it was written and played, was first and foremost. Nonetheless, everyone sensed the potential for the album to strike a chord with rock n' roll enthusiasts and go platinum. Tom Zutaut wouldn't settle for anything less. He believed he found the next great rock band and his reputation as a top A&R rep for Geffen was on the line.

Meanwhie, the band bid farewell to Los Angeles and took their act to the UK, headlining at the pretiguous Marquee in London. After a few more gigs, they joined The Cult as the opening act and toured the world for the next eighteen months, coming back to Los Angeles periodically.

Tom's initial strategy of building mystique around the band backfired. Their

reputation took on a life of its own as they were characterized as out-of-control drug addicts; to hot to handle for mainstream media and against the family values of the corporate conglomerates that could carry them to success. No one would touch them, despite the fact that word-of-mouth sales were on the rise wherever they toured.

In the face of sluggish sales, limited airplay and a record company who was ready to pull the plug on the album, Tom played the last card he had; the goodwill he had earned with his boss, David Geffen. He convinced Geffen to use his influence to get "Welcome to the Jungle" aired on MTV. Geffen got the favor; albeit smaller than what Tom was hoping for.

MTV promised "Welcome to the Jungle" a single airing during the graveyard shift of their programming schedule -- at 2am, Pacific Standard Time. Tom reluctantly accepted his fate and gathered the band to celebrate their four minutes and thirty-three seconds of fame. Tom strolled into work by early afternoon, mostly content with the MTV airing and never expected the news that would greet him at the office.

The band came home from th-eir tour as international superstars, not quite aware of the success "Appetite for Destruction"

had become in the States until they
returned. The album became legendary
and the band, as a solidified unit, held on
for the ride as long as they could.

As the twentieth anniversary of the
release of "Appetite for Destruction"
passes, generation after generation of
fans revere those who were involved in
the making of the album. Tens of millions
of records sold and the album lives on
dozens of "Desert Island" lists around the
world. "Appetite for Destruction" stands
as one of the greatest rock n roll albums
ever produced.

TOM ZUTAUT When the record was
done, after I mastered it, I went and
played it for David Geffen and the
president of the company. I said, "This
is going to be the biggest album in the
history of the label," and they looked at
me like, "Sure kid."

MIKE BARBIERO Axl asked me at the
time if I thought the album had a shot,
and I remember telling him that it was
very original. I remember telling him that
to my ear the songs and performances
were good enough that, though the album
wasn't at all like anything being played on
radio, the band stood a good chance for a
gold record based on word of mouth.

STEVE THOMPSON I think we released
"Welcome to the Jungle" first, which I

thought was an anthem. I was pretty
shocked that it didn't break the way it
should have. "Sweet Child O' Mine" was
not even in the picture. It was a good
song, but to say that I thought that was
the song that was going to break GNR, I
couldn't predict that. I'm usually good at
predicting what songs are going to hit. To
me it was "Welcome to the Jungle."

TOM ZUTAUT I didn't tell anyone at
Geffen about "Sweet Child O Mine," and
I buried that song towards the end of
side-two. I did that because I knew that
promotion people and radio people at
that time very rarely listened past the
first two or three songs. I did not
want that song to be discovered
until later. And my reason was,
that Guns N' Roses needed to start
based on its punk roots. And that
song was way too refined. In some
ways it was almost like a song for
the second album. But I figured,
if we buried it on side-two, we'd
eventually get to it and there would
be enough of a buzz and a base
on the band that we would get an
opportunity to take a shot at a song like
that to mainstream radio. So I didn't tell
anyone that. It was my little secret.

We put the album out and radio stations
were afraid to play them. It seemed like
everyone at radio and MTV was afraid

of the band. They were so dangerous.
And a lot of this was the mystique; this
was my whole mystique theory paying
off. Because of the fact that they weren't
being interviewed all the time, and they
were kind of hidden, people began
inventing stories about them. Their
reputation was a lot worse than it really
was, because people were scared and
they were saying things like, "Oh, they're
a bunch of drug addicts, they'll bite your
head off." We actually had trouble getting
them on the radio. Meanwhile, we put the
band on the road and they opened for
The Cult and they did some Motley Crue
shows.

SLASH The first thing we did after
finishing "Appetite" was we went and
played in England, playing three shows at
the Marquee in London, which is a famous
place. We played London down in Soho.
From that point on, the record came out,
we started opened for the Cult and we
just became sort of an international band.

We were no longer just a local L.A. band and the rest is sort of history.

DUFF Once we completed the album and finished the artwork, we might've played a couple gigs in L.A. and then we were off. We did our first gigs outside of L.A. and they were in London at the Marquee. Then we caught the Colt tour and then we spent the next year and a half on the road. We became a worldwide rock band at that point.

ROBERT JOHN I remember when they were going over to England, Axl and Izzy asked me if I wanted to go. I said yes, but that I would have to quit my job. That was it. I never went back to a nine-to-five job ever from that point on because Guns N' Roses hit. As soon as we went over to England, that was the beginning, at least for me. It opened up a lot of doors. Axl helped me out tremendously with my career, because as doors got opened for him, he made them available for me. I totally appreciate that to this day and thank him for that. I didn't realize how big they became because I was touring with them and it wasn't until I stepped back that I saw it. These guys got huge. We went from watching this band that drew thirty-five people at the Troubadour to this.

TOM ZUTAUT MTV basically said, "we will never play this band because they are drug addicts, they are scary, and the cable operators have threatened to drop MTV off cable." The guys who ran the big cable companies were basically putting pressure on MTV to tone it back. They said, "This is HBO, this is about family entertainment, and MTV, if you cross the line we're going to pull you off the cable network because we're not going to have our cable franchises pissed at us because

of your programming." Now MTV says they will never play Guns N' Roses, they're way too dangerous, and they'll get thrown off the cable networks. We've sold 200,000 units by word of mouth only. People who are buying the record are people seeing them open for Motley or The Cult and they are telling their friends. Honestly, it was like clockwork. They'd go into town and open for somebody, and the next week, spike in sales. I get called into the president of the company's office one day and he looks at me says, "Hey kid it was a great run, but you've got to quit beating up the promotion people. They can't get it on the radio, MTV's not going to play it, and we're done with this record at 200,000 units." So I looked at my half-boss, who was a great guy, and as smart-aleck of

a kid as I was then and as sure of myself with Guns N' Roses, I had to give him some deference. I said, "with all due respect Eddie, this is the biggest rock and roll band in the world, and 200,000 is hasn't even scratched the surface yet. I will not go in the studio and make the next record, I will not stop pushing for this record. It's only just beginning; I don't know how you can say it's over. I'm going to call David Geffen, because I disagree with this decision. I'm not going to accept this decision that we're giving up on this record."

STEVE THOMPSON I remember a meeting we had with David and he sat down and says, "This is not the type of music I listen to, but the people I hire, I expect them to find bands like this." He gave his people the breathing room to be creative. And I remember him pointing to his staff and saying, "You see this guy, you see that guy over there? He's kind of cold right now, but I think in a year or two he's going to come up with something

big. Well, that same person was Gary Gersh; he signed Nirvana. Geffen had the integrity to let his people have the freedom to be creative. That's why people like Tom Zutaut went with their gut. Zutaut would camp out with Guns N' Roses, which is unheard of today. He stayed with them everyday along the way. And to me, I have the utmost respect for that. When they got Guns, they just believed in it. And Zutaut and Geffen spent over a year breaking this band, which is also unheard of today. They were not going to give up on this and it's a good thing they didn't.

TOM ZUTAUT I called David Geffen and David said, "I've never heard you so adamant about something." And I said, "I'm telling you, 200,000 records is a disgrace." And he said, "do you know how many new bands sell 200,000 records?" And I said, "well this band can sell ten million, so it's not enough." So David said, "What's the one thing I can do?" And I said, "Well, you could put the 'Welcome to the Jungle' video on MTV. I mean you're best friends with Fresten the guy who runs it, and they owe you favors. MTV owes you favors." And Geffen's like, "Yeah, I could do that. I'll take care of that and I'll put in a call."

So the next day David Geffen calls me up into his office and he says, "You tricked me!" And I said, "What?" And he said, "Well, first off you didn't tell me that they already, adamantly vowed and sworn to never to play this band on MTV. If you had told me that in advance I might have been able to do better for you." I said, "You're David Geffen, you're the man, they either owe you a favor or they don't." He said, "Next time, don't forget minor details like that, because it's very important when I call somebody to know what I'm up against." I said, "I promise if something like this comes up again, I'll give you all the nitty gritty." And he goes, "Ok, in spite of that, I did get them. They'll play it one time, this Sunday at 5am New York time, 2am L.A. time." I said, "That's it?" And he said, "Look, don't be a schmuck, you could have gotten nothing." And I said, "Alright." So I called the band and said, "Look we'll stay up all night and we'll watch it." It was exciting. Here it was on MTV in all its glory and it looked amazing. So I come into work the next day, not thinking much of anything other than I hope something happened. I took my shot with David Geffen and the

record's over and I don't know what I'm going to do.

STEVEN ADLER When I first saw myself on MTV, I dropped my lighter, I picked it up and I said, "Man, we are the fucking shit!" We became everything we dreamed about, but cooler. Except for Aerosmith. I thought Aerosmith was cooler.

TOM ZUTAUT So the head of promotion was this real excitable guy named Al Corian. Because I was up all night with the band, I probably didn't get in until 1:00pm. With Guns N' Roses, if I could get in by 1:00pm, that was pretty good. I get an urgent message from Al Corian as soon as I get in and I went to his office immediately. And this guy starts babbling, "I've got to tell you, that Guns N' Roses thing -- it's unbelievable. We're going to get it everywhere." He said, "You don't understand, they blew up the switchboard at MTV, I'm telling you the switchboard blew up. They're putting it in heavy rotation. This is amazing." I told this guy for months it was going to be the biggest band in the world. They wanted to drop the record on Friday and now on Monday it's the biggest thing that ever happened. MTV had put the video into heavy rotation, and it explodes, and we go from 200,000 units to a million units practically overnight. If there's anything to be learned by the lesson of Guns N' Roses and "Appetite for Destruction," it's keep it real.

STEVE DARROW By the time GNR hit real big after the videos hit and by the time "Appetite" was on the charts, all the record labels were signing up every band that started coming to town and started playing at the Coconut Teaser and the Troubadour. Everyone was the next Guns N' Roses and none of them became that really.

MIKE CLINK It was a gradual process, watching the album climb the charts. The interesting thing about "Appetite" is that when I finished it, I played it for friends and people in the business and a lot of them said, this is the biggest piece of crap I've ever heard. Fast forward a year later, and everyone's saying they love the record; they've always loved that record.

VICKY HAMILTON I didn't know that they ultimately would sell the amount of records that they ended up selling – what

was it, like 75 million in the end? All I knew was that I loved it and I thought it was great. They were amazing. Still to this day, there aren't bands that can rival what Guns N' Roses did and who knows if there ever will be. Their star burned very fast and bright.

MIKE BARBIERO Anyone who says they anticipated the legacy of this album and the extraordinary sales figures it achieved would be a liar. It was a tremendous feeling to see the album steadily make its way up the charts. It took a really long time, which I came to appreciate more once I had an album that debuted at number one and then steadily fell off.

RON SCHNEIDER When it really hit me was the American Music Awards. They got the number one song or best song of the year for "Sweet Child O' Mine." At the same time, the album went number one. They got up to accept and I think Slash and Duff were there just lit.

STEVE THOMPSON I'm a stickler. Every record I make I want to make it timeless. I don't just want to make it for the present. What I've tried to achieve throughout my whole career has been

to make it contemporary, but at the same time have it hold the test of time like a piece of art. You don't want to make it disposable, just for the moment. "Appetite" was a perfect example of something that remains timeless.

MIKE CLINK Every week people come up to me, telling me how "Appetite" changed their lives. It's affected the generations. I'm a celebrity at my fourteen-year-old daughter's school now

because I did "Appetite." "Emma, did you know that your dad did Appetite?" And she goes "Yeah, so?" It's interesting because even now the kids love it. That's the sign of a great record. Just like those AC/DC records or the Beatles records or Pink Floyd. It's a work of art that stands the test of time and everyone wants to hear it. That's what we set out to do when we made that record; was to make it timeless.

From the collection of Marc Canter these are a partial sample of music magazine cover art about Guns N' Roses.

GIANTS STADIUM

AEROSMITH

AUGUST 16TH 1988

I flew out to the East Rutherford, NJ, for this show at Giants Stadium.

It was an opportunity to see Guns N' Roses perform in a huge stadium setting and see two of my other favorite bands, Deep Purple and Aerosmith. I took some photos at soundcheck, including a shot of Slash taking an onstage bicycle ride. I guess this is where it all began for me; Slash and bicycles.

Video footage for "Paradise City" was shot at this event. I was able to video tape the making of MTV's video for"Paradise City" from the high up in the rafters above the stage.

It's So Easy
Mr. Brownstone
Paradise City
You're Crazy
(acoustic)
Out Ta Get Me
Welcome to the Jungle
Sweet Child O' Mine
Used To Love Her

LOT NO.
9/11
V.I.P.
PARKING

DEEP PURPLE
PLUS SPECIAL GUEST GUNS N' ROSES

Giants
Stadium
AUGUST 16TH

When we were kids, Slash would often give drawings as gifts.

These drawings of members of Aerosmith were some of my favorites and Slash knew that I loved the band.

The ink and pen drawing on the facing page was actually done in two stages. Take a look at the original on enhancedbooks.com.

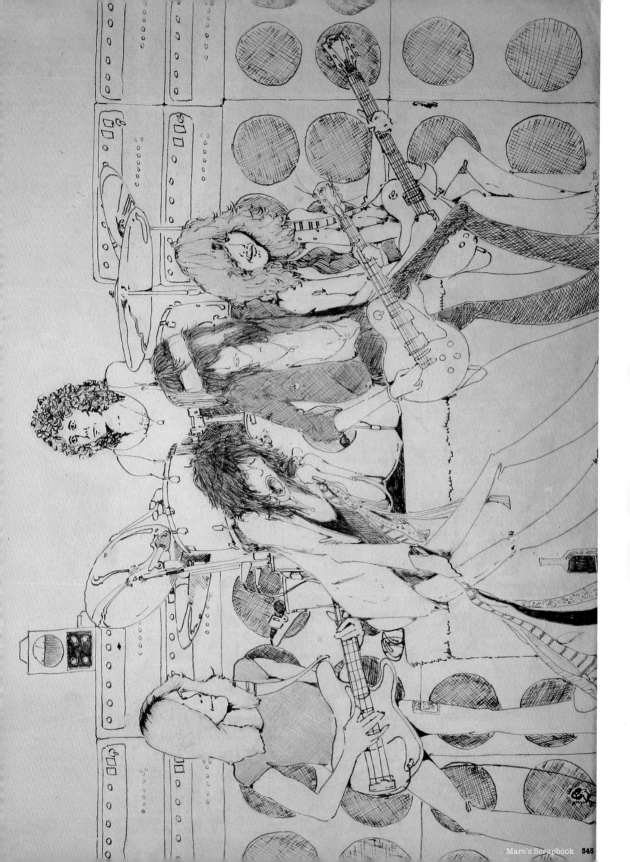

CANTER'S KIBITZ ROOM
FLYER:
A WELL LUBRICATED SLASH
SKETCHED THIS DESIGN
FOR A PROPOSED CANTER'S
T-SHIRT AT MY REQUEST.

12/92 SLASH JAMMING
ONCE AGAIN AT THE
KIBITZ ROOM WITH
VOCALIST JESSICA
TILTON.

THEIR MANAGER, ALAN NIVEN, HAD
GOLD RINGS WITH THE GUNS N' ROSES
LOGO ON THEM MADE FOR EACH OF THE
BAND MEMBERS WHEN APPETITE WENT
GOLD. NOT BEING SOMEONE WHO FELT
COMFORTABLE BEING PART OF A CLUB,
SLASH GAVE ME HIS RING.

SLASH CONTRIBUTING SOME SLIDE GUITAR LICKS TO A TUESDAY NIGHT JAM BEHIND
MORTY COYLES VOCALS AT CANTER'S KIBITZ ROOM 9-8-92

MY WEDDING PHOTO:
SLASH CAME TO MY
WEDDING DRESSED
AS HIMSELF; AXL
PUT ON A SUIT. MY
WIFE LEISA CUT ALL
THE BAND MEMBERS
HAIR AND WENT ON
CUTTING AXL'S HAIR
UP TILL 2001

AFTER SIGNING A FEW PHOTOS FOR A FRIEND, AXL WITH PEN STILL
IN HAND, DECIDED TO FOOL AROUND WITH A LEFTOVER PHOTO.

MY SON ALEX'S BAR MITZVAH WITH A SPECIAL GUEST
PHOTO BY SHEL ROSENTHAL

AXL PIANO PHOTO BY SHANNON PAYNTER
3-4-89 AXL HAD AGREED IN ADVANCE TO PLAY "NOVEMBER RAIN" AS WE WALKED DOWN THE AISLE;
AT THE LAST MINUTE HE SPORTINGLY LET HIMSELF BE PRESSED INTO SERVICE BY A SOMEWHAT BEFUDDLED
WEDDING COORDINATOR TO ENTERTAIN THE GUESTS AS THEY ARRIVED. AMONG THE TUNES HE OFFERED WERE
BITS OF THE SONG THAT WAS EVENTUALLY RELEASED AS "ESTRANGED"